OSTROM'S
TENSIONS

TENSIONS IN POLITICAL ECONOMY

SERIES EDITORS: VIRGIL HENRY STORR and STEFANIE HAEFFELE

ABOUT THIS SERIES

The Tensions in Political Economy series consists of edited volumes of original essays that explore the research programs of key scholars in the tradition of mainline economics. These volumes delve into the tensions in a scholar's work, including real and apparent gaps, shortcomings, and inconsistencies, in order to highlight and encourage contemporary research aimed at providing novel solutions to these tensions and bridging the gap between theory and practice. Through this series, the Mercatus Center at George Mason University aims to further mainline economics by ensuring that these critical examinations of the writings of key figures are made available to students and scholars.

BOOKS IN THIS SERIES

Peter J. Boettke and Solomon Stein, eds., *Buchanan's Tensions: Reexamining the Political Economy and Philosophy of James M. Buchanan*

Roberta Q. Herzberg, Peter J. Boettke, and Paul Dragos Aligica, eds., *Ostrom's Tensions: Reexamining the Political Economy and Public Policy of Elinor C. Ostrom*

TENSIONS IN POLITICAL ECONOMY

OSTROM'S TENSIONS

REEXAMINING the POLITICAL ECONOMY and PUBLIC POLICY of ELINOR C. OSTROM

———

EDITED by ROBERTA Q. HERZBERG,
PETER J. BOETTKE, and
PAUL DRAGOS ALIGICA

MERCATUS CENTER
George Mason University
Arlington, Virginia

ABOUT THE MERCATUS CENTER AT GEORGE MASON UNIVERSITY

The Mercatus Center at George Mason University is the world's premier university source for market-oriented ideas—bridging the gap between academic ideas and real-world problems.

A university-based research center, the Mercatus Center advances knowledge about how markets work to improve people's lives by training graduate students, conducting research, and applying economics to offer solutions to society's most pressing problems.

Our mission is to generate knowledge and understanding of the institutions that affect the freedom to prosper and to find sustainable solutions that overcome the barriers preventing individuals from living free, prosperous, and peaceful lives.

Founded in 1980, the Mercatus Center is located on George Mason University's Arlington and Fairfax campuses.

Mercatus Center at George Mason University
3434 Washington Blvd., 4th Floor
Arlington, Virginia 22201
www.mercatus.org
703-993-4930

Cover design by Jessica Hogenson, Port Ludlow, Washington
Editing and composition by Publications Professionals, Fairfax, Virginia
Index by Connie Binder, Laurel, Maryland

ISBN 978-1-942951-57-5 (hardcover)
ISBN 978-1-942951-58-2 (paper)
ISBN 978-1-942951-59-9 (ebook)

Library of Congress Cataloging-in-Publication Data are available for this publication.

CONTENTS

INTRODUCTION   1
Roberta Q. Herzberg, Peter J. Boettke, and Paul Dragos Aligica

SECTION 1: THEORETICAL TENSIONS
1   BEYOND A PRECARIOUS BALANCE   19
   Michael D. McGinnis

2   AN INTRICATE MOVE TOWARD REALITY   73
   Adrian Miroiu

SECTION 2: PUBLIC ADMINISTRATION TENSIONS
3   "WHAT SHOULD WE DO?"   105
   Peter Levine

4   SOCIAL RECONTRACTING   127
   Adam Martin

5   INSTITUTIONAL COMPLEXITY AND THE PUBLIC CHOICE
   ANALYSIS OF FEASIBLE POLICY CHANGES   147
   Vlad Tarko

SECTION 3: METHODOLOGICAL TENSIONS
6   WHOSE PROBLEMS ARE BEING SOLVED?   181
   Andreas Thiel and Erik Swyngedouw

7   IN PRAISE OF ECLECTICISM   211
   Aurelian Craiutu

CONTRIBUTORS   247
INDEX   249

INTRODUCTION

ROBERTA Q. HERZBERG, PETER J. BOETTKE,

AND PAUL DRAGOS ALIGICA

W ho doesn't love a good fight? Although maybe not everybody loves a fight, serious intellectual challenges help advance entire fields of knowledge. Certainly, Elinor Ostrom and her spouse and collaborator, Vincent Ostrom, enjoyed careers that contested the scholarship of mainstream political economy and public policy in their quest to understand how individuals resolve a variety of social dilemmas. Indeed, Elinor Ostrom even dedicated her seminal book, *Governing the Commons: The Evolution of Institutions for Collective Action* (1990, v), with "To Vincent—For his love and contestation." Through that contestation, they developed new approaches to institutional economics that would shape scholarship across multiple fields.

In 2009, Elinor Ostrom was named corecipient of the Sveriges Riksbank Prize in Economic Sciences in Memory of Alfred Nobel (Nobel Prize in Economics) along with Oliver E. Williamson, with particular recognition for her path-breaking work on institutions organized to address common-pool resource settings. As the Nobel committee notes, Ostrom "challenged the conventional wisdom by demonstrating how local property can be successfully managed by local commons without any regulation by central authorities or privatization" (NobelPrize.org, n.d.). The prize was, in many ways, the ultimate recognition of her influence on fields ranging from institutional analysis to metropolitan service delivery, from federalism and theories of polycentric orders to common-pool resource management and sustainable development.[1] Looking back, the importance of Ostrom's scholarly *oeuvre* seems obvious.[2] Along the way, however, this recognition was anything but obvious, as Elinor and Vincent Ostrom found themselves at odds with mainstream thinking. Elinor Ostrom's willingness to consistently take on accepted approaches with respect and perseverance inspires scholars around the world to engage, to challenge, and, finally, to advance her work.

Among the important truths the Ostroms challenged was the belief that a system of governance based on expert public officials could perform better than and should be a priori preferred to a system based on citizens' self-governance. This challenge, which is frequently a source of tension and debate in fields focused on solving policy problems, helps explain the reactions to their work over the years. Vincent Ostrom faced hurdles early on at the University of Wyoming and the University of California, Los Angeles, as administrators sought to censor or circumscribe the policy implications of his work. Likewise, they both faced pushback from the mainstream of the public administration discipline as they stressed a public choice critique in response to increasing municipality consolidation (Ostrom and Ostrom 2014). Their work on metropolitan service delivery was received as an affront by many peers and professional administrators who sought even greater consolidation. Even Elinor Ostrom's most famous contributions to understanding institutions and common-pool resources faced criticism from scholars and policy experts who had tackled the analytic puzzle of governance from a simpler, even dichotomous, theoretical perspective.

To solve social dilemmas, Elinor Ostrom pressed for a marriage of the more complex empirics of real-world settings to some of the precision and generality of the analytic models popular in the field. She did not just give in when others questioned the difficulty of such an approach. She also did not leave theory behind as she continued to engage and understand existing real-world situations. In her 1984 presidential address to the Public Choice Society, for example, she makes the case for continuing an institutional perspective even as others were turning away from such analysis because it was difficult to generalize with analytic clarity (Ostrom 1986). The critics suggested that such an approach would never be done—there would always be another set of institutional rules to examine, another model to create. But Elinor Ostrom persevered and developed a framework logic to make sense of the wide variety of possible theories and models she explored. Eventually, the Institutional Analysis and Development (IAD) framework became the metatheory for common-pool resources laid out in *Governing the Commons* (Ostrom 1990). In the IAD framework, Ostrom explains actors' decisions in relation to the decision context they face and the policy and resource outcomes that result. The IAD framework lays out the broad relationship between the action and characteristics of the environment, the community, and the rules used to make decisions. It represents her effort at abstract generalization within a complex policy space. She was unwilling to give up either the empirical richness or the analytic advancement, as she deemed both critical to understanding the specific dilemma and advancing the broader knowledge about such problems. Ostrom, as Boettke (2010) argues, treated rational choice as if the choosers were human and institutional analysis as if history matters.

Ostrom argued that many of the shortcomings in policy and institutional design are a function of oversimplifying the problem and forgetting the role that individuals play in policy design and community governance. She suggested at least three dimensions on which simplification leads to incorrect prediction and design (Ostrom 2010b). First, many analysts approached the problem of social dilemmas from the perspective of only two possible solutions—fully privatizing the resource or fully managing it under a single governing entity. For Ostrom, these alternatives were, at most, just two possibilities along a continuum of governing arrangements that incorporate various combinations of both private and public decisions. Second, scholars often focused on a dichotomy in the resource itself—categorizing the resource as a purely private or a purely public good. Again, by broadening how social scientists characterize goods, Ostrom was able to examine hybrid solutions not considered before in the literature. Third, Ostrom contended that the assumption of narrow economic self-interest was insufficient to capture the range of individuals' interests. When we as analysts broaden our lens to incorporate a wide range of rational motivations for action, it is possible to find solutions for a variety of collective problems.

Thus, the Ostroms argued that polycentric arrangements could be superior to more consolidated alternatives for solving policy problems and satisfying citizens' preferences (Ostrom, Tiebout, and Warren 1961; Ostrom 1965, 2006; Ostrom, Parks, and Whitaker 1978). Unfortunately, the Ostroms' work was often deemed irrelevant by public administrators. Metropolitan reformers, in and out of academia, ignored the complexity faced by the individuals whom the Ostroms studied. These reformers continued to press for consolidated so-called UniGov institutions that ultimately faced constraints in identifying, reconciling, and implementing the diverse interests of the residents of those metropolitan areas. By looking for the arrangements that individuals designed for themselves, the Ostroms could recommend institutional forms in which social choices were consistent with individuals' self-interest more broadly understood. Individual interests could be served without constant recourse to force. Not until decades later did the full significance of the Ostroms' critique become clear (Ostrom and Ostrom 2004, Ostrom 2010a). Today, calls for and celebrations of polycentricity and community-based policy differentiation abound, thanks in no small part to the careful theoretical and empirical arguments the Ostroms advanced (Cole and McGinnis 2015a, 2017).

One of the distinguishing features of the Ostroms' work was their programmatic attempt to link theories to practice. Elinor Ostrom argued not only for retaining the powerful tools of political economy theory but also for strengthening theory by incorporating more pragmatic aspects of real-world political and policy problems. She and Vincent Ostrom recognized that their questions of interest went beyond traditional disciplinary boundaries, and so they set out to forge an interdisciplinary approach. They established the Workshop in Political Theory and Policy Analysis at Indiana University (known as the Ostrom Workshop) to carry out this interdisciplinary approach. It would serve as their intellectual home from 1973 until their deaths in 2012.

At the Ostrom Workshop, they used a multiple method approach to challenge existing, general, and oversimplified models and theories to account for the myriad of circumstances citizens actually face. Rather than the stark majority-rule processes underlying most analysis of democratic and collective-choice decisions at the time, the Ostroms identified institutionally complex arrangements that allowed citizens to uncover solutions acceptable to their own community.[3] These analyses focused on the general features of the collective-choice process, rather than a specific set of defined decision rules. Early examples included common-pool resource settings, such as the Los Angeles, California, metropolitan water system (Ostrom 1965) and local fiscal decision-making designed to determine police and other public services in metropolitan areas across the United States (Ostrom, Tiebout, and Warren 1961; Ostrom and Whitaker 1974; Ostrom, Parks, and Whitaker 1978).

Likewise, the clear hierarchy so frequently used to theoretically explain decisions within large organizations and societies seemed inconsistent with the patchwork of polycentric relationships that characterized most policy settings the Ostroms observed. Rather than collapse analysis quickly to an overgeneralized pattern, the Ostroms built frameworks within which a wide variety of institutional arrangements might be carefully considered. They remained committed to rigorous analytic approaches, but they did not allow the rigor to overpower their desire to tackle serious real-world problems that citizens face. In this respect, it is illustrative of the effort the Ostroms made to completely understand what happens within an institutional setting from all perspectives, including the perspective of the participants themselves. The Ostroms characterized this latter approach as "seeing like a citizen" rather than "seeing like a state," an important distinction in institutional analysis of the time (Ostrom 2006; Ostrom 2001).

Across their careers, this approach took many forms—theories of self-governance in Tocquevillian associations (Ostrom 1997); polycentric orders for public services, federalism, and constitutional arrangements of contending powers (Ostrom 2007); empirical examinations of fiscal competition in metropolitan service delivery (Ostrom, Parks, and Whitaker 1978); the theoretical and empirical analysis of institutions that permit individuals to address common-pool dilemmas (Ostrom 1990); and the theoretical development of institutional analysis (Ostrom 2005). As they developed their theoretical focus, the Ostroms did not simply adopt the accepted, mainstream theoretical lenses—either concentrating authority in a sovereign or decentralizing all action to private exchange. They noted the existence of a rich middle ground and sought analytic ways to understand why these complex compromises worked in the real world (Ostrom and Ostrom 2004).

And thus, in the "era of the expert" the Ostroms challenged the tendency to concentrate further authority in expert policymakers, in part because they understood the limits of public officials to determine and deliver optimal policy results. Likewise, they observed many instances in which citizens worked together and performed beyond the low expectations predicted by existing theories. The Ostroms' careful empirical findings in metropolitan services and in common-pool resource settings suggest that citizens can (and do) successfully resolve conflicts, at least some of the time. Rather than write off the realities of self-governance that they observed, the Ostroms chose to develop new, richer institutional theory that could explain under what conditions citizens might successfully self-govern.

The tension between the rigor provided by formal models of institutions and the relevance of specific and complex institutions would set the Ostroms' work apart from many in political science and economics, as Michael D. McGinnis explains in his chapter in this volume (chapter 1). The path the Ostroms advanced is a result of being in constant tension with one or another of the main tenets of the mainstream literature of the day (Ostrom 1998). The Ostroms took the tensions between their work and the conventional wisdom of the mainstream literature seriously, and they built theories and frameworks that provided a richer understanding of the phenomena they studied. In a sense, the work advanced most when they confronted those tensions. The spirit of such an embrace of challenge and tensions inspires this volume. The contributors to this volume identify and consider several tensions or gaps in understanding that remain in Elinor Ostrom's work in an effort to continue advancing its effect.

All of the above introduction suggests reasons that, in the preparation of a volume on Elinor Ostrom's intellectual legacy 10 years after her Nobel Prize in Economics, the very idea of "tensions" emerges so saliently as a core underlying theme. All the chapters in this volume illuminate important aspects of Ostrom's contributions and how they shape our understanding of institutions, constitutions, and the prospects for self-governance and also identify critical tensions that remain to be studied. The theoretical tensions considered range from issues of the cohesiveness of the research program to its comparison with well-accepted theoretical approaches to the evaluation of those specific, unresolved theoretical puzzles posed by the underlying assumptions in the Ostroms' scholarship. Together, they offer a sample of today's wide range of interpretive and critical engagement with the Ostroms' intellectual legacy.

THEORETICAL TENSIONS

The first section focuses on the theoretical tensions raised by the way in which Elinor Ostrom addressed frameworks, theories, and models. In each of the settings examined, Ostrom's research countered the generally predicted results of conventional wisdom. She saw capacity where others saw dilemmas that must be overcome. But the Ostroms' explanations often required a different analytic approach than that of the mainstream (Ostrom 1998). The result was an approach built up from individual institutions to generalized understanding and predictions. While investigating individual dilemmas, Elinor Ostrom developed a way of organizing the components of the decision problem that other scholars could use to understand a variety of collective-choice problems, and that a policymaker could use to shape and advocate for a solution. By discovering a proper theoretical structure, Ostrom enabled analysts to knit together the relevant factors of complex real-world problems and situations. Ostrom (2010b, 646), in the lecture she gave when accepting her Nobel Prize in Economics, explains that, "While the terms frameworks, theories, and models are used interchangeably by many scholars, we use these concepts in a nested manner to range from the most general to the most precise set of assumptions made by a scholar." Frameworks identify common critical factors across institutional settings, while theories and models consider smaller and more precise puzzles within the framework. Theories and models are, thus, building blocks within a broad analytic framework.

A frequent concern with the framework approach is the challenge it poses when trying to simultaneously achieve analytic rigor and policy relevance. These often-conflicting objectives mean that one or the other may be shortchanged, leaving one or both audiences frustrated. The complexity of most institutions leads carefully structured analysis in the tradition of game theory to become difficult to manage. The Ostroms balanced the need for careful theory with the desire to speak to policy analysts and citizens about the consequences of their scholarship. But in creating this balance, the Ostroms often frustrated analysts on both sides. To understand the decision setting, the analyst must give up some of the precision common to the methodology of analytic choice theory in order to have models that may be comprehended and used by policymakers.

The first part of the book explores these and related themes. In a particularly rich analysis, Michael D. McGinnis explores a major tension in the Ostroms' work—the desire to balance rigor in their models with a need for policy relevance, a balance McGinnis terms *strategic rigor*.

The Ostroms developed several different theoretical frameworks to address the questions of institutions. McGinnis pushes beyond the Ostroms' *corpus* to suggest important ways in which their different frameworks—IAD, common-pool resource, and Social-Ecological System—can be linked. McGinnis brings his own approach to concrete application to identify common processes across different decision settings and suggests how these theoretical approaches provide useful insight for policymakers. The complexity of policy situations that overlap and intersect make it difficult to settle on a generalized model applicable in many circumstances, but a framework can provide the focus necessary to produce meaningful comparisons across these different settings. In pressing for this shift, McGinnis suggests how each stage of the traditional policy cycle model might be seen as linked action situations. Such a perspective bridges the Bloomington School tradition with work in classic policy analysis to broaden the audience of understanding for each.

McGinnis also notes that the precision of rigorous mathematical models limits the extent to which policymakers and citizens can take advantage of the insights that the models provide. The Ostroms recognized the value that mathematical theoretical approaches provide to structure analysis on critical similarities and differences across decision settings, but such methods often limit the relevance to only those audiences who understand the formal language. McGinnis argues that the strategic rigor the Ostroms pursued allowed a degree of clarity in the argument made within a policy-relevant framework where rigor and relevance reinforce rather than counter each other.

Starting from similar concerns, Adrian Miroiu uses a philosophy of social science perspective to explore Ostrom's use of frameworks, theories, and models to tease out the differences between each level of analysis and the role it plays in her work. Miroiu explores the tension in interpreting the philosophical foundations of the Ostromian enterprise and suggests that they focus on models that best represent the empirical characteristics of the settings of interest. Ostrom does not give much attention to the syntactic view of theories. As Miroiu (chap. 2, 78) suggests: "Ostrom is more interested in 'operationalizing' the syntax and using it to build models with different empirical, concrete situations than in constructing a consistent set of statements about them." Miroiu goes on to argue that this approach, which he calls "structural realism," may be characterized as a variation of the philosophical approach of "scientific realism." In this case, realism operates at the level of the structural variables, but not necessarily at the detailed level of the empirics. This type of realism provides the continuity across different models that permits Ostrom to generalize about those factors most important in accounting for success.

Miroiu's contribution illustrates an interesting feature of the Bloomington School: the philosophical and epistemological assumptions and implications of the Ostromian perspective are an open domain of investigation and development almost a decade after the founders of the Bloomington School passed away. In the case of the Ostroms' research program, we observe one of the few cases in which the applied work and the empirical analysis were done at the same time as the development and articulation of the philosophical apparatus underpinning them. It differs from many research programs, which often start by programmatically announcing a grand foundational philosophical position (epistemic, ontological, or normative) and then go on to prescribe (in most cases deriving abstractly from that position) what and how it should be done in the social scientific practice. The recent history of social science research features many programs announced through bold philosophical and methodological manifestos, only to then linger in search of ways to generate empirical research that reinforces those positions. The Ostroms' case is different: the two facets developed congruently. The task of the philosopher, as advanced by the Ostroms, is to draw lessons and implications from successful research, either in development or previously conducted, and to contribute to the articulation of the foundational position behind that success. Miroiu's paper engages in that type of exercise, offering a fresh way of approaching and reading the Ostromian enterprise from the point of view of a philosopher of science.

PUBLIC ADMINISTRATION TENSIONS

The Ostroms were always interested in the real-world effects of the problems they studied. It was not enough to solve an analytic puzzle if it did not shine light on potential improvements or possible pitfalls for citizens and policymakers. Contributions to the second section of this volume consider the challenges posed by more specific use of the Ostroms' work in the fields of public administration, public service delivery, and civic participation. The Ostroms challenged the hubris of central administrators who argued for consolidation and expert rule over citizen-based processes (Ostrom 1989). Through this decades-long debate, they kept alive the idea of competing, polycentric arrangements as feasible alternatives to the race to consolidate that dominated public administration theory and practice. Additionally, they were committed to citizen self-governance, especially when many other scholars dismissed the notion that individuals are capable of making decisions and implementing solutions for themselves. But what do the requirements of self-governance and polycentricity impose on citizens? Are these requirements likely to be met? And, if not, what are the consequences in terms of the results predicted by the Ostroms' scholarship? Several of the chapters in this section take on specific arguments in the Ostroms' work on polycentricity, metropolitan service delivery, and local governance to consider some of the challenges that remain.

Peter Levine's chapter examines the viability of citizen self-governance within an Ostromian model. Levine considers whether it is possible to generalize the Ostromian approach to a wider range of collective action dilemmas beyond common-pool resource settings. He argues that Ostrom's approach correctly focuses on individual citizens, but that it may be inadequate to explain citizen governance in at least two different settings. First, in circumstances when citizens are unsettled on the end or ultimate objective, the Ostrom theory is inadequate. In successful commons situations, participants often are highly similar in terms of the desired objective or end state. Each member recognizes that future value from the resource depends on being able to sustain the resource as a source of benefit. The common desire to solve a dilemma serves as the basis for working out an institutional solution. Each resource user may desire greater access relative to other users, but each also shares a view that the resource is valuable as a source of future use that can be affected by current use decisions. These settings, therefore, are more symmetric relative to the ends of the process (although intensity of interest may vary). By contrast, many collective-choice dilemmas emerge because individuals disagree about what the appropriate ends for collective choice should be. When community members face greater disagreement about the desired ends, resolution requires working out both the ends and the process necessary to achieve those ends. In these settings, Levine suggests that the Ostromian approach may fall short.

Second, Levine considers the challenge posed by situations with significant asymmetries in power between individuals and finds that Ostrom's approach provides little insight into how citizens might challenge current authoritarian leadership. Most of the resolved dilemmas Ostrom outlines are characterized by relatively equal positions among participants, or at least the prospect of equality. Levine suggests that an asymmetry of power requires a different form of analysis to explain its outcomes.

Adam Martin's chapter then outlines Elinor Ostrom's important work on metropolitan service delivery to suggest some of the limitations that emerge as a result of contracting across different levels within a polycentric order. Although supportive of the contribution Ostrom made to the dilemma of meeting residents' diverse interests in metropolitan services, Martin suggests that challenges remain in reaching market adjustments once contracts are in place. He contrasts the problem of contracting public services with private market processes to suggest that the transaction costs involved in polycentric public services constrains the ability of residents to make needed adjustments to best serve their changing needs. Ostrom recognized this challenge, but unfortunately many of these concerns remained unresolved in her work.

In contracting, Martin notes four key problems identified by public choice theorists that could complicate the process. First, as a contractor, the polycentric government takes on more of the characteristics of a sovereign, losing the advantage of citizen involvement that keeps governments in check. Second, social contracting creates winners and losers, and losers often are more motivated to act, which exacerbates the problems of public choice that always emerge when there are gains to be had. Third, as power concentrates in larger governments there is an increased incentive for actors at different levels of government to collude to create special benefits at the expense of the broader community. Finally, as power concentrates there is a tendency for government agents to seek to expand their authority and the size of government. By noting these challenges of contracting, Martin suggests new avenues left unexplored by the Ostroms' treatment of polycentricity.

In the last chapter in this section, Vlad Tarko considers the applicability of the Ostroms' IAD framework in relation to other statistical tools—such as factor analysis and cluster analysis—to "provide a more rigorous grounding for mapping out the set of possible institutional (or policy) configurations" (chap. 5, 148). He explores how modern statistical methods might be wed to the logical construct of the IAD framework to explore more closely interrelationships between institutions. In particular, he considers the challenges for institutional analysis associated with the complexity of institutional linkages relevant in most natural settings. The chapter uses data from the Fraser Institute's Economic Freedom of the World index to provide a statistical analysis on institutional quality and to more rigorously evaluate the actual configurations of institutions. Tarko finds that most institutions tend to cluster into a smaller set of areas of the parameter space, which permits the analysts to reduce much of the complexity that emerges from the combinatorial explosion that is possible without such categorization. For explaining causality and giving core meaning to intent, he finds the IAD framework provides a superior analysis as compared with statistical methods on their own, especially when the long tradition of public choice findings is incorporated. Using these methods (statistics and IAD) together allows for a better integration of theory and empirics so as to ensure better description and interpretation of institutional arrangements across systems.

METHODOLOGICAL TENSIONS

The final section of this volume explores the tensions illuminated when the Ostroms' work is viewed from different perspectives. Throughout her career, Ostrom explored a wide range of theoretical perspectives in developing her approach to institutions and collective choice. She never hesitated to explore a different approach that she believed could contribute to understanding some part of a question of interest. As a result, her work was of interest to a wide range of theorists and methodologists outside her theoretical circle. However, the Bloomington School approach might be strengthened by incorporating an even broader theoretical lens than Ostrom considered.

Andreas Thiel and Erik Swyngedouw consider the limitations of Ostrom's work on polycentricity from a perspective centered on the problem of power relations. They engage in a unique exercise, combining the perspectives of Ostrom's work on polycentricity with those of Marxist geography, to show that it is difficult to determine whose interests are included in the design of any given polycentric institution by using the Ostromian approach. At the center of this argument, Thiel and Swyngedouw suggest that the political issues of suffrage and distribution or redistribution within a given polycentric institution are not resolved by action within the institution, but instead by some external factors. They suggest that the polycentric political approach cannot adequately capture the dynamic interests of those excluded historically from the institution, and only by reference to the broader political theory literature can social scientists account for the inequality currently present in these institutions. To explore this issue, they distinguish between "politics" and "the political," reserving the latter for more fundamental issues of how society is ordered. They suggest that the inability to address the critical issue of institutional change when politics is marked by an asymmetry of power limits the generalizability of the Ostroms' institutional approach.

Aurelian Craiutu considers his own experience encountering the Ostromian method as an outsider who examines self-governance in the Tocquevillian tradition. He provides a personal lens into how the Ostroms, along with the entire Ostrom Workshop family, brought people together from many disciplines to create a richer community of scholarship. The Ostroms' interest in Tocquevillian forms of self-governance and association (especially Vincent Ostrom's interest) shaped the way in which they approached institutional analysis and provided a bridge to Craiutu's own work on Tocqueville and moderation. They recognized that diverse communities required diverse ways of organizing how community services and governance might best be carried out. Instead of proposing a single set of policies, the Ostroms focused on classes of rules and decisions that could vary depending on community preferences and cultural context.

Craiutu suggests that these eclectic interests in institutions, methodological approaches, and politics allowed the Ostroms to consider problems that other, more directed, and more precise approaches may find impossible. However, this same eclecticism also limits the extent to which their work has affected broader political theory as deeply as it might otherwise. Additionally, Craiutu notes the empirical challenge posed by the high demands of citizenship that the Ostroms' Tocquevillian approach requires and the realities of modern democracy. It is unlikely that these demands will be met as the Ostroms envisioned, and Craiutu wonders to what extent their optimistic outcomes can be retained if those conditions are not met.

The Bloomington School was built on the idea of relentless contestation as a way of improving scholarship and moving social science forward. The Ostroms and their students and collaborators valued engagement with alternative viewpoints—some of them radically diverging from the Bloomington paradigm—and they constantly revisited their own positions, reconsidering them in the light of new evidence or of the new relevant theoretical developments. It is likely, therefore, that Elinor and Vincent Ostrom would have very much appreciated the contributions to this volume as a way to identify and explore remaining tensions in their work and to improve the applicability and reach of their contribution and its legacy.

NOTES

1. In addition to the Nobel Prize in Economics, Elinor Ostrom received many recognitions, including fellow, American Academy of Arts and Sciences, elected 1991; fellow, American Academy of Political and Social Science, elected 2008; member, American Philosophical Society, elected 2006; fellow, American Association for the Advancement of Science, elected 2001; member, National Academy of Sciences, elected 2001; Elazar Distinguished Federalism Scholar Award, American Political Science Association, 2009; Diamond Jubilee Award for Lifetime Achievement in Political Studies, Political Studies Association of the United Kingdom, 2010; Adam Smith Award, Association of Private Enterprise Education, 2011; Frank E. Seidman Distinguished Award in Political Economy, 1997; president, American Political Science Association, 1996–97; president, International Association for the Study of Common Property,

1990–91; and president, Public Choice Society, 1982–84. Likewise, Vincent Ostrom was professionally recognized many times, including the John Gaus Award for a lifetime of exemplary scholarship in the joint tradition of political science and public administration, American Political Science Association, 2005; Daniel Elazar Distinguished Scholar Award, American Political Science Association, 1991; Robert O. Anderson Award for the vital role in the drafting of the Natural Resource Article in the Alaskan Constitution; editor-in-chief, Public Administration Review, 1963–66; president, Public Choice Society, 1967–69; and corecipient with Elinor Ostrom of the Fund for the Study of Spontaneous Order's Lifetime Achievement Award, Atlas Economic Research Foundation, 2003.

2. Analyses by several of the authors included in this volume expand on the effect of Ostrom's work and the Bloomington School more broadly. Their own books are a testimony to the range and depth of Ostrom's contribution to political economy. See, for instance, Aligica (2014), Aligica and Boettke (2009), Cole and McGinnis (2015a, 2015b, 2017, 2018), McGinnis (1999), Munger (2010), and Tarko (2017).

3. Other communities might produce quite different arrangements and use slightly different institutional rules to achieve consensus.

REFERENCES

Aligica, Paul Dragos. 2014. *Institutional Diversity and Political Economy: The Ostroms and Beyond*. New York: Oxford University Press.

Aligica, Paul Dragos, and Peter J. Boettke. 2009. *Challenging Institutional Analysis and Development: The Bloomington School*. New York: Routledge.

Boettke, Peter J. 2010. "Is the Only Form of 'Reasonable Regulation' Self Regulation?: Lessons from Lin Ostrom on Regulating the Commons and Cultivating Citizens." *Public Choice* 143 (3-4): 283–91.

Cole, Daniel H., and Michael D. McGinnis, eds. 2015a. *Elinor Ostrom and the Bloomington School of Political Economy: Vol. 1, Polycentricity in Public Administration and Political Science*. Lanham, MD: Lexington Books.

———, eds. 2015b. *Elinor Ostrom and the Bloomington School of Political Economy: Vol. 2, Resource Governance*. Lanham, MD: Lexington Books.

———, eds. 2017. *Elinor Ostrom and the Bloomington School of Political Economy: Vol. 3, A Framework for Policy Analysis*. Lanham, MD: Lexington Books.

———, eds. 2018. *Elinor Ostrom and the Bloomington School of Political Economy: Vol. 4, Policy Applications and Extensions*. Lanham, MD: Lexington Books.

McGinnis, Michael D., ed. 1999. *Polycentricity and Local Public Economies: Readings from the Workshop in Political Theory and Policy Analysis*. Ann Arbor: University of Michigan Press.

Munger, Michael, ed. 2010. "Special Issue: Elinor Ostrom and the Diversity of Institutions." *Public Choice* 143 (3-4): 263–352.

NobelPrize.org. n.d. "Elinor Ostrom—Facts." *The Nobel Prize,* https://www.nobelprize.org /prizes/economic-sciences/2009/ostrom/facts/.

Ostrom, Elinor. 1965. "Public Entrepreneurship: A Case Study in Ground Water Basin Management." PhD dissertation, University of California, Los Angeles.

———. 1986. "An Agenda for the Study of Institutions." *Public Choice* 48 (1): 3–25.

———. 1990. *Governing the Commons: The Evolution of Institutions for Collective Action.* Cambridge, UK: Cambridge University Press.

———. 1998. "A Behavioral Approach to the Rational Choice Theory of Collective Action: Presidential Address, American Political Science Association, 1997." *American Political Science Review* 92 (1): 1–22.

———. 2005. *Understanding Institutional Diversity.* Princeton, NJ: Princeton University Press.

———. 2006. "Converting Threats into Opportunities." The 2005 James Madison Award Lecture. *PS: Political Science and Politics* 39 (1): 3–12.

———. 2010a. "The Challenge of Self-Governance in Complex Contemporary Environments." *Journal of Speculative Philosophy* 24 (4): 316–32.

———. 2010b. "Beyond Markets and States: Polycentric Governance of Complex Economic Systems." *American Economic Review* 100 (3): 641–72. Reprinted in Ostrom and Ostrom 2014.

Ostrom, Elinor, and Vincent Ostrom. 2004. "The Quest for Meaning in Public Choice." *American Journal of Economics and Sociology* 63 (1): 105–47.

———. 2014. *Choice, Rules and Collective Action: The Ostroms on the Study of Institutions and Governance,* edited by Filippo Sabetti and Paul Dragos Aligica. Colchester, UK: ECPR Press.

Ostrom, Elinor, Roger B. Parks, and Gordon P. Whitaker. 1978. *Patterns of Metropolitan Policing.* Cambridge, MA: Ballinger.

Ostrom, Elinor, and Gordon P. Whitaker. 1974. "Community Control and Governmental Responsiveness: The Case of Police in Black Neighborhoods." In D. Rogers and W. Halley, eds., "Improving the Quality of Urban Management." *Urban Affairs Annual Reviews* 8: 303–34. Reprinted in McGinnis 1999, 203–31.

Ostrom, Vincent. 1989. *The Intellectual Crisis in American Public Administration,* 2nd ed. Tuscaloosa: University of Alabama Press.

———. 1997. *The Meaning of Democracy and the Vulnerability of Democracies: A Response to Tocqueville's Challenge.* Ann Arbor: University of Michigan Press.

————. 2001. "The Challenge of Modernity: Seeing Like Citizens." *Good Society* 10 (2): 40–41.

————. 2007. *The Political Theory of a Compound Republic: Designing the American Experiment*, 3rd rev. ed. Lanham, MD: Lexington Books.

Ostrom, Vincent, Charles M. Tiebout, and Robert Warren. 1961. "The Organization of Government in Metropolitan Areas: A Theoretical Inquiry." *American Political Science Review* 55 (4): 831–42.

Tarko, Vlad. 2017. *Elinor Ostrom: An Intellectual Biography*. London: Rowman & Littlefield.

THEORETICAL TENSIONS

CHAPTER ONE

BEYOND A PRECARIOUS BALANCE

IMPROVING THE SCIENTIFIC RIGOR AND POLICY RELEVANCE OF INSTITUTIONAL ANALYSES FROM THE BLOOMINGTON SCHOOL

MICHAEL D. MCGINNIS

The Bloomington School of political economy, or institutional analysis, has produced a corpus of research ranging from the highly abstract to the deeply descriptive, from representations of game models and laboratory experiments to historic accounts of the development of water management institutions in specific locations, with many variants in between. Yet, to a remarkable extent, it all fits together as a relatively coherent whole.[1]

Elinor Ostrom and others in the Bloomington School tradition have done institutional analysis in a way that strikes a uniquely productive balance overall between scientific rigor and policy relevance. That point is one of the key topics my colleague Jimmy Walker and I emphasized in our assessment (2010, 299) of Ostrom's contributions to scholarship after she won the 2009 Nobel Prize in Economics:

> The methodological legacy of the research programs that underlie Lin's success includes three key characteristics: insistence on both scientific rigor and policy relevance, openness to multiple techniques of empirical and formal

analysis, and sensitivity to nested levels of analysis. An enduring legacy of her work is that the research literature on CPR [common-pool resources] situations now routinely encompasses field studies, experimental methods, mathematical modeling, statistical analyses, and agent-based simulations, each of which brings unique insights to this common object of study. (Ostrom et al. 1994; Poteete, Janssen, and Ostrom 2010)

However, the balance achieved was rarely good enough to satisfy strong advocates of either rigor or relevance. If the criticism from both sides is left unchallenged, it might undermine the long-term sustainability of the Bloomington School as a recognizable tradition of institutional analysis. In this chapter, I explain the reasoning behind this balance and suggest ideas for future elaboration.

It is generally presumed that rigor and relevance are in constant tension with each other, because highly rigorous models cannot match the level of policy relevance in analyses finely tuned to the complexities of local conditions. I propose ways in which scholars working within the Bloomington School tradition can simultaneously improve their performance in terms of both rigor and relevance. By bringing into play a wider range of relevant actors and institutional obstacles to collective action, while using similar methods to represent the behavior of all these actors, scholars may be able to explain in new ways the logical structure of a specific empirical setting, while still making the simplifying assumptions needed to examine interactions among so many actors with diverse interests and resource capabilities.

This chapter is organized into seven sections. The first section introduces tensions between rigor and relevance and in the study of political institutions and policy analysis more generally, and the second briefly reviews examples of research and policy analyses from the Bloomington School that illustrate various mixtures of analytical rigor and policy relevance. In the third section, I highlight a hidden theme running throughout this body of research and policy analysis. Briefly, an analyst can be said to be engaged in *strategic rigor* whenever both rigor and relevance are considered essential goals, and each goal is pursued in a way that also supports the other goal, thus balancing these seemingly contradictory goals. The fourth section illustrates how this balance is revealed in the research findings that Elinor Ostrom summarized in her most influential work, *Governing the Commons* (Ostrom 1990), and in the Institutional Analysis and Development (IAD) framework of complexly interconnected action situations that guided her investigations. In the fifth section, attention shifts to the Social-Ecological System (SES) framework she developed to organize further research on closely coupled social-ecological systems. I argue that too much of this research has focused on compiling long lists of potentially relevant social and ecological variables and suggest an alternative research strategy in which these variables are interpreted as "pointers" to other sites of interaction, or *action situations*, where the values of those variables have been determined (and thus could conceivably be changed). The sixth section outlines a reinterpretation of the mode of institutional analysis pioneered by Elinor and Vincent Ostrom as a systematic process of zooming in and out of a complex network of interrelated action situations. I argue that both institutional analysts and the participants in the processes those analysts study are, in effect, navigating their way through a dynamic and polycentric landscape of interrelated action situations as they seek better policy intervention. The final section discusses how researchers continue to innovate on the foundations laid by the Ostroms, and it draws out potential connections between that work and the new conceptualization offered here.

My hope is that this chapter can help researchers and practitioners become more confident in their application of what is at best an imperfectly rigorous process of analyzing their own decision processes and the decisions made by individuals and groups most directly affected by policy outcomes. By implementing this mode of analysis in a more systematic manner, both policy analysts and active participants in policy processes could more effectively identify points of intervention that can strengthen the collective knowledge of those processes or improve the outcomes that emerge from those processes, and, in some circumstances, accomplish both goals at the same time.

RIGOR AND RELEVANCE IN POLITICAL SCIENCE AND POLICY ANALYSIS

My home discipline of political science (and especially the subfield of public policy) has a long-standing tradition of controversies concerning the relative importance given to scientific rigor and policy relevance. Many in political science have sought to improve the level of rigor in the analyses of policy settings, even if that comes at a cost to its influence on practical politics. Others have decried the technical jargon that such research seems to require

TABLE 1.1: DISTINGUISHING CHARACTERISTICS OF SCIENTIFIC RIGOR
AND POLICY RELEVANCE

Scientific Rigor	Policy Relevance
Seeks to make new contributions to the existing body of scientific knowledge	Seeks practical suggestions for improvement of existing conditions
Pursues general explanations, which may be based on simplified models or generalizations	Provides contextually rich descriptions, which may be overly detailed or presumed unique
Follows a systematic mode of analysis that should be easily replicable	Clearly communicates conclusions to relevant publics and other audiences
Clearly defines concepts and specific measures and indicators used	Clearly states goals and recommends particular plan of action
May overemphasize technical detail at cost of broader communication	May reinforce biases and undermine more productive open discourse
Ideally, uses all appropriate methods; in practice, relies on a more limited range	Relies on familiar forms of public discourse, political organization, and policy tools
Uses research design to select cases in ways that support valid inference	Selects examples and emphasizes aspects that support policy recommendations
Ideally, investigates full logical implications; in practice, avoids unneeded complexity	Ideally, engages with all parties affected; in practice, tends to adopt one point of view

and advocated for clearer communication to nonacademic audiences.[2] Elinor Ostrom contributed to these debates, arguing strongly in favor of improved rigor in research (see Ostrom 1976, 1982, 2005a, 2005b) and increased efforts to improve civic education by incorporating into educational materials a better understanding of research findings on collective action and self-governance (see Ostrom 1996, 2002, 2006a, 2006b).

Any attempt to review in detail the literature on rigor versus relevance would leave too little space for the core line of argument I develop here, so I base my discussion on an informal list of the primary attributes typically associated with rigorous or relevant modes of policy analysis. Table 1.1 summarizes key characteristics often used to evaluate the quality of research on the grounds of rigor versus relevance. I have arranged these points to highlight the contrast between respective characteristics listed together in the same row.

For an analysis to be deemed rigorous in a scientific sense, all steps of the research process, including the initial statement of the research problem to be resolved and the hypotheses to be examined, need to be clearly stated. All concepts need to be measured, and the procedures for these measures need to be explicitly stated. Researchers need to select cases for comparison in ways that make it more likely that any conclusions they draw from the comparisons can be generalized to a broader population. Doing so requires that the researchers pay careful attention to selecting a research design that will enable them to make valid inferences to broader settings. Researchers should fully develop the logical implications of their preferred and alternative explanations and test these implications in a systematic manner. Because each discipline develops its own set of concepts and shorthand labels for complex procedures to facilitate communication among its members, the resulting technical language or jargon may preclude clear communication to anyone outside that intellectual community.

In sharp contrast, the whole point of policy-relevant research is to contribute to ongoing debates over alternative solutions to problems that the broader public sees. Institutional analysts working to enhance the relevance of their research findings must take great care to make it easy for nonexperts to understand the logic behind their policy recommendations. As a result, they should frame their arguments by using familiar terms from contemporary public discourse and connect recommendations to the policy tools already available to officials in existing political institutions. For policy problems that require more creative solutions, an analyst/advocate should clearly explain how those solutions might be implemented. Ideally, policy analysts will carefully examine arguments on all sides of a particular controversy, but as a matter of practicality, no one researcher can be entirely objective.

These two clusters of desired characteristics need not stand in direct opposition to each other in all settings. Because the results of rigorously conducted empirical research can be used by proponents of different policy responses to evaluate alternative solutions to real-world policy problems, good science can contribute to good policy. But the political reality is that perceptions and interests often matter more than the current level of scientific understanding, especially if scientists studying a particular set of processes do not share a clear consensus. The points listed in the right-hand column of table 1.1 highlight the central importance that policy advocates attach to getting their preferred policies enacted versus the factors in the left column that emphasize getting the science right.

I admit these characterizations of analytical rigor and policy relevance are oversimplified, perhaps to the point of parody. Even so, they serve as bookends for the full range of work found within policy-related disciplines and professions.

Elinor Ostrom participated in research projects that range across the full spectrum, from rigorous formal models and laboratory experiments (Weissing and Ostrom 1993; Ostrom 1998) to highly detailed case analyses (Ostrom 1965, 2011b), but the bulk of her most influential research effectively combined both rigor and relevance, as she understood those criteria. Adherents of the Bloomington School can be found near both sides of this extreme, but a high proportion of this work maintains a balance somewhere in between. The next section highlights examples of various balances found within this tradition.

FINDING BALANCE IN THE BLOOMINGTON SCHOOL

The classic 1961 article by Vincent Ostrom, Charles Tiebout, and Robert Warren (hereafter OTW) introduced the concept of a "polycentric system of governance" to the political science and public policy literature. OTW used this concept to describe the underlying logic behind the high level of complexity and duplication of effort that is evident to any observer of metropolitan areas in the United States. Proponents of urban reform decried this complexity as inefficient and wasteful, and they advocated consolidating governing units into a single comprehensive system at the level of the metropolitan region as a whole.

Vincent Ostrom and his colleagues were not convinced that consolidation was the best solution. They appreciated the benefits of maintaining units at multiple scales of aggregation to provide for all relevant public goods, because different scales of production would be efficient for different specific goods. They offered a conceptually rich framework, one that inspired a long tradition of subsequent research into different forms of metropolitan governance (see McGinnis 1999b; Oakerson 1999; Oakerson and Parks 2011; Feiock 2009). However, their argument here was not stated in a rigorous manner; nor did they pay any attention to how one might measure their core concept of polycentricity, which remains a difficult nut to crack (Carlisle and Gruby 2017; Blomquist, Thiel, and Garrick 2019; Van Zeben and Bobić 2019).

In 1965, Vincent and Elinor Ostrom obtained faculty positions in the Department of Political Science at Indiana University, Bloomington. In 1973 they established the Workshop in Political Theory and Policy Analysis as a home for interdisciplinary research on institutions and public choice (Mitchell 1988; Aligica and Boettke 2009). Elinor Ostrom led the first extended effort to subject the normative assertions made by OTW (1961) to rigorous empirical tests. She led a research team of faculty and students that undertook an extensive comparative analysis of police services in different units in Indianapolis, Indiana, just an hour's drive north of Bloomington. The researchers began by developing multiple measures of different aspects of police services, and they selected communities for study on the basis of sound principles of research design (see the papers collected in McGinnis 1999b).

In short, this team of Workshop researchers concluded that there were indeed advantages to allowing small jurisdictions to control some aspects of police work (or other forms of public services) while assigning other tasks requiring various forms of coordination to larger units. Their findings can be related to the policy of "community policing," but as it turned out, this particular research project did not have much effect on public discourse on this policy area (Boettke, Palagashvili, and Lemke 2013; Boettke, Lemke, and Palagashvili 2016).

Ironically, the OTW (1961) article did not attract much attention from policymakers either, even though its core point about the need for complex networks of governing units now seems so central in the public administration literature and practice on collaborative governance and other forms of cross-sector coordination (McGinnis and Ostrom 2012). An important step toward making this concept more attractive to analysts and practitioners in this area was supplied by Feiock (2009), who developed an Institutional Collective Action (ICA) framework in which the primary actors are conceptualized as public officials acting as agents for public, private, and community organizations operating at different scales. The ICA framework delivers an effective balance between relevance and rigor by providing conceptual clarity to the range of cross-sector collaborations found in different metropolitan areas. For example, Swann and Kim (2018) use this framework to draw explicit practical lessons for public officials charged with the responsibility of managing fragmented governments.

Vincent Ostrom (1953a, 1953b) began his career as an expert on water resource law and policy. As a political theorist, he contributed to the classical liberal tradition of seeing constitutional restraints on the arbitrary abuse of executive power as absolutely critical to the sustainability of democracy. In particular, he expressed deep skepticism toward any effort by national leaders to design comprehensive plans for the future evolution of a complex political economic system, because doing so would require a nearly unlimited cognitive capacity for information gathering and analysis as well as an unreasonably naïve expectation of disinterestedness on the part of the planners (Ostrom 1994, 1997, 2008a, 2008b). But these works did not provide readers much in the way of practical policy advice.

Governing the Commons (Ostrom 1990) is by far the most accessible and influential example of policy-relevant research from the Bloomington School. Other noteworthy examples of policy-focused works in the Bloomington School tradition include Vincent Ostrom (1953a, 1953b, 2008a, 2008b), Elinor Ostrom (1965, 1976, 1992, 2010b, 2011b), Ostrom, Schroeder, and Wynne (1993), Oakerson (1999), Gibson et al. (2005), and Andersson and Ostrom (2008). In addition, Polski and Ostrom (2017), Polski (2017), and McGinnis (2017) go through the steps necessary to apply the mode of institutional analysis to the study of specific policy problems.

Even though the phrase "policy analysis" was included in the original name of what is now known simply as "the Ostrom Workshop," actual policymakers, as traditionally conceived, play surprisingly minor roles in most publications from scholars associated with the Ostrom Workshop. Instead, community leaders and ordinary citizens take center stage, especially in Ostrom's highly influential research on community-based management of common-pool resources (Ostrom 1990, 2010a). Although widely praised for raising general awareness of the ability of self-governing communities located in remote regions of the world to solve complex problems of collective action, this work has been criticized for not taking into account the gross inequities of power that can sharply curtail the effectiveness of local reforms (Clement 2010). Also, Frank Baumgartner (2010, 575), a prominent policy scholar, noted in his contribution to a symposium on *Governing the Commons* that "Elinor Ostrom pays little attention to many issues that I have found central to how policies evolve," yet he praises her PhD dissertation (Ostrom 1965) as an excellent example of policy-relevant analysis. Contributors from other subfields of political science similarly find selected aspects of her research to be compelling, but none have considered her a leader in their own subfield (McGinnis 2011c).

Elinor Ostrom's preferred style of research contributed to her marginality in the discipline of political science. Except for her early research on police services (Ostrom 1976; McGinnis 1999b) and her later experimental research (Ostrom et al. 1994; Ostrom 1998), she rarely stated explicit hypotheses or tested them in any traditionally rigorous manner. Instead, she devoted careful attention to the framework for analysis within which she was working, rather than using those concepts to build a causal theory or formal model (McGinnis

1996, 2011c). She was the primary driving force behind the initial development and subsequent revisions of the IAD framework (Ostrom 1989, 2005b,
2010a), which has become one of the most prominent theoretical perspectives
in scholarly research on public policy (Weible and Sabatier 2017; Cole and
McGinnis 2017). Later in her career Ostrom (2007, 2009) introduced the
SES framework, which fine-tuned the IAD framework to apply more directly
to the study of resource systems.

Ostrom envisioned both frameworks as a means whereby scholars from
multiple disciplines could more effectively communicate with each other as
they used diverse disciplinary and methodological perspectives to better understand complex policy settings. She expected that anyone using the frameworks
as a foundational set of concepts would combine those concepts into different theories or models that specify causal relationships among the concepts
in clearly defined circumstances. As frameworks, they were intentionally
designed to fall short of the gold standard of a clearly specified formal model
or a fully developed causal theory. Even so, it seems to me that Ostrom and
others in this tradition have systematically neglected opportunities to expand
the logical depth or completeness of the IAD or SES frameworks.

For example, when Sue Crawford and Elinor Ostrom (1995) added a delta
parameter to a rational actor's utility function, to represent the intrinsic benefits or costs of following or violating some normative rule, they did not follow
up by explicitly incorporating the actors supervising the socialization processes
through which the individual actors had internalized those normative rules.
Yet Ostrom also faced constraints on the level of complexity that her colleagues would accept in a "mere" framework. For example, in her presidential
address to the Public Choice Society (Ostrom 1986), her introduction of an
"action situation" as a generalization of the formal definition of a game model
was not welcomed by scholars present at that lecture, because her concept was
too complicated to be fully represented using mathematical notation. Similar
concerns about the lack of mathematical or statistical precision in Ostrom's
frameworks were expressed by some economists who criticized her selection as
a corecipient of the 2009 Nobel Prize in Economics.

A unique exemplar of the efforts by Bloomington School researchers to
explicitly connect rigorous and relevant modes of research in a single project can be found in *Rules, Games, and Common-Pool Resources* (Ostrom et
al. 1994). The first part of this book generalizes game models to laboratory
settings in which experimental subjects are allowed to discuss their common

interests and establish institutional procedures for monitoring and sanctioning each other's behavior. The remainder of the book consists of case studies of real-world field settings in which communities of farmers, fishers, or other resource users learned to resolve similar dilemmas through their own efforts. This book highlights the commonalities behind these social dilemmas in natural and artificial settings, but the specific lessons from these very different two modes of analysis were not entirely integrated, beyond their common grounding in the IAD framework.

Elinor Ostrom combined rigor and relevance in a similar manner when she led a multiyear collaborative research project focused on comparative analyses of forested areas. Scholars and students associated with the Institute for Forestry Resources and Institutions (IFRI) developed and field-tested a rigorous method of measuring the characteristics of forested areas and their user communities in Bolivia, Ecuador, Guatemala, India, Mali, Nepal, Uganda, and the United States. The central goal was to understand which combinations of institutional arrangements are most likely to support sustainable development of forestry resources. Rigorous comparison lies at the heart of their method: the coding form includes measures of more than a hundred variables on the physical, economic, and institutional characteristics of specific forested regions. Furthermore, the data and analytical conclusions from the IFRI project were made freely available to local people in a user-friendly form meant to aid local efforts to improve living conditions. However, its broader policy relevance (beyond any effect on the local communities themselves) lies primarily in the contribution these research projects made to the conclusions Ostrom presented in *Governing the Commons*.

Understanding Institutional Diversity (Ostrom 2005b) is the most analytically rigorous explication of the entire analytical apparatus of the IAD framework and how it might best be used as a tool for social scientific research. More traditionally rigorous examples of research from this tradition have been published in social scientific or policy analysis journals, and the ones collected in McGinnis (1999b, 2000) demonstrate the range of rigorous models and statistical analyses that scholars have produced. Poteete, Janssen, and Ostrom (2010) is a more widely accessible overview of the range of interdisciplinary research projects that scholars have built upon the IAD and SES frameworks, with particular attention to practicalities of coordination within teams of researchers.

Precise use of language is essential for purposes of rigor, but it can get in the way of policy relevance. The most important example from the Bloomington

School tradition is the word *provision*, which OTW (1961) took great care to distinguish from the actual *production* of a public good. Provision is typically the responsibility of a public entrepreneur, who needs to arrange for the production or purchase of any collective good to be consumed by the groups that the entrepreneur serves. (Provision does not play such a role in the exchange of private goods, because the purchaser is typically also the consumer.) Or provision can be done by the consumers themselves, as in the common-pool resource setting, where provision includes efforts by resource users to build or maintain infrastructure needed to extract resources from the common pool.

The problem with respect to unclear communication to mainstream policy scholars is that the term *provision* is so close to *service provider*, which generally is used for a person who delivers the services, but who would have to be called a producer in Workshop terminology. Perhaps a better word would have been *provisioning*, in the sense of gathering supplies in preparation for a long journey or some other collective endeavor. Leaders who play this provisioning role also need to find sources of funding and plan how the collective task will be organized as a whole.

Perhaps the biggest obstacle working against the practical influence of this work was that the Ostroms were reluctant to use their research to support any particular position in partisan debates. "No panaceas" was Elinor Ostrom's immediate response to anyone seeking advice on a specific policy problem. Although useful as a summary statement of the Ostroms' underlying attitude, this orientation limited their potential effect on the policy community, which consists of people and organizations endlessly in search of answers. Once her work became widely known, advocates on opposite sides of policy debates used her name to support directly contradictory positions, suggesting that neither side had fully understood her profound appreciation of the intrinsic value of practical problem-solving and the institutional diversity that will naturally result from those efforts (Ostrom 2005a, 2010a; McGinnis 2011c; Cole 2014; Sarker and Blomquist 2019).

In sum, the Ostroms pursued a unique vision of policy relevance. Within the disciplines of political science or policy studies, researchers often decry the lack of attention paid to the results of their research by major policymakers operating at the national or international level. Although both Elinor and Vincent Ostrom did direct some of their work toward those audiences, for the most part they focused on groups and communities of individuals whose own lives were directly affected by policy outcomes. Policy analysts can too easily forget that local communities retain a significant degree of agency even in demanding circumstances.

In a guest editorial in the January 1994 issue of *Research & Creative Activity* (a periodical published by the Indiana University Graduate School), Vincent and Elinor Ostrom succinctly articulated their unique attitude toward policy relevance:

> Once we understood the logic of the use of land and water in paddy agriculture, for example, we came to appreciate the marvel of hillside terraces in Nepal and elsewhere that would justify their being considered among the Wonders of the World. In a contrary way, intelligent people can perversely reduce urban landscapes to rubble. How people think of themselves, structure their relationships with others, and pursue the opportunities that they see as available to them may make the difference between a sustainable and meaningful way of life and one reduced to rubble. Working with others to gain mutual advantage under changing conditions of life requires substantial use of knowledge, moral sensitivity, skills, and intelligence in the exercise of self-organizing and self-governing capabilities. (Quoted in McGinnis 1999a, 25.)

The consequences of their unique perspective are evident throughout their many research projects. In their analysis of metropolitan political systems, OTW (1961) directed analysts to consider the nature of the myriad working relationships with private firms and community leaders who were often most directly involved in the actual production of local public goods. In her PhD dissertation, Elinor Ostrom (1965) focused on the actions of public entrepreneurs serving on local water boards or in community organizations, because their efforts were instrumental in resolving contamination of groundwater in that part of southern California. The 1970s Workshop project on police services demonstrated the critical importance of coproduction—that is, the positive effects of situations in which citizen recipients of public services actively participate in producing those services (McGinnis 1999b).

In *Governing the Commons* Elinor Ostrom clearly articulated the importance of understanding how local communities manage common resources critical to their own survival. Most of them have minimal support or encouragement from public officials or foreign aid agencies. Although the title of a later work, *The Samaritan's Dilemma* (Gibson et al. 2005), highlights the tensions between the conflicting interests of donor and recipient governments in the distribution of assistance, the bulk of the research by that research team focused on how seemingly mundane patterns of employee rotation and advancement shaped the incentives facing lower-level agents within the Swedish International Development Agency. When the team examined how this assistance actually worked out in field settings, they concluded that the core actors in the whole process were contractors (typically Swedish construction firms) hired to build and (perhaps) maintain these projects. In the end, they stressed the need to involve local communities in all aspects of the process from initial proposal to construction and especially to long-term maintenance, to give members of those communities a more meaningful sense of ownership over these projects. Finally, although Elinor Ostrom (2010b, 2012) acknowledged that international agreements can play a positive role in policy responses to global climate change, her recommendations focused instead on encouraging other actors to do whatever they could by direct action, especially local municipalities and individual consumers.

This quick survey of highlights from the Ostrom oeuvre is far from complete, but one consistent message is clear: policy analysts need to pay careful attention to the actual and potential contributions by individuals and groups acting primarily on a local level. To be blunt, this presumption is not a widely shared one within the disciplines of political science or economics.

STRATEGIC RIGOR AND THE RIGOR-RELEVANCE BALANCE IN THE BLOOMINGTON SCHOOL

To understand the unique balance between analytical rigor and policy relevance that characterizes research and policy analysis in the Bloomington School, we need to look closely at the origins of the IAD framework. The first overview of the IAD framework (Kiser and Ostrom 1982) was published as the concluding chapter in an edited volume, *Strategies of Political Inquiry* (Ostrom 1982). This volume also included Ostrom's introductory essay (with the imposing title "Beyond Positivism") and five colloquium papers or distinguished lectures presented in Bloomington during 1978–81. The concluding chapter was written by Ostrom and Larry Kiser, then a postdoc trainee at the Ostrom Workshop. Although Ostrom describes this chapter as an overview of a book-length manuscript she and Kiser were working on, it took her another two decades to complete a full-length volume on the IAD framework (Ostrom 2005b).

In "Beyond Positivism," Ostrom takes as her point of departure a general malaise among political scientists at the time, namely the noticeable lack of any significant accumulation of empirical knowledge after decades of concentrated applications of state-of-the-art scientific methods. Rather than using this malaise as a tool in an ongoing disciplinary debate between the relative merit of quantitative versus qualitative research methodologies, she viewed this situation from a more fundamental vantage point. She argued that the basic problem was that political scientists were too eager to mimic positivism's success at finding explanations in the natural sciences by using the covering law model. But she thought it was simply not reasonable to seek a comparable level (or type) of rigor from the social sciences. Her justification of this position (1982, 14) is worth quoting in some detail.

> Since scholars were trying to find empirical regularities, the major focus for political scientists doing research was on questions of method—of how to operationalize variables adequately and of the proper kind of statistical test to use to assert relationships between variables. These are essential questions of an empirically based political science. But their dominance during the past several decades places the questions of how to describe political relationships in a quantitative manner above how to gain an adequate understanding of the processes involved in the relevant world of inquiry.

In that quotation, Ostrom acknowledges that ensuring valid measurements is an essential prerequisite for the validity of any scientific-based understanding of political processes, but she also points out (1982, 17–18) that too many scholars were too willing to discard traditional wisdom too cavalierly.

> During the 1960s many political scientists accepted, for example, the frequently repeated statement that "political structure doesn't matter." . . . The fact that political variables accounted for a small proportion of the variance in government expenditure levels after economic and social variables had first been entered in multiple regression equations was taken as "proof" that institutional variables did not matter and should not be the subject of a mature science.

Her critique (1982, 18) was based on a sophisticated understanding of both the power and the limitations of any single form of analysis.

The way a process is conceptualized should affect the analytical techniques to be used for estimating statistical parameters in empirical models of that process. Multiple regression techniques were first developed to examine the independent effect of land, labor, and fertilizer in agricultural productivity. Since each of these variables was conceptualized as *independent* and its effect on productivity was *additive,* the general linear model underlying multiple regression was the appropriate theoretical language for stating how these variables would be related to a dependent variable. I seriously doubt that one could find many statements in Hobbes, *The Federalist,* or Tocqueville that conceptualized the effect of institutions in a manner similar to that of fertilizer added to labor and land to produce corn. (Italics in original; internal citations omitted.)

Ostrom concludes that more recent researchers, using different kinds of analytical methods, have empirically demonstrated the significant effects of different institutional arrangements in determining outcomes. After encouraging students and scholars to develop familiarity with a wide range of analytical methods, Ostrom uses examples from the other contributors to demonstrate the effectiveness of nontraditional methods. In particular, Ostrom (1982, 20) draws from Boynton (1982) a general organizing principle for rigorous analysis of social settings:

Boynton's chapter can be viewed as an inquiry into what is the "right type of law" for social scientists. The right type of law, he argues, is highly specific and relates a limited number of variables to each other under stated conditions. The conditions of a theory state the values of other variables that must be closely approximated for the posited theoretical relations to hold among explanatory variables. The "other" variables condition the type of relationships among the explanatory variables stated in the theory. Boynton urges social scientists to try to understand the logic of relatively contained situations where the conditions structuring a situation are specified. His notion, therefore, of theory pertains to the organizing principles used to understand particular types of situations structured in specific ways.

Characteristically, Ostrom concludes her essay on an optimistic note. After admitting that the limited utility of covering laws in social settings will make the accumulation of knowledge in the social sciences a slow and difficult process, she encourages us to accept that "the cumulation we do achieve will be limited in scope to specific types of theoretically defined situations rather than sweeping theories of society as a whole" (Ostrom 1982, 26). She was comfortable with that more limited goal, and the IAD framework she and Kiser introduced in the concluding chapter of that volume was explicitly designed with all these considerations in mind.

I use the phrase *strategic rigor* to encapsulate the balanced combination of rigor and relevance that the Ostroms' work exemplifies. It is rigorous in that researchers should be as systematic as possible in their examination of all factors relevant to a fuller understanding of a particular policy setting. Using *strategic* as a modifier implies that this systematic process must be guided by an overarching goal. As typically understood, the primary goal of scientific research is the accumulation of empirically verified knowledge, as a step toward a more complete understanding of the phenomenon under study. I am convinced that the Ostroms had a different goal in mind—namely, the identification of effective levers of change that could help enable individuals and groups directly affected by that policy setting to find ways to make improvements in their own condition.

Improved scientific knowledge can be a means toward that end, but should not be the primary consideration. We, as scientists and policy analysts, should never ignore the contributions toward positive change that can be made by the traditional array of policymakers: political leaders, public officials, legislators, judges, and other external stakeholders. But we should always be wary of any claims made by analysts or by partisans that they have found the perfect solution to a policy problem. This is why Vincent Ostrom reacted so strongly against "central planning," and why Elinor Ostrom so frequently cautioned that "there are no panaceas."

If the ultimate goal is to learn enough to help communities improve their own circumstances, then we should definitely be interested in learning how that community got into its current situation, as well as what plans it already has discussed for making potential improvements. Thus, we need to investigate the historical background for the current situation and should be open to learning from the people themselves. In addition, we should communicate our conclusions to people in a form they will be able to understand and use. All this may sound simple, but each implication deserves additional explication.

When it comes to history, we will need to understand not just how the current situation has changed over time but also the broader trends or changes in other policy areas that have affected the policy outcomes that concern us. To identify which possible connections to other policy settings we should investigate, we can take clues from the people involved, as well as from our own familiarity with similar kinds of situations in other contexts.

To be able to communicate clearly with the participants affected by the policy we are investigating, we need to remain open to understanding what their goals are—that is, what aspects of the current situation most concern them. Because different stakeholders will emphasize different concerns, we need to take special precautions to make sure that in our efforts to draw out the big picture we do not rely too heavily on our own ideological biases as we force complex details to fit our own expectations. It's critical to realize that the goal in this process of strategic rigor is not to prove ourselves or our policy allies correct, but instead to select an effective path through the many analytical choices open to us.

As policy analysts, we should never expect that the members of any community will always be able to come to a consensus on their primary goals, nor should we expect them to agree with us on any priority goals we might posit for them. In an earlier volume in this series, Levy and Peart (2018) identify the former consideration as "the endogeneity of group goals," which they characterize as a foundational principle of the Virginia School of public choice. They also discuss competing interpretations of whether or not economists should see themselves purely as "truth seekers" or as compromised by private interests as any other policy actor. I realize that many policy analysts are driven by strong policy preferences, but I hope that we can all work to limit the effect of our own ideological preconceptions on the implications of our own analyses.

Institutional analysts should never lose sight of the complexity of competing interests that coexist in any vibrant community. Nor should they be surprised if participants in those policy deliberations reach out to seemingly remote levers of policy change. Analysts need to remain open to exploring leads suggested by community members even if those leads do not make sense within the context of their own scholarly disciplines. For example, whereas a social scientist might seek an explanation focused on identifying the underlying power structure of a situation, or seek a better understanding of the foundational structure of the relevant system, participants are likely to be much more interested in identifying practical options for change, even if they require tracing out a convoluted path connecting seemingly disparate policy settings.

One downside of relying so heavily on pursuing many potentially effective levers for policy reform is that different analysts may end up with quite different conclusions. In other words, the process of strategic rigor may itself demonstrate the path dependence so commonly observed in all types of institutional arrangements. But this is just another reason for institutional analysts to remain humble, by offering their conclusions as provisional suggestions, rather than the final word.

In *Governing the Commons,* Elinor Ostrom framed her famous "design principles" explicitly as tentative clues toward improving the prospects for sustainable solutions, rather than as established facts that can be directly generalized to other policy settings. Institutional analysts would all do well to follow her example. In the remainder of this chapter, I suggest guidelines for institutional analysts hoping to follow her example of strategic rigor in a more effective manner.

LINKING THE IAD FRAMEWORK AND *GOVERNING THE COMMONS*

The IAD framework provided the analytical foundation upon which Elinor Ostrom built a multidisciplinary collaborative research program on community-based management of natural resources for which she was named a corecipient of the 2009 Nobel Prize in Economics. The Nobel committee placed particular emphasis on her research as reported in her highly influential 1990 book, *Governing the Commons.* Although Ostrom makes no explicit use of IAD in that book, she does use an informal discussion of its basic components to frame her overall mode of analysis (Ostrom 1990, 45–57). A closer examination of how the IAD framework shaped her analysis helps illustrate how the IAD framework can be used in practice.

As shown in figure 1.1, the IAD framework represents institutional processes by a series of boxes within which different variables or processes are located. At the heart of the IAD framework is an *action situation,* an abstraction of decision environments in which individuals and corporate actors interact with each other by making choices that jointly determine the outcomes of some particular aspects of a policy question. Individual choices and collective outcomes are influenced by the beliefs and incentives of the relevant individuals, as shaped by the responsibilities and social expectations

FIGURE 1.1: INSTITUTIONAL ANALYSIS AND DEVELOPMENT (IAD) FRAMEWORK

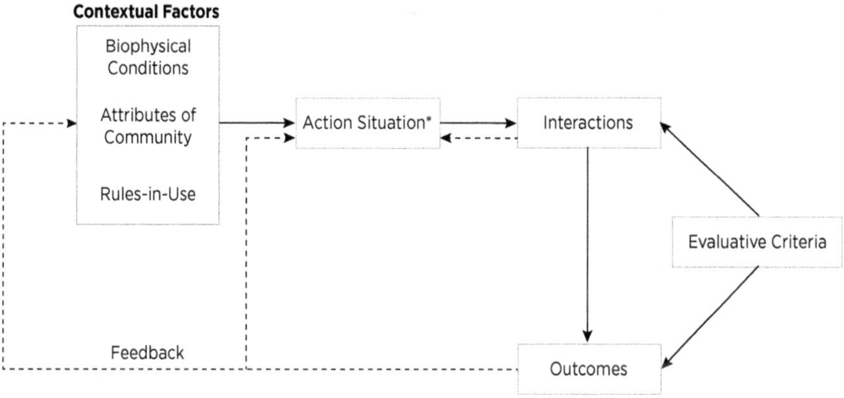

*Earlier versions separated an action situation into actors and an action arena.
Source: Adapted from Ostrom (2010a, 646).

attached to any official position they may hold, and by the information available to them.

The specific nature of the problem faced by actors within a particular action situation is shaped by a list of preexisting *contextual conditions*, grouped for analytical purposes into three categories: (a) the "nature of the good" under consideration, including all relevant biophysical conditions; (b) the social ties and cultural attributes that characterize the individuals interacting on that policy problem; and (c) the existing configuration of laws, regulations, rules, norms, and shared understandings held by the participants to be relevant to deliberations on that policy area. Outcomes from an action situation are evaluated by the relevant actors (some of whom may not have been involved in the original decision). Then feedback from these outcomes and evaluations can reinforce or induce changes in these contextual conditions, which in turn sets the stage for the next iteration of that action situation. In sum, the outcomes from one action situation may change the values of the contextual factors relevant for other related action situations. This means that the contextual conditions are *endogenous* to the never-ending cycles of collective action in many interlinked action situations.

The IAD framework differentiates among three different types (or levels) of action situations, which are referred to as different arenas of choice, or conceptual levels of analysis: (a) *operational-choice* settings in which the choices of the relevant actors directly affect tangible outcomes, (b) policy-making or *collective-choice* settings in which actors shape the rules that constrain actors in operational-choice arenas, and (c) *constitutional-choice* settings in which decisions are made concerning which actors have standing in different choice situations as well as which kinds of alternative institutional mechanisms are available to them as they make their collective deliberations and operational-level choices (Ostrom 2005b, 58–62). In all types of action situations, biophysical, legal-institutional, and sociocultural factors interact in complex ways to shape patterns of interactions and outcomes.

Each action situation denotes a nexus where decision makers jointly confront important decisions about a particular policy concern. As is typical in strategic interactions, potential outcomes are differentially valued by actors with only partial control over the final determination of results. Ostrom (1986, 2005b) explicitly frames an action situation as a generalization of standard game models. To define a game, modelers must specify the actors involved, the information available to them, their options for choice, and how these individual choices jointly generate various outcomes. Similarly, an action situation is configured by interlocking "working components," which she relates (2005b, 188) in the following manner:

> *Participants*, who can either be individuals or any of a wide diversity of organized entities, are assigned to *positions*. In these positions, they choose among *actions* in light of their *information*, the *control* they have over *action-outcome linkages*, and the *benefits and costs* assigned to actions and outcomes. (Italics added.)

The specific nature of each italicized component will have been determined by processes occurring in other settings for strategic interaction—that is, in other action situations, which may be occurring at the same or different levels of choice. Although published descriptions of most applications of the IAD framework include a version of figure 1.1, which can convey the sense of a single action situation existing by itself, the analysis contained in that research tradition has always relied on making connections to other, related action situations (McGinnis 2011b).

Concurrent action situations interact in subtle ways. In particular, the contextual factors that define any given action situation will themselves have been determined by outcomes generated by other action situations. Ostrom

FIGURE 1.2: A NETWORK OF ADJACENT ACTION SITUATIONS

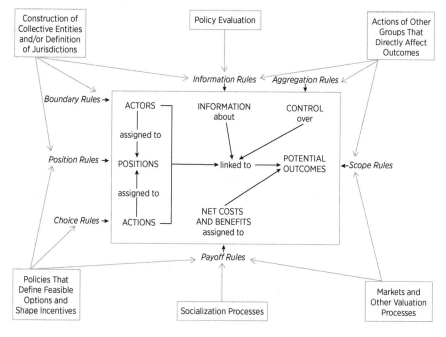

Source: McGinnis 2011b, 54. Interior figure is taken from Ostrom (2005b, 189).

and Ostrom (2004, 134) illustrate how processes of constitutional choice can shape the general context under which collective policy decisions are made, and the outcomes generated by action situations at the collective-choice level can determine the specific conditions under which operational choices are implemented. Individual and collective processes of evaluation are also very important in connecting outcomes to the conditions that will be in place for later decision points. Although evaluative criteria are placed in a box off to the side of figure 1.1, a more complete representation would show that these criteria were determined by processes of collective or constitutional choice occurring in other action situations, and that those criteria are themselves subject to revision in light of experience.

Elsewhere (McGinnis 2011b, 54), I offered a revised representation of the IAD framework in which different kinds of collective- or constitutional-choice processes can influence the working components that constitute an action situation at the operational level. Figure 1.2 shows how a single action situation (including the internal working components as described earlier) may be connected to a series of "adjacent" action situations, each of which has the effect of setting the values for one or more of those working components. I am pleased to say that Elinor Ostrom liked this concept of action situation adjacency so well that she took it into account by revising the representation of the action situations located in the center of the figures she adopted for later versions of the SES framework (Ostrom and Cox 2010; McGinnis and Ostrom 2014).

Each action situation denotes a nexus of strategic interaction in which a group of decision makers jointly confronts important decisions related to some particular policy concern. To use the IAD framework, analysts need to give separate consideration to each of these critical decision nodes. They face the difficult challenge of understanding how multiple action situations interact to jointly produce policy outcomes.

The following sentences from Ostrom (2005b) demonstrate just how profound the implications of this conceptualization of multiple interconnected action situations are for institutional analysis:

▶ Rarely do action situations exist entirely independently of other situations (p. 55).
▶ Where one draws the boundaries on the analysis of linked situations depends on the questions of interest to the analyst (p. 58).
▶ An institutional theorist must self-consciously posit the kind of information participants possess, the relevant preference structure of the participants, and the process they use for choosing among actions. Assumptions about information, preferences, and choice mechanisms are thus the essential components [that] need to be specified in order to generate hypotheses about interactions and outcomes that can be tested in a particular type of action situation or linked set of action situations (p. 99).
▶ To dig under that situation, however, to think about changing it, one needs to know a lot about the underlying structure leading to the social dilemma (p. 189).

Because no action situation sits in isolation but is instead embedded in complex networks of adjacent action situations, there is no such thing as an institution-free context (Cole, Epstein, and McGinnis 2014). Thus, no policy reform can be applied to a completely blank slate. Policy advocates necessarily introduce purposeful interventions into an already complex ecosystem of institutional arrangements.

Inevitably, the resulting networks of adjacent action situations are complex. Even so, this complexity does not prevent participants from engaging in efforts to change the conditions under which they are interacting. For example, actors dissatisfied with the outcome of any particular action situation could engage in "level-shifting strategies" (Ostrom 2005b, 62–64) to seek to influence the outcomes of the collective- or constitutional-choice processes where the basic contours of the focal action situation were established. Because there may be no logical limit to deployment of this strategy, and because each of the working components in any one action situation have been determined by outcomes from adjacent action situations, anyone seeking to use the IAD framework to understand the implications or improve the outcomes of a fully articulated network of action situations may be overwhelmed by the immensity of the analytical task.

However, it is not necessary to know everything about everything before one can make a decision regarding any one specific thing. Thus, it is not necessary to know the entire network of adjacent action situations, so long as the analyst can identify critical deficiencies in the current understanding of the situation, and follow the trail of connections to locate the appropriate and most effective point of intervention.

The primary value to researchers of the IAD framework is the guidance it provides concerning the kinds of factors that need to be examined in situations of pervasive endogeneity, by structuring the types of questions researchers should ask as they work their way through the complexities of those policy settings (Cole and McGinnis 2017). In a self-organized community of resource users who live in a remote area and rarely experience interference from outside actors, the relevant network of adjacent action situations could distill down to a small number of tightly interwoven action situations. It is one reason why this mode of analysis has proven so useful for analysts studying community management of common resources and other forms of self-governance.

By highlighting the configural nature of causal relationships in social settings, this framework implies that the effects of any policy intervention will ramify throughout complex institutional ecologies in ways unlikely to be immediately apparent. In that way, IAD forces policy analysts to dig deeper into the underlying nature of the problem. IAD also sensitizes analysts to follow through the likely consequences of any policy intervention on the subsequent incentives facing relevant actors and institutional processes.

Although Elinor Ostrom intended IAD to be generally applicable, in practice it tends to be most frequently used for certain kinds of policy settings (Heikkila and Cainey 2017). Individuals who find themselves in situations in which they have the capacity to work together to meaningfully shape the conditions under which they interact are likely to find it easier to move from operational decisions to reconsideration of collective choices or to renegotiation of fundamental questions concerning their own societies, and back again. As a consequence, analysts working within this tradition tend to focus on the problem-solving aspect of policy problems and downplay the extent to which policy outcomes are driven by external actors with sufficient power to get strict constraints on feasible policy outcomes. However, Clement (2010) has expanded the IAD framework in a natural manner by adding two categories of contextual variables to highlight the consequences of the social-economic foundations for political power and the ways in which public discourse can be shaped to favor the interests of influential actors.

It should be obvious by now that anyone who thinks the IAD framework is a method as clearly defined, demarcated, and rigorously established as the interpretation of statistical regression is sure to be disappointed. Frameworks offer only a starting point for analysis, and each analyst has to make many decisions along the way to put this framework to use.

To help acquaint new students or others not yet familiar with the concepts and terminology introduced into the field of institutional analysis by the Ostroms and their colleagues, I put together a glossary or guide that provided brief explanations or definitions of these terms, and some sense of how more complex concepts might be applied in practice (McGinnis 2011a). To serve the particular needs of graduate students taking the first-year introductory seminar in institutional analysis, which required students to prepare a term paper applying these methods to a subject matter of their own choosing, I prepared a guide to the steps of analysis that need to be involved. Even in this short overview, the problem remained that the whole thing often seemed overwhelming, with too much needing to be considered from the beginning, before any real progress could be made on better understanding the nature of that policy setting.

To help make the steps more concrete, I wrote a version of that research guide as it might have been applied to the design principles that Ostrom used to summarize her findings in *Governing the Commons* (McGinnis 2017). I'd like to draw upon a few observations from that guide.

The IAD framework directs analysts to focus their attention on a small number of key action situations in which resources, rules, and communities mutually influence each other. In figure 1.1 it looks like an exogenous set of contextual variables determines the values of the working components of an action situation, which then generates patterns of interactions and outcomes. I think a more appropriate interpretation would be to emphasize that the IAD is directed toward identifying a common set of *processes*, rather than variables.

Ostrom was rigorous in her collection of data for the many case studies that she and her collaborators investigated in many pieces of research. But there came a point in *Governing the Commons* when she admits that she simply had to adopt a less rigorous mode of analysis, more integrative and intuitive in nature. I argue that when Ostrom was working her way toward her famous list of design principles for sustainable community-based management of natural resources, she concentrated her attention on four critical, or *focal*, action situations in her case studies: (a) appropriation, (b) provision, (c) rulemaking, and (d) monitoring and sanctioning. Other related action situations were treated more superficially, such as the processes through which new organizations are constructed (or constitution-making; see Ostrom 1989), dispute resolution, evaluative processes, and the slow accumulation of indigenous knowledge. By framing her analyses of these cases through the lens of her IAD-based mindset, she was able to peer deeply into the underlying structure of these interwoven processes.

Further, the IAD framing worked so well in this analysis because, in most of the cases she examined, the same actors were directly involved in all four focal action situations, as well as most of these supplementary (or adjacent) action situations. Each of the design principles specify attributes of one or more of these action situations, attributes that were exhibited by some cases and not others. Also, this range of focal and supplemental action situations covers arenas of choice at each of the operational, collective, and constitutional levels. Finally, each design principle explicitly connects to factors from one or more of the three categories of contextual variables.

Consider what might be the case if the core processes of rulemaking, monitoring, and sanctioning are dominated by different agencies within a national government. Several problems can be expected: the rules may be poor fits to local circumstances, monitors may be easily bribed by those seeking to violate the rules, and sanctioning may be implemented so harshly that it deepens distrust between local community members and government officials. On the other hand, if all three of those processes point to an array of activities through which local community members are able to participate directly in rulemaking, monitoring, and sanctioning, then several of Ostrom's design principles are likely to be satisfied. To take one example, if the magnitude of a sanction is determined by people from the local community, they are more likely to show mercy toward fellow citizens who went outside the rules because they found themselves under extreme pressure to do so, but who would like to remain a valued member of that community. If sanctioning is done remotely, then there is likely to be little, if any, consideration of the need to maintain a viable sense of community.

Typically, comparative case studies result in conclusions concerning which explanatory variables can be inferred to have the strongest influence on the outcomes of those cases. In *Governing the Commons,* the primary outcome variable concerned the long-term sustainability of institutional arrangements for managing those resources. Other researchers, in related projects, identify a relatively small number of variables that proved especially important as determinants of stable regimes of resource management. To take a frequently cited example, Agrawal (2001) lists 30 variables as being the "key enabling conditions" for the successful operation of common property institutions. More recently, in the Social-Ecological System Meta-Analysis Database (SESMAD) project, resource management, and international relations researchers worked together to identify the factors most conducive to successful collective action among actors engaged in local or global policy settings (Cox 2014; Epstein et al. 2014; Fleischman et al. 2014).[3]

For Elinor Ostrom, the critical factor was not the values of the variables per se. Rather, it was the extent to which the overall configuration of institutional arrangements satisfied conditions in what she described as design principles (Ostrom 1990; Cox, Arnold, and Villamayor-Tomás 2010). For her, the essence of institutional analysis lies in appreciating the configural nature of the effects of what may seem to be isolated variables, but whose effects cannot be understood without understanding the configuration of their interactions.

REVEALING ECOLOGIES OF GOVERNANCE WITH THE SES FRAMEWORK

In collaboration with colleagues from different disciplines, Elinor Ostrom (2007, 2009) led the development of a complex analytical framework intended to provide a more comprehensive approach to the study of closely coupled systems of complex human-environment interactions, or social-ecological systems. This Social-Ecological System (SES) framework was designed to give equal weight to both the social and ecological sides, whereas the IAD framework focused its attention on the social-institutional side of policy problems.[4]

The SES framework was originally optimized for application to a relatively well-defined domain of common-pool resource management situations in which *resource users* extract *resource units* from a *resource system.* The resource users also provide for the maintenance of the resource system according to rules and procedures determined by an overarching *governance system* and in the context of *related ecological systems* and *broader social-political-economic settings.* The processes of extraction and maintenance were identified as among the most important forms of *interactions and outcomes* that were located in the very center of this framework.

The IAD and SES frameworks are closely related, but it's safe to say that the SES framework has been having a much broader effect. One critical contribution of the IAD framework is its insistence that no action situation occurs in isolation; instead, each action situation points outward to other action situations in which the defining components of that focal action situation have been determined (McGinnis 2011b). A graphical representation of this recognition of the concurrent operation of multiple, overlapping action situations lies at the very center of the SES framework as Elinor Ostrom presented it during her Nobel Prize in Economics lecture (Ostrom 2010a), reproduced as figure 1.3 in this chapter.

In practice, however, most researchers have tended to focus on identifying lists of variables to be included in the first-tier categories of resource users, resource units, resource systems, and governance systems (Partelow 2018). The action-situation-based category of interactions and outcomes has received considerably less attention, despite its central location in all SES figures. Too few analysts using the SES framework follow the lead of the IAD framework by carefully identifying the small number of critical processes that should

FIGURE 1.3: SOCIAL AND ECOLOGICAL SYSTEM (SES) FRAMEWORK

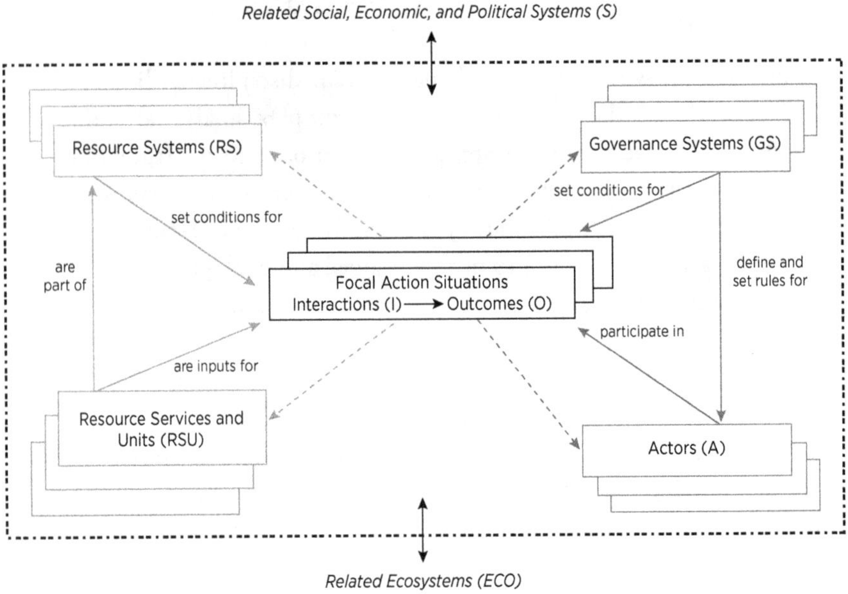

Related Social, Economic, and Political Systems (S)

Resource Systems (RS)

Governance Systems (GS)

set conditions for

set conditions for

are
part of

define and
set rules for

Focal Action Situations
Interactions (I) ⟶ Outcomes (O)

participate in

are inputs for

Resource Services and
Units (RSU)

Actors (A)

Related Ecosystems (ECO)

Note: Solid arrows show direct link and dashed arrows show feedback.
Source: Adapted from McGinnis and Ostrom (2014).

serve as the focal points of their analysis, and then building outward from that foundation.

Many researchers rely on the SES framework to help them generate a list of variables as the end product for their analysis, but these lists should be seen as only an initial step in a longer process of investigation. It is those later steps that could make the difference in efforts to improve both the rigor and the relevance of this mode of analysis.

Variables identified as critical contextual determinants of a focal action situation should be understood as *pointers* to *other* adjacent action situations, specifically to those action situations in which the values of those variables have been determined. Each contextual variable may point to a distinct action situation that determined its current value, or several variables may have been determined in the same action situation (or within densely interconnected ones). In either case, following these variables to their sources will force analysts to address the deeper foundations of the policy setting to which their attention was first drawn.

Once an institutional analyst has identified the dynamic processes through which the key elements of a policy setting have been shaped, that analyst can also begin to identify a range of opportunities for policy intervention. Further pursuit of this same mode of analysis will reveal other layers of action situations that shape the likely outcomes of any attempted intervention, thus providing the basis for explicit comparisons among the relative merits of alternative pathways toward meaningful change to the focal action situations.

These comparisons will themselves require the application of systematic analysis, and this analysis constitutes an action situation in its own right, one that is focused on individual and collective processes of evaluation. Among the critical factors to be considered when evaluating each candidate for policy intervention are (a) the collective action and other transaction costs that would be involved in inducing the desired change at the point of intervention, and (b) the likely effect of those particular changes on the policy outcomes of primary interest. One would also have to consider the possible consequences of coordinated interventions at different points, but the critical point is that all these factors can be understood as further applications of the same analytical process.

I want to push this idea of "treating variables as pointers" a bit further. Many of the variables included in SES analyses relate to certain attributes of actors or collective processes. Those variables, in effect, point toward the collective-choice situations that assigned specific individuals to fill roles in that organization or toward the constitutional-choice situations that those organizations established. For individual attributes, long-term, often-hidden processes of socialization and professional training have shaped an individual's perceptions and preferences, indeed his or her basic identity. When the attributes refer to organizational actors, then attention should be directed to constitutive processes of the establishment and evaluation of organizations. In sum, *actor attributes* should also be treated as *pointers* that direct our attention toward those sites of collective action in which the values of those attributes were determined, and thus to sites where those attributes might be changed.

For many institutional analysts, the primary attribute of concern is each actor's incentives to prefer some outcomes or actions over others. It's often said to be important to "get the incentives right," which in this context I interpret as a realization of the need to investigate where those actor incentives came from in the first place. In other situations, it's even more critical to "get the institutions right." Although many others have drawn this same distinction among incentives, institutions, and outcomes, I think a case can be made that the mode of institutional analysis pioneered by Elinor Ostrom brings a logical coherence to understanding both the process of research through which institutional analysts can best ply their trade and the most effective processes of political practice that the actors they study are most likely to employ.

I'm suggesting a shift of worldview under which social scientists seeking to understand some puzzling aspect of human behavior, or policy advocates seeking reforms that could improve policy outcomes, are both understood as looking out upon a complex, multidimensional, multilayered landscape of interconnected sites of interaction among humans and their environment. Although scientists or advocates may initially be focused on concerns about understanding or changing some of the outcomes they observe, their gaze must necessarily move both deeper within critical sites of interaction to trace out the connections that shape those outcomes, and outward to related and interconnected sites of interaction. The conditions of those focal action situations were determined by those sites of interaction and might be changed by concerted action.

Fischer (2018, 138) summarizes the nature of a social-ecological system in a compellingly succinct phrase: "nested sets of coevolving social and natural subsystems connected through feedbacks, time lags, and cross-level interactions." This definition highlights the primary importance of dynamic change in establishing, maintaining, or changing the outcomes that emerge from the operation of an SES.

Although Fischer's analysis was explicitly focused on actual forest landscapes, I think exactly the same interpretation could be applied to analytical landscapes as a much broader concept. The systems analysis literature uses the term *analytical landscape* to denote an abstract multidimensional parameter space that exhibits an array of peaks and valleys. States within a given region (or valley) will tend toward a local equilibrium (the equivalent of the lowest point in a physical valley), and effort will need to be exerted (in this case, changes made in the values of some parameters) to move the state into a different region, after which the process will reach a new local equilibrium.

For my conceptualization of an *institutional landscape* defined by interconnected action situations of operational, collective, and constitutional choice, a valley corresponds to the operation of an action situation when all changes in its parameters are being driven endogenously. Also, the outcome from that action situation will eventually reach an equilibrium that may be dynamic rather than resting in any single point, or state. Within that range of the underlying space of parameters, the focal action situations may exhibit such a regularity of behavior that they may come to be seen as a mechanism pushing policy deliberations toward expected outcomes. For example, under some circumstances we should indeed expect to see a common resource degenerate into what Hardin (1968) famously labeled the "tragedy of the commons." However, under different circumstances (that is, under different values for working components in the focal action situations), a quite different mechanism would seem to be in operation, resulting in, for example, the sustainable regimes of community-based management of common-pool resources that Elinor Ostrom's research has enabled us to understand.

Moving from one focal action situation to an adjacent one, as would be the case for communities pausing to collectively reevaluate their current operational processes in hopes of reaching a mutually desirable improvement in those outcomes, would be analogous to pushing a ball up a hill and seeing where it ends up. In this case the outcome of that second (adjacent) action situation might move the associated operational-level action situation (the initial focal point of interest) into a different region of the parameter space, where its subsequent dynamics may differ significantly from before. But it took effort to change the relevant parameters, or in this case to engage in the deliberation or other forms of collective action to accomplish that goal. For action situations stuck in a particular valley, there may be different hills that might be climbed in this institutional landscape in hopes of arriving at a new outcome, and these hills may differ significantly in the transaction costs entailed in such analytical trips. This view could lead to a more realistic evaluation of the extent to which communities are able to revise the conditions of their own governance, under different sets of circumstances.

An institutional analyst of the Bloomington School must navigate through this landscape of interconnected action situations when embarking upon a journey of discovery or reform. The IAD and SES frameworks were designed to help analysts choose their path to most effectively navigate their way through the institutional landscape to their desired end. That end could be an improved scientific understanding of the relevant social and ecological phenomena or practical proposals for effecting desired changes in the outcomes of these interconnected processes.

Admittedly, the guidance provided by these frameworks tends to be rather vague and unspecified, leaving the quality of the outcome at the mercy of the skill and discernment of those analysts directly involved in directing this analytical journey. Elinor Ostrom has given analysts compelling examples of the outcomes that such a journey can generate, most memorably in *Governing the Commons*. In other works, especially *Understanding Institutional Diversity* and her coauthored volume *Working Together*, she tried to explain how the IAD and SES frameworks helped her see her own way to a deeper understanding of the ability of communities to manage resources critical to their own survival.

The key to understanding how this mode of analysis works is, first, to realize that any one action situation is necessarily embedded within a complex network or system of intertwined action situations (McGinnis 2011b). Second, we need to understand how an institutional analyst primarily concerned with understanding the dynamics within a focal action situation chooses which other action situations are so closely intertwined as to constitute an equally important status as co-focal action situations. We also need to understand which secondary (or adjacent) action situations are worthy of further investigation so we can better understand the sources of the context within which these focal situations occur, or to most effectively intervene to improve the policy outcomes those focal action situations generate. In effect, institutional analysts are faced with a wide range of paths through these landscapes, and in the next section I suggest one way of understanding the nature of those choices.

NAVIGATING INSTITUTIONAL LANDSCAPES IN A POLYCENTRIC SYSTEM

Workshop students and visiting scholars often ask me how they might use the IAD framework in their seminar papers. I would encourage them to ask questions like the following: If the current procedure biases the process toward undesirable outcomes, what changes in collective-choice procedures might give participants access to more effective policy responses? What changes in constitutional-choice procedures might result in a better fit between those making policy decisions and those affected by their decisions? Which actor positions (or roles) have incentives that generate perverse effects, and where in the system could reformers intervene to help change those incentives? Is it a question of understanding the nature of the good or the relevant resources in a new way? Or how might we help participants incorporate other normative criteria in their evaluative processes?

In short, they should start their analysis by identifying a focal action situation (or at most a few of them), learn how the relevant collective and constitutional-choice arenas shaped that action situation, and then think deeply about the processes through which those conditions might be changed. To me, this process of zooming in and out of interrelated action situations is the way institutional analysis should be done.

In my guide to the terminology and analytical concepts used in the Bloomington School (McGinnis 2011a), I argue that the concepts of the IAD framework, the SES framework, and polycentric systems of governance all tie together as a single coherent worldview, or mode of thinking, or analytical perspective. Yet each highlights different aspects of the overall picture.

The IAD framework is focused on the physical, social, and institutional context within which collective action occurs and policy outcomes are realized. It presumes that no one action situation exists in isolation and insists that policies live within a complex ecology of strategic interactions.[5] The SES framework explicitly incorporates the nested, multilevel complexity of ecological systems and suggests that, to be sustainable, institutional arrangements must somehow match that complexity in a productive manner. As scientific knowledge expands, so does the range of potentially policy-relevant concerns. Also, as public entrepreneurs bring to the political agenda new issues and concerns related to the environment and the sustainability of access to needed resources, then the demands on scientific knowledge expand ever further. In effect, biophysical conditions, scientific knowledge about those conditions, human communities, and the range of public policy are complexly coevolving.

The IAD and SES frameworks are naturally congruent with a particular understanding of governance, namely, *polycentric governance*. Originally introduced by Ostrom, Tiebout, and Warren (1961) as a vision that embraced the potentially positive consequences of governmental fragmentation in US metropolitan areas, this conceptualization inspired empirical analyses of police services and other aspects of metropolitan governance (McGinnis 1999; Oakerson 1999; Oakerson and Parks 2011). The most widely known application of polycentricity to real-world settings remains the work of Elinor Ostrom (1990, 2010a), who concluded that community-based commons management was likely to be sustainable only if its rules were nested within a broader system of polycentric governance that allowed for alternative mechanisms of collective decision-making and conflict resolution at all levels of aggregation.

Elsewhere, I define *governance* as the "process by which the repertoire of rules, norms, and strategies that guide behavior within a given realm of policy interactions are formed, applied, interpreted, and reformed" (McGinnis 2011a, 171). My basic point is that governance should be understood as a *process*, and that both government officials and nongovernmental actors can play critical roles in that process. In an ideal-typical system of polycentric governance, a diverse array of public and private authorities with overlapping domains of responsibility interact in complex and ever-changing ways. Each decision center typically addresses only a few pivotal action situations, but uncoordinated processes of mutual adjustment among related action situation/decision centers can, in some circumstances, generate the resilient patterns of social ordering that can support and sustain capacities for self-governance (Cole and McGinnis 2015a, 2015b; Blomquist, Thiel, and Garrick 2019).

The mainstream literature on public policy is all about the strategic choices made by political leaders. For me, much of politics is driven by strategic calculations by political actors that follow, loosely, the process of strategic rigor I introduced earlier in this chapter. Applying the IAD or SES frameworks to an empirical setting is all about searching for places where policy interventions could be most effective, or to identify those critical junctures that can contribute the most to deepening our understanding of the relevant processes. Participants in policy settings do much the same thing, but in a more informal manner.

For the Ostroms, institutional analysis and governance are not done only by outside experts. In many settings, members of a community are personally engaged in analytical self-reflection on the institutional context within which they find themselves and actively participate in the coproduction of governance. The analytical path through the complex landscape of interconnected action situations that I have outlined is a path that has always been, and will continue to be, trod by those individuals whose lives are most directly affected by the outcomes of these interconnected processes. They know that they can either attack a problem directly or instead adopt a more indirect approach.

For example, rather than making a rule that prohibits actions with collectively undesirable outcomes, it may be more effective to find a way to convince a recalcitrant individual that it would be in his or her own self-interest to make a minor sacrifice to serve the common good. And then it might be useful to set up a way to monitor that person's behavior and to establish a schedule of graduated sanctions as well as some mechanisms to resolve the disputes that will inevitably arise. In some circumstances, the path through this institutional landscape will lead to conditions that satisfy Ostrom's design principles. In other cases, more tragic results may be observed. Success in collective action may always be possible, but it is never inevitable.

Many action situations were created by groups seeking to cope with newly emerging challenges or those that recur on a regular basis. And these actors can strategically link action situations together in chains of decisions, some of which are repeated so frequently that they come to be seen as quasi-automatic mechanisms that can set constraints within which policy participants operate, as well as open up new opportunities for them to realize joint aspirations. For example, some sequences of action situations take the form of legally required processes or standard operating procedures found in any formal organization.

For analytical purposes, researchers and policy analysts can think of a policy process as a path through a complex network of linked action situations, with the outcome from any one node affecting the likely outcomes from subsequent decision nodes. Some action situations will have only trivial consequences, but for many decisions of interest any one action situation may have significant implications for later decisions, including ones to be made by other sets of actors. In effect, each *consequential* action situation constitutes a mini-critical juncture that shapes the opportunities and probabilities of subsequent steps, thereby imposing a form of path dependence at the micro level.

In terms of the IAD framework, any collective decision to intervene in an ongoing policy process constitutes either a new action situation to be added to the existing system, or is a particular realization of a form of intervention that had already been incorporated into that system. Interventions frequently seek to influence the outcome of a focal action situation in an indirect manner, by effecting changes in other action situations that set values on the factors that shape which outcomes are generated by that focal action situation. Many interventions are intended to change the beliefs, identities, incentives, or behavior of the actors making decisions in a focal action situation or ones closely adjacent to it.

Policy participants weave their ways through complex ecologies of action situations along multiple paths, which may proceed in a logical sequence, or become trapped in endless repetition, or double back upon themselves. When we as analysts study how a particular community attempted to address some difficult problem, we need to identify the sources of the contextual conditions that defined the focal action situation(s) that generated the unfortunate outcome. Some path of decisions must have led that community into that conundrum, and other paths might enable them to secure a more satisfactory future. Some important decisions may lie too far in the past to be remediable at this late date, but more recent critical junctures should be more easily identifiable. We should be able to imagine how some of those decisions might have come out differently and how to see a path toward a more preferred outcome, one that could be realized through concerted action.

What the Ostroms have provided us, and what I am trying to clarify in this chapter, is that this analytical process of finding one's way through complex landscapes of adjacent action situations can be understood as a systematic process of search for more effective points of intervention, as well as for more fundamental determinants of policy outcomes. But is it sufficiently systematic to count as being rigorous? I claim that this strategically rigorous process of analytical pathfinding may be the most rigorous method available when we confront the deep complexity of social settings, and especially those found in closely coupled social-ecological systems.

One common problem with Bloomington School institutional analyses is that they can generate a long list of potentially relevant variables. There may be no limit to the extent of complications, because more than one participant (and often multiple potential interveners) are traversing analytical paths of this same type, coming up with competing interventions that may counteract each other or interact to generate totally unexpected or unintended outcomes. But if we treat these variables as pointers toward the sites of interaction where those values were determined, and actor attributes as pointers toward sites where those attributes were shaped, then we have identified a potentially manageable set of options for policy intervention, along with a mode of analysis that can be used to compare their likely consequences. It's not as rigorous as a computer programmed to calculate the values of specific metrics, but it is systematic in the sense of moving forward toward better outcomes and deeper understanding.

To fully realize the potential in this approach, we need to say something more specific about the *process* through which groups shift gears from operational-level to collective- or constitutional-level choices, or choose to direct their attention to institutional, physical, or social changes. It's important to directly acknowledge the strategic nature of the way participants and reformers move through the complex landscape of interconnected action situations at all levels of analysis. Most importantly, we need to be able to make judgments concerning which paths through the institutional landscape are easier to follow or more effective in realizing change.

In hopes of clarifying my recommendations, here is an example of how a process of strategic rigor might work, in outline form:

1. Institutional analysts and/or participants in policy processes begin their efforts by using the IAD-SES frameworks to lay out the general structure of the broader institutional and biophysical landscape of interconnected action situations and other determinants of relevant contextual factors. They should identify a few focal action situations with direct influence on the policy outcomes of primary concern to them, and then work their way through the relevant institutional landscape (that is, the network of adjacent action situations) to find effective points of potential intervention for improving policy outcomes or increasing our understanding of the relevant dynamic processes in play.

2. As institutional analysts, we should be able to make a preliminary determination of which actors are likely to be the most dissatisfied with current outcomes, as well as those actors with leverage over promising levers for change. As dissatisfied public entrepreneurs look around to identify effective targets, they may need to insert themselves into ongoing action situations or develop new ones of their own design to try to change the conditions that have been generating the problem, as they see it.

3. By knowing the relative manipulability of alternative points of leverage, we should be able to compare, in general terms, the magnitude of the costs of collective action that disenchanted public entrepreneurs would face in any effort to move different policy levers. In other words, we should be able to say something meaningful about the menu of strategic choice options available to participants in these policy settings, and about the relative magnitude of the transaction costs facing different actors or coalitions contemplating concerted manipulation of different combinations of targeted action situations.

4. In effect, we would be making probabilistic claims about the results that public entrepreneurs are likely to arrive at through their own processes of observation and diagnosis of the strategic situation at hand. If their efforts are successful, then we could start over again, by identifying those relevant actors who are likely to be most dissatisfied by the newly established

equilibrium outcome. We could then evaluate the likely choices and possible rates of success of alternative entrepreneurs or interest coalitions—that is, those who are going to be left unsatisfied by the new equilibrium.

5. Meanwhile, other processes will also be at work, including natural dynamics of ecological change, as well as global markets and other exogenous processes. We need to remember that it's not all about choice, and that some factors will change for reasons not directly attributable to human action, or for reasons that were not intended by those actors.

For comparative purposes, analysts might peruse the event sequences that occurred in different settings, to check if the path historically traced out in those cases seems reasonable, based on their analysis of the relative appeal of alternatives. At best, this process could generate a rough estimate of equilibrium distributions over outcomes likely to occur for a given set of parameters, with the specific outcomes determined by some randomized process. Some of these parameter values may adjust automatically, especially on the ecological side of the SES ledger, but major changes are likely to require conscious collective action by interested parties.

This process may seem to leave us with an unreasonably open-ended form of analysis, but that seems to me to be an inevitable consequence of the radical extent of endogeneity and breadth of agency presumed in the basic structures of the IAD and SES frameworks.

EXPLORING NEW WAYS FORWARD

Both the IAD and SES frameworks continue to inspire applications to new policy settings (Cole and McGinnis 2017; Heikkila and Cainey 2017; Schlager and Cox 2017; Gari et al. 2018; Partelow 2018). As I suggested at the beginning of this chapter, there remain, within the conceptual and analytical tool kit of the Bloomington School, unrealized opportunities to improve both the scientific rigor and the policy relevance of the conceptual apparatus built into these two frameworks.

Consider, for example, a comment from Elinor Ostrom's introduction to her 1976 edited volume *The Delivery of Urban Services* that Vlad Tarko (2017, 32 and 108) deemed sufficiently important to quote twice in his intellectual biography of her: "Failure, in many cases, leads to adoption of another program—one often based, as was the first, on inadequate analysis of the strategic behavior of the different actors. Failure seems to breed failure" (Ostrom 1976, 7).

This sequential compounding of policy failures can too easily be taken as an ideologically grounded dismissal of the potentially beneficial consequences of policy reform or other forms of planning. Alternatively, this "failure" could be framed as encouraging institutional analysts to develop a carefully specified model of the circumstances under which this kind of compounding would occur, which could then serve as the basis for evaluating the range of remedies available to those trying to break out of this vicious cycle. To my knowledge, no researcher working within the Bloomington School tradition has examined in any detail the conditions under which such a compounding of policy failures would most likely occur.

Why not? Presumably, the IAD framework could have been used to help explain why the road from the good intentions of public entrepreneurs so often leads to compounded policy dilemmas. Why has the Ostrom tradition never fully engaged with the mainstream literature on public policy to a sufficient extent to be able to ask that kind of question, or to engage in a full-fledged interrogation of the types of arrangements among action situations that could generate such perverse effects?

In *The Samaritan's Dilemma* (Gibson et al. 2005), Elinor Ostrom and her collaborators did identify examples of this kind of cascading failure in their interviews with policymakers at the national and local levels. In this case, the researchers used the IAD framework primarily to organize the set of questions they asked participants and to clarify what would be required for local communities to truly take over ownership of a development project from the international donors. This effort represents a promising start on one way to enhance both the rigor and the relevance of research in the tradition of the Bloomington School. I discuss several other promising leads below.

By strategically exploring the relevant institutional landscapes, institutional analysts may find that the IAD and SES frameworks can offer a secure foundation for further development of some of the most interesting recent developments within the Bloomington School. Consider, for example, Elinor Ostrom's work with Sue Crawford to include a delta parameter in a rational actor's utility function, to represent the intrinsic benefits or costs of following or violating some normative rule. The institutional grammar that Elinor Ostrom and Sue Crawford first introduced in the mid-1990s is finally starting to bear some fruit. Initial investigations, such as Basurto et al. (2010) and Siddiki et al. (2011), analyzed single institutional statements, but were not able to aggregate these results into useful characterizations of rule clusters.

So far, in the literature using these tools there has been little attention paid to actors responsible for the socialization processes through which those normative values had been internalized by the individual actors. This kind of socialization played a critical role in Tocqueville's understanding of the foundations of a sustainable democracy, but not so much in applications of the IAD framework. Closer examination of the action situations in which agents of socialization operate (and are themselves socialized into playing those roles) might provide the basis for a more natural formal representation of the critical role of organizations as actors within action situations. Technically, organizations can act only through the choices of their agents, but if agents in any long-lasting organization are regularly socialized into the worldview widely shared within that organization and are responsive to the incentives attached to that position, no matter who fills it, then the behavior of that organization can, for many analytical purposes, be treated as if it is a long-lived actor pursuing a relatively consistent set of goals. The extent to which a specific individual's own values or interests deviate from that positional norm could, at least conceivably, be measured and the implications of increased deviations could be derived.

More recent work, such as the analysis of different forms of payment for ecosystem services in Lien, Schlager, and Lona (2018), is showing potential for drawing useful connections to the broader literature on policy tools or instruments. The landscape navigation mode of analysis within the context of the IAD and SES frameworks suggested here might help make that connection. If attributes of the specific components of particular rules are treated not merely as variables, but as pointers toward the collective- and operational-level arenas of choice in which those attributes were first determined or subsequently modified, that might provide one way to begin knitting together individual rules into broader systems of interlocking action situations. That is, detailed analyses of the attributes of specific rules might serve as clues leading to a better understanding of the collective-choice action situations in which multiple rules are clustered together to support a new form of policy instrument.

I consider it promising that the analytical perspective I lay out in this chapter shares a great deal in common with the work of other scholars, some of whom have been directly associated with the Ostrom Workshop and others who, to the best of my knowledge, have not. For examples, consider Kimmich and Villamayor-Tomás (2019) and Oberlack et al. (2016, 2018). In each of these papers, the authors identify a few core processes at work in the substantive area of policy they are studying and then step back to examine the factors that are most influential in determining the nature of those processes. Oberlack et al. (2016) set up a three-step sequence with core processes, the primary outcomes of those processes, and the "activating factors and facilitating processes" that shape both core processes and outcomes. The labels may be different, but the underlying logic is remarkably congruent with both the IAD and SES frameworks.

Consider also the diagnostic approach to the study of institutions for water governance advocated by de Loë and Patterson (2018, 567): "A *diagnostic approach* is a structured process of context-specific inquiry into both the biophysical and human aspects of a problem situation. Diagnostic approaches should provide systemic but strategic ways of identifying and evaluating external factors in particular situations." They advocate explicit adoption of a "*user-oriented perspective* (i.e., thinking [as] an analyst, who could be a research, policymaker, or practitioner), and give specific regard to the challenge of suitably capturing relevant external factors" (de Loë and Patterson 2018, 568). Their approach to institutional analysis is especially pertinent to Bloomington School concerns in their explicit focus on the critical problem of determining the appropriate scale at which a given policy setting should be understood, and more specifically, on the problem of where to draw the boundary between core elements of a social-ecological system and exogenous effects from outside that system. They use the term "action situation" to refer to the relatively coherent whole that encompasses the primary components of the empirical setting under investigation.

As de Loë and Patterson (2018) acknowledge, there are no clear and fast rules for making these boundary choices. They recommend that the problem should initially be framed as "tightly" as possible, and then go on to encourage analysts to "critically reflect" on the boundaries they are provisionally considering. They posit a process of sequential consideration of potential extensions by first "looking inward" to more fully understand the internal structure of that action situation and "spiraling outwards" to consider social and environmental factors that are closely tied to those core components, and encourage repetition of movements in both directions. They assert that "This spiraling approach is important because it allows for progressively expanding the scope of analysis while continuing to re-visit each key SES variable category in light of previous reasoning" (de Loë and Patterson 2018, 571).

In another recent work, Heikkila and Andersson (2018) emphasize the importance of taking a diagnostic approach to contextually specific institutional design. They make the important point that even though the possibility of sustainable self-governance is more viable than generally realized, it is not always the best solution. In short, they encourage other scholars to use the IAD framework as a basis for diagnosis, and to focus their attention on design considerations that are particularly crucial for the relevant contexts.

Villamayor-Tomás et al. (2015), Webster (2015), and Fischer (2018) devise more explicitly dynamic frameworks for the study of social-ecological systems, in ways that suggest potential extension of a dynamic variant of the SES framework to incorporate important aspects of the policy stages heuristic that remains so influential among public policy scholars. Webster introduces an "action cycle" as a simplified generic version of a policy cycle, in which a problem generates signals that may or may not trigger a response on the part of the policymakers. Villamayor-Tomás et al. (2018) represent food and energy production processes as "value chains" that effectively consist of sequences of action situations of resource extraction, production, distribution, and consumption.

Fischer (2018, 139 and 141) treats "feedbacks, time lags, and cross-level interactions" as the "core processes that govern forest landscapes" and offers a succinct statement of the crucial importance of considering time lags, because "society's governing institutions often function on different spatial and temporal scales than natural systems." This concern with the process of finding the right spatial and temporary boundary for an action situation (see de Loë and Patterson 2018) ties in nicely with broader concerns about the importance of institutional fit to effective forms of adaptive governance.

Frankly, I find the degree of correspondence among the basic logics of these separate approaches to research to be quite remarkable, and a reminder of just how many diverse forms of inspiration scholars may draw from the work of a single Nobel laureate.

These papers and articles inspired me to propose that a "policy cycle" (broadly understood as including stages of problem definition, agenda setting, policy selection, implementation, and evaluation) might be represented as a sequence of relatively distinct action situations, one for each of these stages, which typically operate in something like a linear progression, but with the important caveat that stages can be skipped and reversions to earlier stages may occur at any time. In effect, a policy cycle would consist of multiple sites of interaction (or action situations) arranged in an overlapping manner, with each of them consisting of a series of sequential action situations, some of which (especially at the operational level) occur over a regular time sequence (like quarterly business reports or seasonal changes throughout a year), others (collective level) occur at regular intervals (fixed election cycles, for example), and still other combinations of action situations are formed and dissolved in a very irregular manner. The regular repetition of foundational operational-level choices and fixed points for policy implementation or evaluation would be supplemented by irregularly timed creative efforts by participants to resuscitate long-dormant decision arenas or to invent new ones.

In *Understanding Institutional Diversity*, Ostrom (2005b) details an analytical perspective meant for application to all forms of institutional arrangements. This ambitious goal required her to suggest ways to identify the core foundational components of the action arenas or action situations that occur within all sites of collective action; to develop distinctions between the closely interrelated concepts of norms, rules, and strategies; and to offer a taxonomy of how those concepts might be categorized into distinct types. Not surprisingly, the resulting framework was very complex. Elinor Ostrom (2005b, 256–57) realized this complexity required justification:

> This complexity of language has not been introduced lightly. A scholar should also keep analysis as simple as possible—given the problem to be analyzed. Just as important, however, is developing a mode of analysis that enables scholars, policymakers, and participants in ongoing processes to grapple with the problems they face by digging through the layers of nested systems in which these processes exist When one is analyzing what is operationally a relatively simple system using a relatively simple language for analysis, one may not need the full language system developed in this volume. Most common-pool resources, and many other policy fields, however, are complex systems and not simple systems. Thus, we need a consistent, nested set of concepts that can be used in our analysis, research, and policy advice in a cumulative manner.

In short, these frameworks should be as complex as they need to be to find an effective balance between the cognitive requirements of analytical simplicity and the need to accept the reality of the overwhelming complexity of institutional diversity found in the real world (Ostrom 2005a). Ideally, these frameworks are both simple and complex enough to deliver suitable rewards in terms of both analytical rigor and policy relevance.

In my opinion, the single most important contribution made by the Ostroms and others working within the Bloomington School tradition has been to demonstrate the remarkable ability of local communities to creatively craft solutions to practical problems. Ostrom was fond of saying that, in contrast to the lesson conveyed by Hardin's "tragedy of the commons," she preferred to presume that communities are rarely trapped within social dilemmas from which they cannot escape but are typically positioned to take action to improve their own situation. The Ostroms never claimed that this capacity was limitless, and yet the most common line of criticism has been to say that they were too optimistic about the ability of ordinary citizens to govern themselves in the technically complex societies in which we all now live. I admit this criticism may be a fair one, but I would counter with the point that some minimal degree of optimism may be required to accomplish difficult tasks of collective action. Perhaps they were merely overreacting against dominant themes of powerlessness in the scientific and policy communities—after all, unremitting pessimism seems a lousy way to run either a social movement or a scientific discipline.

As public entrepreneurs navigate through multidimensional landscapes of potential institutional change, they will sometimes run up against barriers they can't break through. Those actors who control access to the sites of constitutional deliberation that determine the distributional consequences of collective decisions may not be willing to listen to new voices, or to consider adopting new modes of decision-making. Scholars from the Bloomington School have often been accused of not realistically taking into account the inequities imposed by asymmetric power relations, but there is no reason such inequities need to be neglected (see Clement 2010). Because, in practice, the range of possibilities for community-based action is not unlimited, the IAD framework needs to be able to incorporate these limits in some fashion.

The IAD framework forces institutional analysts to think creatively while searching through the entire framework to identify potentially relevant factors before they settle on a particular theoretical perspective or build a specific formal model. Once we realize that participants in any social dilemma game are simultaneously participating in adjacent action situations, and that they may draw upon resources and capabilities developed or reinforced in those adjacent games for use in addressing their core problem, then game players (or action situation participants) may be able to find some way out of their dilemma.

I'd like to finish this chapter with an observation of the fundamental similarity facing institutional analysts and the problem-solving individuals they study: both must navigate complex institutional landscapes as they simultaneously use and revise the ever-changing polycentric settings within which they live. The analytical perspective on institutions provided by scholars from the Bloomington School can help us, whether we are citizens seeking better access to public goods, active participants in policy processes, or anyone engaged in evaluation of those processes, to more fully appreciate the foundational connection between self-governance and the forms of institutional analysis that the Ostroms exemplified in their own lives. They were pioneers who blazed new paths through polycentric institutional landscapes and who encouraged others to follow them in that ennobling journey.

ACKNOWLEDGMENTS

I would like to thank my Indiana University colleagues Dan Cole and Aurelian Craiutu for their comments on earlier versions of this chapter, and the IU College of Arts and Sciences for research support. I am especially indebted to the organizers and participants in the 2018 symposium held at the Mercatus Center for their extensive comments and excellent suggestions for revisions, and for a fascinating round of discussions. Naturally, none of these individuals or organizations are responsible for any remaining errors.

NOTES

1. For overviews, see Ostrom, Tiebout, and Warren (1961); Mitchell (1988); McGinnis (1996, 1999a, 1999b, 2000, 2011a, 2011c); Ostrom (1990, 2005b, 2010a); Aligica and Boettke (2009); Poteete, Janssen, and Ostrom (2010); McGinnis and Walker (2010); V. Ostrom (2011, 2012); Aligica (2014); Sabetti and Aligica (2014); Cole and McGinnis (2015a, 2015b, 2017, 2018); and Tarko (2017).

2. For a range of perspectives on the question of rigor in political science, see Easton 1969; Singer 1972; Boynton 1982; Putnam 2003; Stoker, Peters, and Pierre 2015. Also, Jacobs and Skocpol (2006) offer a different way of integrating rigor and relevance by focusing on doing rigorous research that could contribute to partisan debates on public policy at the national level.

3. Other efforts more directly focused on formalizing or testing the distribution of research inspired by Ostrom's design principles, including Frey (2017) and Gari et al. (2018).

4. Although the IAD and SES frameworks tend to be considered separately, Cole, Epstein, and McGinnis (2019) argue that these two frameworks should be seen as special cases of a broader integrative framework. For a different perspective on the relationship between these two frameworks, see Schlager and Cox (2017).

5. For the closely related concept of an ecology of games, see Long 1958; Lubell 2013; Lubell, Robins, and Wang 2014; Berardo and Lubell 2019. The latter is an introduction to a special issue of *Policy Studies Journal* in which contributors explicitly connect research tradition to the concept of polycentricity, which lies at the very heart of the Bloomington School.

REFERENCES

Agrawal, Arun. 2001. "Common Property Institutions and Sustainable Governance of Resources." *World Development* 29 (10): 1649–72.

Aligica, Paul Dragos. 2014. *Institutional Diversity and Political Economy: The Ostroms and Beyond*. New York: Oxford University Press.

Aligica, Paul Dragos, and Peter J. Boettke. 2009. *Challenging Institutional Analysis and Development: The Bloomington School*. New York: Routledge.

Andersson, Krister P., and Elinor Ostrom. 2008. "Analyzing Decentralized Resource Regimes from a Polycentric Perspective." *Policy Sciences* 41: 71–93.

Basurto, Xavier, Gordon Kingsley, Kelly McQueen, Mshadoni Smith, and Christopher Weible. 2010. "A Systematic Approach to Institutional Analysis: Applying Crawford and Ostrom's Grammar." *Political Research Quarterly* 63 (3): 523–37.

Baumgartner, Frank R. 2010. "Beyond the Tragedy of the Commons: A Discussion of *Governing the Commons: The Evolution of Institutions for Collective Action*." Review Symposium, *Perspectives on Politics* 8 (2): 575–77.

Berardo, Ramiro, and Mark Lubell. 2019. "The Ecology of Games as a Theory of Polycentricity: Recent Advances and Future Challenges." *Policy Studies Journal* 47 (1): 6–26.

Blomquist, William, Andreas Thiel, and Dustin Garrick, eds. 2019. *Governing Complexity*. Cambridge, UK: Cambridge University Press.

Boettke, Peter, Jayme Lemke, and Liya Palagashvili. 2016. "Re-evaluating Community Policing in a Polycentric System." *Journal of Institutional Economics* 12 (2): 305–25.

Boettke, Peter J., Liya Palagashvili, and Jayme S. Lemke. 2013. "Riding in Cars with Boys: Elinor Ostrom's Adventures with the Police." *Journal of Institutional Economics* 9 (4): 407-25.

Boynton, George R. 1982. "On Getting from Here to There." In *Strategies of Political Inquiry*, edited by Elinor Ostrom, 29-68. Beverly Hills, CA: SAGE Publications.

Carlisle, Keith M., and Rebecca L.B. Gruby. 2017. "Polycentric Systems of Governance: A Theoretical Model for the Commons." *Policy Studies Journal* (August): 1-26.

Clement, Floriane. 2010. "Analysing Decentralised Natural Resource Governance: Proposition for a 'Politicised' Institutional Analysis and Development Framework." *Policy Sciences* 43: 129-56. Reprinted in Cole and McGinnis 2017.

Cole, Daniel H. 2014. "Learning from Lin: Lessons and Cautions from the Natural Commons for the Knowledge Commons." In *Governing Knowledge Commons*, edited by Brett M. Frischmann, Michael J. Madison, and Katherine J. Strandburg, 45-68. New York: Oxford University Press. Reprinted in Cole and McGinnis 2018.

Cole, Daniel H., Graham Epstein, and Michael D. McGinnis. 2014. "Digging Deeper into Hardin's Pasture: The Complex Institutional Structure of 'The Tragedy of the Commons.'" *Journal of Institutional Economics* 10: 353-69. Reprinted in Cole and McGinnis 2018.

Cole, Daniel H., Graham Epstein, and Michael D. McGinnis. 2019. "Combining the IAD and SES Frameworks." *International Journal of the Commons* 13 (1): 1-32.

Cole, Daniel H., and Michael D. McGinnis, eds. 2015a. *Elinor Ostrom and the Bloomington School of Political Economy: Volume 1, Polycentricity in Public Administration and Political Science*. Lanham, MD: Lexington Books.

———. 2015b. *Elinor Ostrom and the Bloomington School of Political Economy: Volume 2, Resource Governance*. Lanham, MD: Lexington Books.

———. 2017. *Elinor Ostrom and the Bloomington School of Political Economy: Volume 3, A Framework for Policy Analysis*. Lanham, MD: Lexington Books.

———. 2018. *Elinor Ostrom and the Bloomington School of Political Economy: Volume 4, Policy Applications and Extensions*. Lanham, MD: Lexington Books.

Cox, Michael. 2014. "Understanding Large Social-Ecological Systems: Introducing the SESMAD Project." *International Journal of the Commons* 8 (2): 265-76.

Cox, Michael, Gwen Arnold, and Sergio Villamayor-Tomás. 2010. "A Review of Design Principles for Community-Based Natural Resource Management." *Ecology and Society* 15 (4): 38. Reprinted in Cole and McGinnis 2015b.

Crawford, Sue E. S., and Elinor Ostrom. 1995. "A Grammar of Institutions." *American Political Science Review* 89 (3): 582-600. Reprinted in McGinnis 2000 and Ostrom 2005b.

Easton, David. 1969. "The New Revolution in Political Science." *American Political Science Review* 63 (4): 1051–61.

Epstein, Graham, Irene Pérez, Michael Schoon, and Chanda L. Meek. 2014. "Governing the Invisible Commons: Ozone Regulation and the Montreal Protocol." *International Journal of the Commons* 8 (2): 337–60.

Feiock, Richard C. 2009. "Metropolitan Governance and Institutional Collective Action." *Urban Affairs Review* 44 (3): 356–77. Reprinted in Cole and McGinnis 2017.

Fischer, Alexandra Paige. 2018. "Forest Landscapes as Social-Cultural Systems and Implications for Management." *Landscape and Urban Planning* 177: 138–47.

Fleischman, Forrest D., Natalie C. Ban, Louisa S. Evans, Graham Epstein, Gustavo Garcia-Lopez, and Sergio Villamayor-Tomás. 2014. "Governing Large-Scale Social-Ecological Systems: Lessons from Five Cases." *International Journal of the Commons* 8 (2): 428–56.

Frey, Ulrich J. 2017. "A Synthesis of Key Factors for Sustainability in Social-Ecological Systems." *Sustainability Science* 12: 507–19.

Gari, Sirak Robele, Alice Newton, John D. Icely, and Maria Mar Delgado-Serrano. 2018. "An Analysis of the Global Applicability of Ostrom's Design Principles to Diagnose the Functionality of Common-Pool Resource Institutions." *Sustainability* 9: 1287.

Gibson, Clark, Krister Andersson, Elinor Ostrom, and Sujai Shivakumar. 2005. *The Samaritan's Dilemma: The Political Economy of Development Aid.* New York: Oxford University Press.

Hardin, Garrett. 1968. "The Tragedy of the Commons." *Science* 162: 1243–48.

Heikkila, Tanya, and Krister Andersson. 2018. "Policy Design and the Added-Value of the Institutional Analysis Development Framework." *Policy & Politics* 46 (2): 309–24.

Heikkila, T., and P. Cainey. 2017. "Comparisons of Theories of the Policy Process." In *Theories of the Policy Process,* edited by Christopher M. Weible and Paul A. Sabatier, 4th ed., 301–27. Boulder, CO: Westview Press.

Jacobs, Lawrence R., and Theda Skocpol. 2006. "Restoring the Tradition of Rigor and Relevance to Political Science." *PS: Political Science & Politics* 39 (1): 27–31.

Kimmich, Christian, and Sergio Villamayor-Tomás. 2019. "Assessing Action Situation Networks: A Configurational Perspective on Water and Energy Governance in Irrigation Systems." *Water Economics and Policy* 5 (1): 1–29.

Kiser, Larry L., and Elinor Ostrom. 1982. "The Three Worlds of Action: A Metatheoretical Synthesis of Institutional Approaches." In *Strategies of Political Inquiry*, edited by Elinor Ostrom, 179–222. Beverly Hills, CA: Sage Publications. Reprinted in McGinnis 2000.

Levy, David M., and Sandra J. Peart. 2018. "Limits on the Application of Motivational Homogeneity in the Work of Buchanan and the Virginia School." In *Buchanan's Tensions:*

Reexamining the Political Economy and Philosophy of James M. Buchanan, edited by Peter J. Boettke and Solomon Stein. Arlington, VA: Mercatus Center at George Mason University.

Lien, Aaron M., Edella Schlager, and Ashly Lona. 2018. "Using Institutional Grammar to Improve Understanding of the Form and Function of Payment for Ecosystem Services Programs." *Ecosystem Services* 31: 21–31.

Loë, Rob C. de, and James J. Patterson. 2018. "Boundary Judgments in Water Governance: Diagnosing Internal and External Factors That Matter in a Complex World." *Water Resources Management* 32: 565–81.

Long, Norton E. 1958. "The Local Community as an Ecology of Games." *American Journal of Sociology* 64 (3): 309–23.

Lubell, Mark. 2013. "Governing Institutional Complexity: The Ecology of Games Framework." *Policy Studies Journal* 41 (3): 537–59.

Lubell, Mark, Garry Robins, and Peng Wang. 2014. "Network Structure and Institutional Complexity in an Ecology of Water Management Games." *Ecology and Society* 19 (4): 23.

McGinnis, Michael D. 1996. "Elinor Ostrom: A Career in Institutional Analysis." *PS: Political Science & Politics* 29 (4): 737–41.

———, ed. 1999a. *Polycentric Governance and Development: Readings from the Workshop in Political Theory and Policy Analysis*. Ann Arbor: University of Michigan Press.

———, ed. 1999b. *Polycentricity and Local Public Economies: Readings from the Workshop in Political Theory and Policy Analysis*. Ann Arbor: University of Michigan Press.

———, ed. 2000. *Polycentric Games and Institutions: Readings from the Workshop in Political Theory and Policy Analysis.* Ann Arbor: University of Michigan Press.

———. 2011a. "An Introduction to IAD and the Language of the Ostrom Workshop: A Simple Guide to a Complex Framework." *Policy Studies Journal* 39: 163–77.

———. 2011b. "Networks of Adjacent Action Situations in Polycentric Governance." *Policy Studies Journal* 39: 45–72.

———. 2011c. "Elinor Ostrom: Politics as Problem-Solving in Polycentric Setting." In *Maestri of Political Science,* edited by Donatella Campus, Gianfranco Pasquino, and Martin Bull, vol. 2, 137–58. Colchester, UK: ECPR Press. Reprinted in Cole and McGinnis 2015a.

———. 2017. "The IAD Framework in Action: Understanding the Source of the Design Principles in Elinor Ostrom's *Governing the Commons*." In *Elinor Ostrom and the Bloomington School of Political Economy, Volume 3: A Framework for Policy Analysis*, edited by Daniel H. Cole and Michael D. McGinnis, 87–108. Lanham, MD: Lexington Books.

McGinnis, Michael D., and Elinor Ostrom. 2012. "Reflections on Vincent Ostrom, Public Administration, and Polycentricity." *Public Administration Review* 72 (1): 15–25. Reprinted in Cole and McGinnis 2015a.

————. 2014. "Social-Ecological System Framework: Initial Changes and Continuing Challenges." *Ecology and Society* 19 (2): 30.

McGinnis, Michael, and James Walker. 2010. "Foundations of the Ostrom Workshop: Institutional Analysis, Polycentricity, and Self-Governance of the Commons." *Public Choice* 143 (3–4): 293–301.

Mitchell, William C. 1988. "Virginia, Rochester, and Bloomington: Twenty-Five Years of Public Choice and Political Science." *Public Choice* 56: 101–19.

Oakerson, Ronald J. 1999. *Governing Local Public Economies: Creating the Civic Metropolis*. Oakland, CA: ICS Press.

Oakerson, Ronald J., and Roger B. Parks. 2011. "The Study of Local Public Economies: Multi-Organizational, Multi-Level Institutional Analysis and Development." *Policy Studies Journal* 39: 147–67.

Oberlack, Christoph, Sébastien Boillat, Stefan Brönnimann, Jean-David Gerber, Andreas Heinimann, Chinwe Ifejika Speranza, Peter Messerli, Stephan Rist, and Urs Wiesmann. 2018. "Polycentric Governance in Telecoupled Resource Systems." *Ecology and Society* 23 (1): 16.

Oberlack, Christoph, Laura Tejada, Peter Messerli, Stephen Rist, and Markus Giger. 2016. "Sustainable Livelihoods in the Global Land Rush? Archetypes of Livelihood Vulnerability and Sustainability Potentials." *Global Environmental Change* 41: 153–71.

Ostrom, Elinor. 1965. "Public Entrepreneurship: A Case Study in Ground Water Basin Management." *PhD Dissertation*. Los Angeles: University of California, Los Angeles.

————, ed. 1976. *The Delivery of Urban Services: Outcomes of Change*. Urban Affairs Annual Reviews, vol. 10. Beverly Hills, CA: Sage Publications.

————. 1982. "Beyond Positivism." In *Strategies of Political Inquiry*, edited by Elinor Ostrom, 11–28. Beverly Hills, CA: Sage Publications. Reprinted in Sabetti and Aligica 2014.

————. 1986. "An Agenda for the Study of Institutions." *Public Choice* 48: 3–25. Reprinted in McGinnis 2000, Sabetti and Aligica 2014, and Cole and McGinnis 2015b.

————. 1989. "Microconstitutional Change in Multiconstitutional Political Systems." *Rationality and Society* 1: 11–50.

————. 1990. *Governing the Commons: The Evolution of Institutions for Collective Action*. Cambridge, UK: Cambridge University Press.

————. 1992. *Crafting Institutions for Self-Governing Irrigation Systems*. San Francisco: ICS Press.

————. 1996. "Civic Education for the Next Century: A Task Force to Initiate Professional Activity." *PS: Political Science & Politics* 29 (4): 755–58.

————. 1998. "A Behavioral Approach to the Rational Choice Theory of Collective Action." *American Political Science Review* 92 (1): 1–22. Reprinted in McGinnis 2000, 89–113, and Sabetti and Aligica 2014.

————. 2002. "Policy Analysis in the Future of Good Societies." *Good Society* 11 (1): 42–48. Reprinted in Cole and McGinnis 2018.

————. 2005a. "Doing Institutional Analysis: Digging Deeper than Markets and Hierarchies." In *Handbook of New Institutional Economics*, edited by Claude Ménard and Mary M. Shirley. Berlin: Springer-Verlag, 819–48.

————. 2005b. *Understanding Institutional Diversity*. Princeton, NJ: Princeton University Press.

————. 2006a. "A Frequently Overlooked Precondition of Democracy: Citizens Knowledgeable about and Engaged in Collective Action." In *Preconditions of Democracy*, edited by Geoffrey Brennan, The Tampere Club Series, vol. 2, 75–89. Tampere, Finland: Tampere University Press. Reprinted in Cole and McGinnis 2015a.

————. 2006b. "Converting Threats into Opportunities." *PS: Political Science & Politics* 39 (1): 3–12. Reprinted in Cole and McGinnis 2015a.

————. 2007. "A Diagnostic Approach for Going Beyond Panaceas." *Proceedings of the National Academy of Sciences USA* 104: 15181–87.

————. 2009. "A General Framework for Analyzing Sustainability of Social-Ecological Systems." *Science* 325: 419–22.

————. 2010a. "Beyond Markets and States: Polycentric Governance of Complex Economic Systems." *American Economic Review* 100: 641–72. Reprinted in Sabetti and Aligica 2014 and Cole and McGinnis 2015a.

————. 2010b. "Polycentric Systems for Coping with Collective Action and Global Environmental Change." *Global Environmental Change* 20: 550–57.

————. 2011a. "Background on the Institutional Analysis and Development Framework." *Policy Studies Journal* 39: 7–27.

————. 2011b. "Reflections on 'Some Unsettled Problems of Irrigation'." *American Economic Review* 101 (1): 49–63.

————. 2012. "Nested Externalities and Polycentric Institutions: Must We Wait for Global Solutions to Climate Change before Taking Actions at Other Scales?" *Economic Theory* 49 (2): 353–69.

Ostrom, Elinor, and Michael Cox. 2010. "Moving Beyond Panaceas: A Multi-Tiered Diagnostic Approach for Social-Ecological Analysis." *Environmental Conservation* 37 (4): 1–13,

Ostrom, Elinor, Roy Gardner, and James Walker, with Arun Agrawal, William Blomquist, Edella Schlager, and Shui Yan Tang. 1994. *Rules, Games, and Common-Pool Resources*. Ann Arbor: University of Michigan Press.

Ostrom, Elinor, and Vincent Ostrom. 2004. "The Quest for Meaning in Public Choice." *American Journal of Economics and Sociology* 63: 105–47. Reprinted in Sabetti and Aligica 2014.

Ostrom, Elinor, Larry Schroeder, and Susan Wynne. 1993. *Institutional Incentives and Sustainable Development: Infrastructure Policies in Perspective*. Boulder, CO: Westview Press.

Ostrom, Vincent. 1953a."State Administration of Natural Resources in the West." *American Political Science Review* 47 (2): 478–93. Reprinted in McGinnis, 1999a.

———. 1953b. *Water and Politics: A Study of Water Policies and Administration in the Development of Los Angeles*. New York: Johnson. Reprint Corp. 1972 [1953] (Los Angeles, CA: Haynes Foundation, 1953, Monograph no. 8 in *Metropolitan Los Angeles: A Study in Integration*).

———. 1994. *The Meaning of American Federalism: Constituting a Self-Governing Society*. San Francisco: ICS Press.

———. 1997. *The Meaning of Democracy and the Vulnerability of Democracies: A Response to Tocqueville's Challenge*. Ann Arbor: University of Michigan Press.

———. 2008a. *The Intellectual Crisis in American Public Administration*. 3rd ed. Tuscaloosa: University of Alabama Press. (1st edition 1973; revised edition 1974; 2nd edition 1989).

———. 2008b. *The Political Theory of a Compound Republic: Designing the American Experiment*. 3rd ed. Lanham, MD: Lexington Books. (1st edition 1971, Blacksburg, VA: Center for Public Choice, Virginia Tech (Virginia Polytechnic Institute and State University); 2nd edition 1989, Lincoln: University of Nebraska Press).

———. 2011. *The Quest to Understand Human Affairs, Vol. 1: Natural Resources Policy and Essays on Community and Collective Choice*, edited by Barbara Allen. Lanham, MD: Lexington Books.

———. 2012. *The Quest to Understand Human Affairs, Vol. 2: Essays on Collective, Constitutional, and Epistemic Choice*, edited by Barbara Allen. Lanham, MD: Lexington Books.

Ostrom, Vincent, Robert Bish, and Elinor Ostrom. 1988. *Local Government in the United States*. San Francisco: ICS Press.

Ostrom, Vincent, Charles M. Tiebout, and Robert Warren. 1961. "The Organization of Government in Metropolitan Areas: A Theoretical Inquiry." *American Political Science Review* 55: 831–42. Reprinted in McGinnis 1999b and Cole and McGinnis 2015a.

Partelow, Stefan. 2018. "A Review of the Social-Ecological Systems Framework: Applications, Methods, Modifications, and Challenges." *Ecology and Society* 23 (4): 36.

Polski, Margaret M. 2017. "Extending the Institutional Analysis and Development Framework to Policy Analysis and Design." In *Institutional Diversity in Self-Governing Societies: The Bloomington School and Beyond*, edited by Filippo Sabetti and Dario Castiglione, 25–47. Lanham, MD: Lexington Books.

Polski, Margaret M., and Elinor Ostrom 2017. "An Institutional Framework for Policy Analysis and Design." In *Elinor Ostrom and the Bloomington School of Political Economy: Vol. 3, A Framework for Policy Analysis,* edited by Daniel H. Cole and Michael D. McGinnis, 13–47. Lanham, MD: Lexington Books. [Reprint of a previously unpublished Working Paper, Ostrom Workshop, 1999.]

Poteete, Amy, Marco Janssen, and Elinor Ostrom. 2010. *Working Together: Collective Action, the Commons, and Multiple Methods in Practice.* Princeton, NJ: Princeton University Press.

Putnam, Robert D. 2003. "APSA Presidential Address: The Public Role of Political Science." *Perspectives on Politics* 1 (2): 249–55.

Sabetti, Filippo, and Paul Dragos Aligica, eds. 2014. *Choice, Rules and Collective Action: The Ostroms on the Study of Institutions and Governance.* Colchester, UK: ECPR Press.

Sarker, Ashuthosh, and William Blomquist. 2019. "Addressing Misconceptions of *Governing the Commons.*" *Journal of Institutional Economics* 15 (2).

Schlager, Elinor, and Michael Cox. 2017. "The IAD Framework and the SES Framework: An Introduction and Assessment of the Ostrom Workshop Frameworks." In *Theories of the Policy Process,* edited by Christopher M. Weible and Paul A. Sabatier, 4th ed., 215–52. Boulder, CO: Westview Press.

Siddiki, Saba, Christopher M. Weible, Xavier Basurto, and John Calanni. 2011. "Dissecting Policy Designs: An Application of the Institutional Grammar Tool." *Policy Studies Journal* 39 (1): 79–103.

Singer, J. David. 1972. "The 'Correlates of War' Project: Interim Report and Rationale." *World Politics* 24 (2): 243–70.

Stoker, Gerry, B. Guy Peters, and Jon Pierre, eds. 2015. *The Relevance of Political Science.* New York: Palgrave Macmillan.

Swann, William L., and Seo Young Kim. 2018. "Practical Prescriptions for Governing Fragmented Government." *Policy & Politics* 46 (2): 273–92.

Tarko, Vlad. 2017. *Elinor Ostrom: An Intellectual Biography.* London: Rowman & Littlefield.

Van Zeben, Josephine, and Ana Bobić. 2019. "Introduction: The Potential of a Polycentric European Union." In *Polycentricity in the European Union,* forthcoming. Cambridge, UK: Cambridge University Press.

Villamayor-Tomás, Sergio, Philipp Grundmann, Graham Epstein, Tom Evans, and Christian Kimmich. 2015. "The Water-Energy-Food Security Nexus through the Lenses of the Value Chain and the Institutional Analysis and Development Frameworks." *Water Alternatives* 8 (1): 735–55.

Webster, D. G. 2015. "The Action Cycle/Structural Context Framework: A Fisheries Application." *Ecology and Society* 20 (1): 33.

Weible, Christopher M., and Paul A. Sabatier, eds. 2017. *Theories of the Policy Process,* 4th ed. Boulder, CO: Westview Press.

Weissing, Franz J., and Elinor Ostrom. 1993. "Irrigation Institutions and the Games Irrigators Play: Rule Enforcement on Government and Farmer-Managed Systems." In *Games in Hierarchies and Networks: Analytical and Empirical Approaches to the Study of Governance Institutions*, edited by Fritz W. Scharpf, 387–428. Frankfurt: Campus Verlag; Boulder, CO: Westview Press. Reprinted in McGinnis 2000.

CHAPTER TWO

AN INTRICATE MOVE TOWARD REALITY

ELINOR OSTROM AND SCIENTIFIC REALISM

ADRIAN MIROIU

In a review of the state of political science as a discipline at the beginning of the 1980s, Elinor Ostrom (1982) noted the dominance of the focus on data collection and analysis, coupled with the neglect of attempts to develop new theoretical insights. For Ostrom, this concentration of efforts in political science had at least two limits. First, scholars failed to acknowledge a correct relation between data and theory. Data, she argued, are not the starting point of the attempts to understand reality; on the contrary, "the development of theory precedes the choice of appropriate methods to test a theory" (Ostrom 1982, 19).[1] A second limit, which has a metatheoretical nature, was researchers' (usually tacit) acceptance of the prevailing view developed by the philosophers of science on what a political theory should look like. For many researchers, the so-called received view of theories, or the syntactic view (Suppe 1974), came to be largely endorsed. According to that view, a theory is identified with a logically connected set of propositions, formulated in a carefully constructed language. The theory can be confronted with reality: in conjunction with statements of antecedent conditions, it gives explanations or predictions of empirical phenomena (Hempel and Oppenheim 1948). That view of theories has many shortcomings. Unfortunately, wrote Ostrom, although alternatives exist—and she mentioned works by authors like Thomas Kuhn, Imre Lakatos, and even Jurgen Habermas—the received view "has not been replaced with another dominant philosophy of science."

However, she was partly wrong. In the decade before her paper was published the received view of theories was powerfully rejected from multiple perspectives by the philosophers of science, and some of its main champions, Carl Hempel, for example, even abandoned it (Suppe 2000). The so-called semantic view of theories, which asserts that theories are not linguistic entities but (structured) collections of models, won the war and revivified the debates on the relation between theory and reality.

In this chapter, I argue that Ostrom's theoretical endeavor was in line with these developments. The structure of my argument is as follows. The first section introduces the semantic view of theories, in the context of Ostrom's well-known triadic conceptual scheme: frameworks, theories, models. According to this view, theories are structured collections of models. In the second section, I argue that the main piece in Ostrom's picture of scientific inquiry is the concept of model. I first identify the main characteristics of models, and then I discuss the structure of the collections of models that researchers develop. This discussion will bring me to discern the characteristics and the role of a neglected concept Ostrom added to complement the triadic scheme: theoretical scenarios. Finally, I argue that the focus on models is consistent with a semantic conception of theories. In the third section, I turn to the philosophical idea of scientific realism: how our conceptual constructs relate to the empirical world. I argue that Ostrom's view on models, theories, and frameworks can be interpreted as a sophisticated type of realist position called *structural realism*.

THE SEMANTIC APPROACH

The Three Levels Approach

The study of complex configurations of rules, argues Ostrom, is done not only by appealing to different theoretical approaches, to be found in distinct disciplines, but also at three "levels of specificity": frameworks, theories, and models.[2] These theoretical concepts range from the most general to the most detailed types of assumptions, so they can be placed at certain points on the same continuum. Frameworks are the most general. Placed at the other end of the continuum, models make very specific assumptions useful in the analysis of a concrete situation (Ostrom 2005a, 27).

A closer examination of the three concepts shows that Ostrom tended to attach to frameworks a law different from that of theories and models. I would identify at least four dimensions that set frameworks apart from both theories and models. First, while theories and models have "theoretical roles," frameworks are situated at a metatheoretical level: their language is rich enough to provide a common base for talking about different theories, so frameworks make us able to compare the theories. "They attempt to identify the universal elements that any theory relevant to the same kind of phenomena would need to include" (McGinnis and Ostrom 2014). Two important aspects are involved here. On the one hand, the capacity of frameworks to offer a comparative evaluation of theories avoids the danger conceptualized by Kuhn (1970) that different theories are encapsulated in mutually incomparable worlds. On the other hand, the fact that frameworks are capable of playing this metatheoretical role means that frameworks are sophisticated enough to allow their use in comparing theories. One can reconstruct in frameworks at least those significant components and parts of the theories that make comparisons possible in terms of theories' descriptive, explanatory, and predictive capacities.

Moving to a second distinction, besides their "diagnostic role," frameworks have an explanatory one. They do not directly explain empirical phenomena, but "isolate the immediate structure affecting a process of interest to the analyst for the purpose of explaining regularities in human actions and results, and potentially to reform them" (Ostrom 2011, 11). Theories are expected to produce their explanation within the structure provided by frameworks. As Vincent Ostrom (1997, 105) notes, a framework is necessary to specify the features that need identification in any analytical effort, and thus opens the way to formulating theoretical explanations. The framework brings together heterogeneous elements that can be used to conceptualize different patterns of order in human societies.[3] By taking into account the multidimensional facets characteristic of the artifactual nature of human reality, the framework offers the possibility to achieve general explanations.

Third, when addressing practical questions of reform and transition, "theory" must be used in the plural but "framework" in the singular; analysts need one framework and a family of theories (Ostrom 2007, 26). The immense diversity of regularized social interactions cannot be captured by a single theory that provides a "universal model of rational behavior." But if analysts move to the level of frameworks, they can retain "the assumption of a universal framework composed of nested sets of components within components for explaining human behavior" (Ostrom 2005a, 7). So, frameworks, but not theories, are the entities that select the universal building blocks that help explain phenomena (e.g., the ways in which individuals craft the structure of their interactions). In this third sense, frameworks are not situated only at a metatheoretical level, for they make claims about structural features of reality. I argue below that this role of a framework in relation to theories and models allows us to advance a (scientific) realist interpretation of our theoretical constructs.

Fourth, a framework organizes "prescriptive inquiry"; it "helps to identify the elements (and the relationships among these elements) that one needs to consider for institutional analysis" (Ostrom 2005a, 28). Besides its diagnostic role (descriptive and explanatory) based on identifying a set of universal building blocks, a framework also works as a heuristic device. It can also be understood as a methodological instrument to build, apply, and compare theories. As Aligica (2014, 75) summarizes, referring to the Institutional Analysis and Development (IAD) framework, "the 'instrument' the Ostroms and their associates put forward is both a conceptual framework and a manual for operating it." In this methodological understanding of frameworks, a core criterion for evaluating them is the capacity to guide action and put in order and investigate the protean institutional diversity and complex systems characterized by heterogeneity and pluralism (Aligica 2014, 100).

However, if one regards the dimension of specificity as fundamental, do theories and models also have, in a smaller or larger degree, the characteristics of frameworks? I think that in Ostrom's view at least some models play the type of roles usually attached to frameworks. They are the ideal models believed to express the paradigm case of a theory: the Copernican model of the solar system, the perfectly competitive market, Hardin's pasture, Arrow's conditions on social welfare functions, or McKelvey's conditions underlying his chaos theorem (Ostrom 1990, 24; 2009a, 523; Anderies, Janssen, and Ostrom 2004). I discuss them in more detail in the second section, Models. For now, let us only note Ostrom's diagnostic of the correct attitude we may have toward them: they are perplexing "impossibility results." For example, Arrow's impossibility theorem can be interpreted in the sense that social choice theory has been destroyed; and Hardin's example looks to entail the impossibility of avoiding the "tragedy of the commons." But in dealing with these issues, both Sen (1977, 1999) and Ostrom (2009a) opted for a different attitude: rather than dismissing or accepting impossibility results without question, they chose to engage with them, not to resign. They regarded the results as valid only in very special models, which incorporated specific assumptions, and took a methodological attitude: instead of despair, they examined the underlying assumptions of these models (e.g., assumptions about human rational behavior) and also focused on the empirical conditions under which different voting rules or institutional arrangements make major differences in outcomes (Ostrom 2009a, 523).

On Theories

The second level of analysis is that of theories. During her entire career Elinor Ostrom did not spare efforts to emphasize the crucial role of theories in advancing scientific research: "Political science of the twenty-first century will advance more rapidly in acquiring well-grounded theories of human behavior and of the effect of diverse institutional arrangements on behavior" (Ostrom 1998, 17). In what follows, I assume that we have chosen a default framework—the IAD framework; another example is the related Social-Ecological System (SES) framework (Ostrom 2009b). All theories I shall use as examples are compatible with this framework. Theories, argues Ostrom (2007, 25), select for further analysis a subset of variables in a framework and make more specific assumptions. They have at least three functions: they (a) diagnose a phenomenon, (b) explain its processes, and (c) predict outcomes. But a more fundamental question about theories is this: what kind of entities are they? The answer has a negative part and a positive one. Here, I argue that, in Ostrom's conception, theories are not linguistic entities; Ostrom did not champion the syntactic view of scientific theories. The positive part of the answer will be given in the next section.

It was already noted that, according to the received or syntactic view, theories can be properly characterized as sets of sentences formulated in a more or less formalized language, sometimes axiomatized in first-order logic. However, in institutional theory the appeal to a less formalized language is also important: "whether individuals use a written vernacular language[4] to express their ideas, develop a common understanding, share learning, and explain the foundation of their social order is also a crucial variable of relevance to institutional analysis . . . . Without a written vernacular language, individuals face considerably more difficulties in accumulating their own learning in a usable form to transmit from one generation to the next" (Ostrom 2007, 43).

But a more rigorous, even formalized language is crucial to analyze institutions. The article Ostrom wrote with Sue Crawford (1995) clearly formulates the structure of the language in which we analyze rules. A large part of the article is devoted to developing the syntax of this language. To construct well-formed statements of this language, we require a number of components: attributes, aim, conditions, deontic operators,[5] and an "or else" clause. By appealing to different collections of these components, the analyst can construct statements that express strategies, norms, or rules.

The advocate of the syntactic view of theories may be disappointed to find in the article no further attempt to construct a collection of general statements on the types of relevant rules—that is, a linguistic theory of institutions. I believe there are two reasons why Crawford and Ostrom did not proceed in that direction. First, the objective of the two authors was to detect the "grammar" of institutions: not the surface statements describing rules, but the deep structures built into the collective action situations. So, the study of syntax is only a first step in the attempt to detect which components of the grammar are involved in each case, and how the common understanding of the participants is structured. Second, the grammar is relevant in the construction of models used to analyze a specific situation. The grammar generates a structural model of the situation. The analyst determines which components of the grammar are involved. Then the model can be constructed by appealing to one of the theories accepted; for example, one can construct simple models of such situations by using game theory. A game is not a linguistic object, although of course some (descriptive and deontological) statements are used to describe them. Games are mathematical abstract objects (Ostrom, Gardner, and Walker 1994, 75).

We can easily note that this focus on structural features of empirical settings has few things in common with the traditional topics studied by the proponents of the syntactic view of theories. Ostrom is more interested in "operationalizing" the syntax and using it to build models to deal with different empirical, concrete situations than in constructing a consistent set of statements about them or, more specifically, in searching for criteria to distinguish between "theoretical" and "observational" terms, as the champions of the received view used to focus on.

Even when such topics appear in Ostrom's studies, their significance is different. Take the example of the distinction between observational and theoretical terms of a theory. The terms *organization* and *institution*, argues Ostrom (2007, 22; 2005a, 18), have different logical properties. Because organizations are located in buildings, which are quite visible, *organization* might be categorized as an observational term. But "institutions themselves are invisible," so *institution* clearly is not observational: "because institutions are fundamentally shared concepts, they exist in the minds of the participants and sometimes are shared as implicit knowledge rather than in an explicit and written form. One of the problems facing scholars and officials is learning how to recognize the presence of institutions on the ground" (Ostrom 2007, 23).

Here is a difficult problem: one can only conclude that *institution* is non-observational, but one has yet no argument to state that it is a theoretical term; that is, it has a descriptive, explanatory, or predictive role in the theory. Being nonobservational is not synonymous with being theoretical. Van Fraassen (1980), for example, argued that terms can be observational or nonobservational, and theoretical or nontheoretical, and that these two distinctions should not be conflated. To argue that *institution* works as a theoretical concept, one can start with an important remark by Ostrom (2014, 11–12): in constructing models (e.g., in a formal game-theoretical analysis), rules and norms are not represented in the game. The reason is that rules and norms are regarded as exogenous factors that create the structure of the model itself, not as components of the model.[6] So when the analyst finds that a model fits a specific situation, "it is always a challenge to determine what the rules structuring patterns of interaction are." What then can the analyst do? She needs to observe and compare the behavior of the players in different models to determine the rules involved. This is a strong argument, in my view, that *institution* can be regarded as a theoretical concept of the theory: theoretical concepts enable the researcher to develop many possible applications of the theory, describe their cross-connections, and thus explain phenomena. As some authors have argued, the mark of a theoretical concept of a theory is that it requires that when we apply the theory we take into account not only the internal structure of its models but also the factors that determine the structure of the models, resulting in a large set of models of the theory (see, e.g., Sneed 1971). Institutions structure patterns of interaction within and across different organizations and situations. Although usually institutions are invisible, because they are "deeply buried under the regularities of observed behavior" (Ostrom 2005b), they are explanatory factors, and much of what analysts see results from them.

MODELS

The Pivotal Role of Models

At this point I can move to the positive part of the answer to the question, What type of entities are theories? Ostrom (2005a, 2007) usually states that models differ from theories in that models make much more specific and precise assumptions about a limited set of parameters and variables that "help the analyst to deduce specific predictions about likely outcomes of highly simplified structures." When appealing to models, analysts may focus on a limited set of outcomes. Given the particular problems at hand, they must develop well-tailored models and avoid applying them inappropriately to the "study of problematic situations that do not closely fit the assumptions of the model" (Ostrom 2005a, 29).

Ostrom makes another important point: multiple models are compatible with more theories included in a framework. That statement means that a model can be constructed by relying on some theory and making some very specific assumptions, and that same model can be constructed if one starts from another theory and then presumably makes some other very specific assumptions. This claim is problematic because there is no guarantee that the two procedures yield the same entity. It is possible that, in fact, we face two similar entities, which nevertheless are quite different in their theoretical assumptions and structure. Although the two entities may entail the same results, it cannot be inferred that they are identical. In Ostrom's perspective, I believe that a way out is to appeal to the concept of a framework: it ensures that there is some common ground that collects together different theories and identifies compatibilities. Frameworks are able to extract common elements of diverse theories by organizing them in a specific way.

Although Ostrom (2007, 25) warns not to confuse theories and models, apart from their degree of specificity, she does not advance other criteria to distinguish them. One may even be confused by assertions such as "Models are very specific working examples of a theory" (2010b, 659). Theories vary in their capacity to apply rigorously to concrete cases (Ostrom and Cox 2010).

Some are very vague and suggest only a general type of solution. For example, some suggest that the key to successfully manage natural resources consists of devising ideal governance types or property regimes. Usually, economic and environmental policy analyses and their related fields have been dominated by this approach in the form of the state-market dichotomy. At the other end, some theories are extremely precise in their applications and lack flexibility to correctly apply to distinct cases. If such theories are available, governments will tend to homogenize the diversity of contexts to which they apply their policies and management practices.[7] These too-rigorous theories are closely attached to extremely well-specified contexts and so cannot be successful in accounting for other cases; not surprisingly, they can be identified with models. Because, as noted above, the main dimension in distinguishing theories from models is specificity, the contrast, argue Ostrom and Cox (2010, 5), comes to be between "excessively general theories" and "excessively precise models."

A note of warning is necessary at this moment. Ostrom repeatedly gives the example of models of the individual used in institutional analyses. *Homo economicus* is a well-established formal model, developed in game theory and neoclassical economics, and based on precise and rigorous assumptions. But researchers must be careful not to confuse this type of "model" with the theoretical models that define a theory and that will be described later in more detail. *Homo economicus* is a model only in the sense that it is a set of claims based on some specific assumptions the researcher makes when approaching a situation. In a sense, because it is used in more theories, it is a very general concept. In Ostrom's use, calling *homo economicus* a model is just a means to indicate the specificity of its assumptions.

However, specificity is not the only reason that the borderline between theories and models is not sharp. To see why, I move from the old "received view" of theories, which was based on the idea that theories and models are entities of quite different types (theories are linguistic entities, models are not), and adopt a semantic view of theories.

It is usually assumed that models are abstract entities. In natural sciences, models are usually formulated in formal terms as mathematical structures. Their main characteristic is that they apply to concrete, particular situations. Ostrom's assertion that a model is a working example of a theory expresses not only the idea that models are more specific than theories and therefore are more appropriate to apply to concrete situations, but also that theories are entities of the same type as models. They both are abstract conceptual means to deal with some problems. A model is theory in action in the sense that it is theory applied to a specific situation.

A fundamental point I want to make is that Ostrom's assertion suggests that theories are even more closely connected with models: theories can be individuated simply by giving the class of their models.[8] For this reason, theories need not be distinguished from models by invoking other criteria. Theories are not collections of connected statements but (well-structured) families of models.

In arguing for this conclusion, I was guided by the so-called semantic conception of theories. This conception was developed by authors such as Suppes (1962), van Fraassen (1980), Sneed (1971), Cartwright (1983), Giere (1999), and Suppe (1974, 2000). The core claim of this conception is that theories can be understood by appealing to the notion of a model. Theories are not sets of statements; rather, they are structured collections of models. Therefore, in the semantic conception the language in which the theory is expressed is not the primary concern of the analysts. The models of a theory are diverse and cannot be reduced to one grand model. Some of them are intended, some are new and surprising. Some of them satisfy certain restrictions, others do not; for example, not all the models of Newton's mechanics satisfy the law of gravity. It is important to note that a collection of models that identifies a theory is structured. Models are located in a well-defined logical space (van Fraassen 1980), and they are connected in different ways. These connections[9] are essential for characterizing the main concepts of the theory (Sneed 1971). Moreover, there are different types of models of a theory, and they are hierarchically arranged. Applying a theory to a concrete situation requires the appeal to different kinds of models, nested in complex structures (Suppes 1962).

More recent work on models questioned their dependence on theories and argued that models, not theories, are central in scientific inquiry. Of course, models are involved in a theory's use. Models can explain and predict points in a theory and be used in experiments. But in many cases models are constructed without relying on a theory, and they are also used in observation, instrumentation, and experimental design without reference to theories. Models are autonomous and mediate between theory and reality (Morgan and Morrison 1999; Morgan 2012; Morrison 2015). First, neither the theory nor the empirical data completely determine models. Second, models function as instruments. That characteristic means that models can be used to fulfill more different theoretical functions; moreover, an instrument is something independent of the objects it operates on. Third, models function as a means of intervention: one learns from them not just by contemplating them but also by building and manipulating them in applications. Morgan and Morrison (1999, 32) argue that models may also function as investigative instruments: they help analysts produce a representation of the reality: "models typically represent either some aspect of the world, or some aspect of our theories about the world, or both at once."

I believe that the first three characteristics of models as independent instruments can be easily detected in Ostrom's conception. She repeatedly noted that in the construction of a model more theories are sometimes needed, and that models must fit the particular conditions of the situation they are to deal with. For example, the study of common-pool resources did not confirm the universal usefulness of a single model, but it raised the tough tasks of further developing theories and building new models. Ostrom (1990, 2) even defined herself as a casual modeler. She used models to fulfill a variety of functions: to diagnose, predict, or reform. Sometimes analysts develop model variants to explore the way in which changes in the assumptions produce differences in predicted behavior. Moreover, Ostrom (2011, 7) argues that the use of well-tailored models lets analysts analyze policy processes and outcomes. They undertake systematic, comparative institutional assessments and provide recommendations of reform. To have a model is to use it.

The fourth, investigative function of models is more problematic. Ostrom (2007, 26) argues that a role of theories is to aid in the accumulation of knowledge from empirical studies. If, for example, a researcher studies the structure of action situations, she constructs and makes use of some formal games (i.e., models) and tries to see how rules relate to the structure of action situations, thereby affecting the way individuals behave and achieve outcomes. In this way, the analyst develops a cumulative body of knowledge about the effects of rules (Ostrom, Gardner, and Walker 1994, 40).

However, the idea behind this fourth function of models is not only that they produce a better empirical adequacy but also that analysts get a better representation of some aspects of the world. As I have mentioned, I think that in Ostrom's view this claim is correct.

The Realm of Models

The family of models of a theory is extremely diverse and presumably cannot be fully determined. Because "no one can undertake a *complete* analysis of all of the potential rules that they might use" (Ostrom 2005a, 255), it is always possible to face the need to develop another new model of the theory. For Ostrom, an enduring effort was to argue for a stronger claim: that this diversity is also irreducible. Therefore, she rejected all "blueprint approaches," based on the actors' inclination to "propose uniform solutions to a wide variety of problems that are clustered under a single name based on one or more successful exemplars" (2005a, 274). The paradigmatic example in this sense is the "only solution" (or the "panacea") approach, which Ostrom rejected: in that approach, one would recommend one of two ideal solutions, either the state or the market, to solve a commons dilemma. Oversimplified, idealized policy prescriptions are equally formulated by both centralizers and privatizers (Ostrom 1990; Ostrom and Cox 2010).

Ostrom's rejection of these approaches has two components. First, she argues that one can dig deeper than both hierarchies and markets. Individuals solve problems by devising an extraordinary set of alternative institutional arrangements that are neither markets nor states. Second, she clarifies the role and place of ideal models. Let me spend some more time on this second component.

I shall start with an analogy: Ostrom (2010b) notes that there is no normative theory of justice that can unambiguously be applied to all settings. She refers to Sen's book *The Idea of Justice* (2009), where the author contrasts two traditions in the study of justice, both stemming from the Enlightenment: what he calls the "transcendental institutionalism," exemplified by authors like Hobbes, Locke, Rousseau, Kant, and, in the past decades, by Rawls, Dworkin, Gauthier, and Nozick, and the "comparative tradition," to be found in the works of, for example, Adam Smith, the Marquis de Condorcet, Bentham, Wollstonecraft, Marx, or Mill. For the authors in the transcendental tradition, the focus is on determining the nature of "the just" and on identifying "perfect" justice. Their main aim is to define and characterize the model of an ideal society. Second, they consider that the character of the society depends fundamentally on the institutions in them, and therefore they concentrate primarily on getting the institutions right.

The work of Rawls (1971, 1999) is paradigmatic of this tradition. He argued that the main task of a theory of justice is to provide a picture of an ideal, perfect society. To evaluate a particular society is to contrast it with the ideal society and determine the distance between it and the ideal state of justice. One cannot embark on the study of real societies if the ideal society is not already given: "nonideal theory presupposes that ideal theory is already on hand. For until the ideal is identified, at least in outline—and that is all we should expect—nonideal theory lacks an objective, an aim, by reference to which its queries can be answered" (Rawls 1999, 89–90).

The authors in the comparative tradition are not much impressed by ideal models. Instead, they try to remove manifest injustice from the actual world. They are concerned with social realizations: what society would result from actual institutions, actual behavior and other influences, rather than presuming compliance by all players with ideal requirements. Sen devoted his book to a deep criticism of the different characterizations of perfectly just institutions. For him, ideal arrangements are of course possible, and even useful in some contexts. But they are not prerequisites for understanding real-world societies and the policy recommendations one would want to advance to remove inequities in contemporary societies.

I think Ostrom can be unambiguously included in the comparative tradition. Her criticism of the prominent and special role of ideal models is in line with Sen's own position. As Aligica (2014, 33) writes, in Ostrom's work "the accent is moved from grand principles and general designs to social processes and contextual analysis. . . . We are increasingly taking distance from the Rawlsian and Habermasian hypothetical arrangements or the neoclassical economics models and their assumptions."

Consider one of her favorite examples: Hardin's pasture as an ideal model. Its logic looks to be compelling. Therefore, policymakers tended to accept Hardin's model and thought their conclusions made it obligatory to take positive action to impose rules on the users of the common-pool resources (CPRs) in their domain (Ostrom 2009a). Moreover, in certain (both experimental and field) settings, Hardin's predictions that individuals involved overharvest the common-pool resource are confirmed. So, we come to the first fundamental aspect of Ostrom's view: ideal models do fit some situations,[10] where they correctly describe the individuals' behavior. They are not utopic—that is, mere idealized models that actually do not (and even cannot) fit any situation at all. They can describe actual behavior of individuals,[11] not only the behavior they would have if situated in ideal conditions like idealized markets or idealized states (Ostrom 1990, 216).

This aspect is as important as a second one: Ostrom emphasized that the focus on ideal models was misleading. There are many other types of models that fit much better real-world situations. Now, if we put together these two aspects, it follows that in Ostrom's view ideal models are accepted, but not with a special and privileged role in the configuration of a theory. They are just models among others. While her main arguments were directed to showing that we must avoid assuming that only ideal models are to be promoted, room still exists to let ideal models help the growth of knowledge. When first proposed, they opened new avenues of theoretical thinking, and at the end of the day they are able to adequately describe some actual cases.

From Models to Scenarios to Theories

Researchers develop models in two main types of situations: when they analyze field settings and when they perform laboratory experiments.[12] Their degree of specificity is very large, which means that they are intended to apply to one situation, or to a family of very similar situations. Models are abstract entities: when, for example, one develops a model of a small group of entrepreneurs who use a common-pool resource, the representatives of these entrepreneurs in the model are abstract actors. Moreover, in highly formalized models (e.g., in agent-based models), their representations may even consist of decision-making algorithms.

Constructing models is a complex enterprise because usually the move from one model to families of models and to (causal) theories is smooth and sometimes difficult to notice. To see this, consider an example given by Ostrom (1998). Given a small group of farmers who are to use a common-pool resource (a creek for irrigation that runs by their relatively flat properties), a number of very precise assumptions and simplifications must be made to build a model of this situation. Thus, we assume that the farms are approximately the same size, that all the farmers expect to continue farming into the indefinite future, that their benefits from using the CPR are proportional with the number of working days spent maintaining it, and that the benefits of participating in a successful collective action are greater than the individual costs of participating, but also that free riding is objectively attractive.

A second step is to identify the structural variables that affect the likelihood of the farmers' collective action. They include (a) the size of the group, (b) the symmetry or the asymmetry in the resources and interests of the farmers, (c) the possibility of (face-to-face) communication, (d) the cost of providing the public good, (e) the time horizon of expected cooperation, and (f) the capacity for monitoring the behavior of the members of the group and so on.

Third, a specific model is defined by restricting the structural variables to a certain range of values. For example, suppose we have a small number of actors (this makes room for better communication within the group), small size of the farms, symmetry of assets and resources, a long time horizon, and a low-cost production function. Given the structure of the model and the restrictions of the structural variables, one can predict some ways in which the actors will behave. In our case, the prediction is that many of the individuals in the situation will succeed in cooperating and overcoming the dilemma.

Fourth, the model is tested. Substantial evidence from the field is consistent with this explanation (Ostrom 1998). But also, if the model is used to design an experiment, this prediction is also supported (Ostrom, Gardner, and Walker 1994; Walker et al. 2000).

At this point the researcher meets a new challenge. The models can be manipulated in different ways: one may change one variable at a time, and so get a new model; then another variable can be changed to get another model, and so on. The result is the development of a cumulative and coherent family of models that can then be used together to construct more sophisticated formal models as well as to design empirical testing (in field and laboratory settings, as well as in computer simulations).

These families of models so assembled are called "theoretical scenarios" by Ostrom (1998). Scenarios are buffer conceptual constructs, situated between models and theories. Starting with some baseline model, a scenario investigates the class of models that result when a variable is changed. Unfortunately, the notion of a theoretical scenario has not received much attention, as compared with frameworks, theories, and models.[13] But it is important for two reasons. First, the role of the scenarios is to help construct a (rough) coherent causal theory, able to explain data and make accurate predictions. Second, because in the construction of a theory more scenarios are involved, the semantic definition of a theory becomes more sophisticated: it consists not simply of one collection of rather autonomous models but of a structured set (of families) of models.

THE WAY TO STRUCTURAL REALISM

The semantic conception of theories gave a new impetus to the realist/anti-realist debates in the philosophy of science. Scientific realists claim that some components of our theoretical constructs can be related, one way or another, to the world. Anti-realists, on the other hand, refuse to give concepts of truth or correspondence a role in scientific theorizing and practice. Van Fraassen, one of the main champions of anti-realism, considers that the aim of science is not truth, but empirical adequacy: "science aims to give us theories which are empirically adequate; and acceptance of a theory involves the belief only that it is empirically adequate" (van Fraasen 1980, 12). Because models are not linguistic entities, truth cannot be meaningfully predicated about them. Models can only be useful or not useful, adequate or not, correct or not. They fulfill, or not, the purpose for which they were intended (Giere 1999). Models are not intended to have a representational role; rather, their proper place is in the use of knowledge.

The "map" metaphor offers a telling argument in this sense. According to it, theoretical models are like maps. Neither models nor maps are linguistic entities and thus cannot be true or false. Just like maps, models "have limited accuracy and represent only certain features of a real-world system. Most importantly, model assessment cannot take place without understanding the purpose for which the model was designed and used" (Clarke and Primo 2012, 60–61).[14] Clearly, this understanding of the nature of models tries to make a realist position highly implausible and to render instrumentalism as a more accurate picture of our philosophical attitude toward theories.[15]

It would seem natural to interpret the instrumentalist position toward theories and models as based on a pragmatist philosophy. Referring directly to Ostrom's views, Aligica (2014, 182) aptly formulates this interpretation: "once engaged in a conceptual reconstruction of the philosophical assumptions and implications of the Ostroms' work, we soon realize that it coalesces almost naturally around pragmatist ideas, more so than around any other competing perspective. This is true not only when it comes to matters of social philosophy or views about the nature and significance of governance processes. It seems to be true also when it comes to methodology and epistemology." The pragmatist perspective succeeds in making sense of Ostrom's view on the role of frameworks and of the theories compatible with them in policy analysis, as intrinsically linked to action. Moreover, many texts of Elinor Ostrom support the pragmatist perspective.

However, in this third part of the chapter, I try to advance a different, complementary perspective on Ostrom's view, rooted in the realist/anti-realist debates and centered on the representational character of theories. I reexamine Ostrom's view on theories and argue that it can be well captured as a sophisticated type of realist position called structural realism (as presented in the chapter introduction). It should be emphasized that the pragmatist and the realist perspectives are not incompatible. In fact, some prominent realists[16] do not hesitate to locate themselves in the pragmatist camp and regard the perspective of the pragmatist philosopher John Dewey as pivotal.

Reference, Truth, and Structure

Models are subjects of evaluation. Two types or procedures are traditionally used.[17] First, models can be evaluated comparatively: given a set of relevant criteria, one model is better than another. For example, a more complicated model that makes use of more parameters, equations, and so on may better fit the data compared with a simpler model. In the more complex case of agent-based models, good statistical performance is a crucial, although not sufficient, criterion. But the simpler model can be better in the sense that it is not too specific and can be applied to more datasets. Second, models can be evaluated by testing them against some standards. One external standard or criterion, relevant especially in situations when models are used in policy analysis, is the coherence of the behavior of the model with the understanding of the relevant stakeholders about the targeted system. The coherence, even coincidence, is in many cases crucial for the acceptance of the recommendations proposed by the analysts. But internal coherence is also important: is the model plausible given the researcher's understanding of the processes? Third, a model must be coherent with the theory or the theories used by researchers, in the sense that it complies with the theory's assumptions and consequences, and even in a stronger sense that the construction of the model is based on that theory. Moreover, models must enhance our understanding of empirical observations. Coherence with the theory turns models into explanatory tools, and a better understanding of the empirical data helps increase the capacity of the theory to predict new facts.

A fourth criterion is of special relevance here. It concerns the issue of the fit between models and the real world. Although "we never know for sure whether a model describes the empirical world," we want to "test which model gives a better description of the real world" (Janssen and Ostrom 2006, 7). Here we meet a fundamental question, What explains the success of a model and consequently the success of one theory, but also the lack of success of another theory? Can we understand why the model is doing so well?

Scientific realism as a philosophical view offers a clear answer: it is the representational character of the theory[18] and of its models that explains its success, its empirical fit. Realism properly concerns theories.[19] Putnam (1975, 69–70) gave the following very simple and also elegant definition of realism (about a theory *T*): "a realist (with respect to a given theory . . .) holds that (1) the sentences of that theory . . . are true or false; and (2) that what makes them true or false is something external—that is to say, it is not (in general) our sense data, actual or potential, or the structure of our minds, or our language, etc."

Because the concept of truth occurs essentially in its definition, realism posits a "correspondence" relation between some components of the theory and items in the external world. In the syntactic conception of theories, the standard move is to take realism to entail that the observational and theoretical terms of the theory genuinely refer to items in the world, and that the items in the world have the properties attached to them by the theory *T*. The most challenging claim of standard realism is that scientific theories (at least the best ones) correctly describe the nature of those unobservable entities that cause the phenomena we observe. That is why, as Putnam famously put it, realism "is the only philosophy that doesn't make the success of science a miracle"; that is, it explains why science is successful.

Scientific realism comes in many versions. Some of them make stronger claims while some are more moderate. In what follows, I introduce a moderate version called structural realism. According to it, accepting a theory does not necessarily commit analysts to accepting that it tells them the nature of the unobservable world; the theory only says something about the form or structure of the external world.[20] The claim of standard scientific realism, which is that the unobservable objects that cause the empirical phenomena are correctly described by our best theories, is too strong. The "correspondence" between theories and the external world is not local; it does not concern the nature of the objects in the world and their properties. One cannot know which objects and events are in the world. Possibly individuals cannot even know the first-order structure of the world—that is, the first-order properties or relations of the objects and events in the world. Structural realists give a different description of the relation between theories and the external world. Their claim is that people should commit only to the mathematical or structural content of theories: we *can* know the characteristics of this structure—that is, determine the second-order properties of the world.

This view also has important applications when studying theory change:

> The rule in the history of physics seems to be that, whenever a theory replaces a predecessor,[21] which has however itself enjoyed genuine predictive success, the "correspondence principle" applies. This requires the mathematical equations of the old theory to re-emerge as limiting cases of the mathematical equations of the new. . . . The principle applies purely at the mathematical level, and hence is quite compatible with the new theory's basic theoretical assumptions (which interpret the terms in the equations) being entirely at odds with those of the old. (Worrall 1996, 160)

So, in the shift from one theory to a successor one, there is continuity, but it is one of structure, not content. The reference of a theory's terms does not need to be preserved.

As an illustration, consider again the map metaphor of models preferred by nonrealists. One famous example they give is that of the London Underground maps. Their argument is that the maps do not describe the "real" characteristics of this objective system, for the role of the maps is not to give a true description of the Underground, but to be useful for people who use it. Look, for example, at the South Kensington station on the Green line. On some maps[22] it is positioned horizontally to the West of Victoria station; in others it is positioned somewhere to the northwest of it. The distance between the two stations is quite different on different maps. So, it is argued, maps have only a practical role; they are more or less useful, but they are not representational.

A structural realist can well accept this argument. But she adds that one should not search for a "correspondence" with reality by considering map by map. Rather, the correspondence is to be found at the level of the entire family of such maps because the configuration of the stations system is what matters for structural realism. For example, on all the maps, the South Kensington station is situated on the Green line between Victoria station and the Gloucester Road station. This betweenness is a structural property of the London Underground that is "truly" described by its maps. We cannot claim that something is the case in the real world by simply contemplating a single model, or more models considered separately. We can only infer that the fact that the South Kensington station is on the Green line between Victoria station and the Gloucester Road station is objective (i.e., it represents a feature of the real world) by comparing the maps of the London Underground and noticing that they all display a relevant invariant.

Structural realists focus on the abstract forms, patterns that are invariant in the different applications (models) of theories. They are not interested in detecting specific, individual items in the external world and their characteristics. Rather, they want to identify the relational structure of the external world and show when two empirical systems are isomorphic.[23]

The argument to be developed in the next subsection can be introduced with the following passage, in which Ostrom summarizes her scientific creed. In it, we find a remarkable analogy with the structural realist perspective described above: "I do not view our primary enterprise as one of explaining individual events. Rather, given the number of conditions that affect most political choices, our normal task is to understand structures and resulting processes and how specific combinations of elements affect the likely outcomes of these processes" (Ostrom 2006, 6).

Structural Realism and Ostrom's View

In this picture of the relation between theoretical constructs and reality, let us replace maps with models of empirical systems in which a group of participants use a common-pool resource. The core components of these models consist of the rules actually used. Which are the characteristics of the set of these models? Or, having in mind the definition of theories in terms of sets of models, the question may be rephrased as, What type of theories would account for these many empirical systems? These theories would include at least some universal claims or conjectures about the world and an explanation of the observable behavior of the participants.

Now, one can distinguish between two main types of answers. The first, which is explicitly rejected by Ostrom, consists of trying to identify a universal set of formalized rules that gives optimal results for every type of problem. This answer assumes that the empirical systems and so their theoretical models are diverse but homogeneous enough to let us construct a general grand model: all specific models of the theory consist, then, in simple designs such as private property, government ownership, or community organization. Under these assumptions, the blueprint thinking works. A unique solution can be advanced for all problems; it consists of, first, framing an ideal model and, second, constructing other models on this pattern.

Suppose also that the researcher accepts a semantic conception of theories. Under these two conditions, just like the person who uses a map of the Underground to travel in London, a realist would try to identify which components of a model correspond to items in the external world. However, as Ostrom (1990; 2005a) forcefully argued, the realist's attempts are doomed to fail because the relative homogeneity assumptions are not correct. At least in the case of the governance of CPR systems, the diversity one can find is so vast that a set of rules that works best in some circumstances may totally fail in others.[24] There is no way to construct a complete isomorphism between models and reality.

Ostrom (1990, 6–8) warned analysts to always keep in mind a sharp distinction between empirical settings and their theoretical models. For example, when a simple game-theoretical model is built to analyze the behavior of a group of individuals jointly using a resource in a natural setting, these individuals are represented in the model as individual rational agents.[25] When using the model, the analyst claims that there is a similarity between the two classes of individuals. In general, attention is called to similarities between some variables in a natural setting and the corresponding variables in its model. In this sense, the model describes certain characteristics of the world as it is. "What makes these models so interesting and so powerful is that they capture important aspects of many different problems that occur in diverse settings in all parts of the world" (Ostrom 1990, 6). However, although analysts are tempted to conclude that many other similarities are present, it is dangerous to believe that models are fully isomorphic to the empirical setting they represent. This danger is best seen if we focus on ideal models. Such models, as for example the well-known prisoner's dilemma game, entail that the rational actors representing the many individuals who jointly use a CPR in a natural setting will, in the model, jointly produce a suboptimal result. When the model is supposed as a full representation of the real setting, it has been frequently concluded that the real individuals are in fact helpless, "caught in an inexorable process of destroying their own resources" (Ostrom 1990, 8). But this conclusion is correct only in a few very specific cases. For although some variables of the model have similar counterparts in the world, we cannot conclude that such similarities exist for all the variables in the model. The model does not succeed in fully describing the world as it is. This conclusion is very general and concerns all the models that analysts build. It is then doubtful to consider that, in the same way as single maps, single models are the adequate entities we can appeal to in order to claim adequate correspondence with reality.

Now we arrive at the second type of answer, explicitly endorsed by Ostrom (2005a, 258). This theoretical account of the empirical world it indicates is far more abstract. Ostrom describes it as follows. She starts by studying a large collection of robust, self-governing CPR systems; having in mind something close to the first answer, she tries to identify the specific rules used by these systems. But she is unsuccessful: "rules that were observed varied dramatically from one system to the next," and she is not able to "identify any particular rules consistently associated with robust governance of common-pool resources." The conclusion is to "give up the idea that specific rules might be associated with successful cases" (Ostrom 2010b). How to deal with this puzzling situation? Her answer is that instead of a highly unsuccessful search for a unique and optimal set of rules, the researcher should make a move upward to a new level of generality and study the ways in which such sets of rules can be designed. She moves from studying specific rules to studying collections of such rules. Instead of studying what the models built around a simple, ideal one have in common, she acknowledges the existence of a large variety of classes of models and tries to find out what these classes have in common. What readers get then is a more abstract theory:[26] its primary attention is on the structure of situations (Ostrom 2005a, 137) or on the "grammar" of the institutional arrangements.

This move has two dimensions, an epistemological and an ontological one. On the epistemological dimension, Ostrom argues for the crucial role in the institutional theory of what she calls design principles.[27] These principles do not describe specific sets of rules; rather, they picture the structural characteristics of such sets of rules. In this sense, design principles can be conceived as similar to regularities, laws, or generalizations that scientific theories usually seek. They are "derived" somehow inductively from field settings and "describe structural similarities" among robust self-organized systems (Ostrom 2005a, 257). They "characterize" these robust institutions (Ostrom 1990, 90). Design principles characterize broader institutional "regularities" among the systems that were sustained over a long period of time and were absent in the failed systems (Ostrom 2005a, 252). So, the focus on the design principles, understood in this way, makes sense of the representational intention of theories.

The ontological dimension of this abstract conception of theories concerns their claims about the external world. The abstract institutional theory turns the focus from governance systems to *systems of governance systems* (from sets of models to *sets of sets of models*). At the level of this system of governance systems, analysts have an overarching interconnected collection of rules that define the structure of this complex setting. If interpreted as regularities, design principles can be viewed as components of this structure. Moreover, since, as argued in the Models section, no model of governance systems enjoys a privileged place, the theory entails that this system of governance systems must work in a decentralized way and get structured as a result of evolutionary interaction of its components.

The reality just described has a name: polycentric systems.[28] So, if we want to identify some (at least partial) isomorphism with reality, it should be conceived as holding between a theory compatible with the IAD framework and the structural characteristics of polycentric systems. The idea is not to search for items in the external world that would correspond to some theoretical constructs, but to find a correspondence between the conceptual structure put forth by the theory and structural traits of the world. Clearly, this is a structural realist interpretation of Ostrom's conception of institutional theory.[29]

CONCLUSION

At this point my argument is completed. I have argued that in Ostrom's view, a methodological understanding of the triadic scheme frameworks/theories/models (or possibly a quadratic one obtained by adding "scenarios") can be adequately developed at the level of the frameworks. However, theories, under the semantic conception, can also be reconstructed as representational instruments. Of course, a realist faces the difficulty of giving a meaningful understanding of what "representation" is. The standard realist approach, according to which representation consists in a local correspondence between components of the theory and items in the world (objects, events, or—in the case of institutional theory—specific systems of rules), does not work when one tries to apply it to Ostrom's work. But this fact does not mean that Ostrom held an instrumentalist position. My argument is that her position can be interpreted as a sophisticated realist position called structural realism.

NOTES

1. Fifteen years later, she noted a radical change in political science: "theory becomes an ever more important core of our discipline" (Ostrom 1998, 17). However, Ostrom (2006) cautiously warned that a symmetrical threat—"the counterproductive search for universal laws of human behavior"—must also be avoided.

2. In the Models section, I argue that Ostrom's approach should include a fourth component: theoretical scenarios. These are buffer conceptual constructs, situated between models and theories (Ostrom 1998).

3. In this sense, a framework differs from universal, ideal models, which, as we shall immediately see, are usually presumed to apply in all contexts and under all circumstances (Ostrom 1997, 102).

4. In this passage Elinor Ostrom quotes from Vincent Ostrom (1997, 228). In his book Vincent Ostrom also argues that researchers cannot focus only on facts and neglect the role of theory.

5. This component is analyzed in the so-called deontic logic: a formalized theory of the structural properties of normative operators (i.e., expressions like "obligatory," "permitted," "prohibited," and so on). The two authors refer to deontic logic in the context of the interdefinability of these operators.

6. To put it another way, more familiar for the philosophers of science, game-theoretical models represent only the empirical content of the theory's application to particular settings. Theoretical components of the theory intervene only in determining the structure of models and the connections between them.

7. These cases define the so-called blueprint approach I shall shortly discuss in the next section.

8. If a model is included in two such classes, it follows that the two theories are mutually consistent.

9. Sneed calls them "constraints." For example, in classical particle mechanics one such constraint is that a particle should have the same mass in all the models in which it appears. In social choice theory, the so-called anonymity condition states that a social welfare function must have the same value in all the profiles that differ only in that the individual preferences are permuted among voters and so on. These constraints were alluded to above when I argued that institution is a theoretical concept.

10. For example, those created in a laboratory (Ostrom 2005a, 70). Moreover, "in some field settings, the classical theory of individual behavior generates empirically confirmed results. In highly competitive environments, we can assume that the individuals who survive the selective pressure of the environment act as if they maximized their individual utility dependent on a key variable, such as profits, associated with survival in that environment" (Ostrom 2012, 59).

11. This finding shows that ideal models of the type Ostrom discusses are different from idealized models used, for example, in natural sciences, which cannot in principle be exemplified in the real world. Giere (1999, 90) gives the following example. Think of Newton's Laws of Motion plus the Law of Universal Gravitation around the year 1900 (when both Einstein's relativity theory and quantum theory did not yet exist). As a matter of fact, no two bodies in the universe could be said to satisfy in their motions these laws, because there are other things in the universe and they also exert gravitational attraction. Moreover, the gravitational field is not homogeneous, and so the conditions necessary to apply the laws are never satisfied.

12. A third, and extremely important, type of model was also investigated by Ostrom and her collaborators: agent-based models—that is, computational representations of autonomous agents who interact with each other at a micro level, leading to broader-level patterns (Poteete, Janssen, and Ostrom 2010; Schwab and Ostrom 2008).

13. But see, for example, Aligica (2014, 16), who notes the heuristic role of the theoretical scenarios as alternatives to grand generalizing.

14. Ostrom also uses the metaphor of the maps. But I believe that her use of the metaphor does not support an instrumentalist interpretation of her position. She writes, for example, that IAD consists of "a series of nested conceptual maps of the explanatory space that social scientists can use in trying to understand and explain the diversity of human patterns of behavior" (Ostrom 2005a, 8). Here, "nested conceptual map" refers to the ways in which we may use the conceptual instruments (frameworks, theories, models) in the process of "zooming in" or "zooming out," not to the relation between the conceptual instruments and the external world.

15. However, some authors, Giere (1999), for example, forcefully argued that conceiving models as maps does not necessarily entail nonrealism.

16. For example, R. Giere (1999, 2006) and H. Putnam (1998).

17. In what follows, I shall appeal to arguments developed in Janssen and Ostrom (2006), and Poteete, Janssen, and Ostrom (2010).

18. As different from the primarily methodological role of frameworks.

19. Some authors add "discourses."

20. In the case of theories in natural sciences, this structure is usually given in a mathematical format.

21. The realist view of theories is in sharp contrast with the Kuhnian incommensurability thesis. For realists, the transition from a theory to a successor one is ensured because reference is preserved. We may note that in Ostrom's conception, the commensurability of theories is a consequence of the methodological role of frameworks. Moreover, combining this view on frameworks with realism gives a further argument that we can apply to different theories, each with its own language and assumptions, if certain invariants can be identified.

22. See, for example, https://www.londoncitybreak.com/tube.

23. Here, I only outlined structural realism and tried to avoid the many complications facing its more detailed elaboration.

24. As Ostrom (2005a, 124) notes, when the irreducible heterogeneity of real-world situations is recognized, the classic model of noncooperative game theory becomes a special case. And although "many new models have been posed in an effort to devise another general model of human behavior," it turns out that "none of these general models are yet sufficiently well supported by experimental and field data that we can just substitute a new general model for the old classical general model."

25. A similar distinction is explicitly made by Rawls (1999, 30–31): "We must not confuse rational and reasonable real citizens with their representation as rational parties in the (reasonably construed) original position."

26. It is analogous, for example, to move from the study of the theorems of first-order predicate logic to the study of that logic's structural properties (compactness, completeness, Löwenheim-Skolem, etc.).

27. Ostrom defines a design principle with reference to its capacity to ensure the robustness of a governance system—that is, its long-enduring success in sustaining the CPRs. However, the connection between robustness and performance is complex: robust design often involves a tradeoff between maximum system performance and robustness (Anderies, Janssen, and Ostrom 2004). This tradeoff leaves open the possibility to either design new principles that would account for the efficiency of governance systems, or construct Ostrom's principles in a much more general manner (Wilson, Ostrom, and Cox 2013).

28. This picture of polycentricity is indebted to Aligica and Tarko (2013).

29. The possibility of matching theory and reality should not be surprising, because empirical phenomena are not independent of our conceptual tools. "The presence of order in the world," writes Ostrom, "is largely dependent upon the theories used to understand the world" (2016, 104). Our theoretical tools not only try to describe but also constitute the world as a cosmos, an ordered and legible reality. See also in this sense Vincent Ostrom's self-characterization as a dweller in Plato's Cave who cannot see the direct light of Truth. For him, "what we presume to be true is expressed and mediated through the conventions of language and the experiences that human beings share in talking with, relating to, and working with one another" (Ostrom 1997, 8).

REFERENCES

Aligica, Paul Dragos. 2014. *Institutional Diversity and Political Economy*. Oxford, UK: Oxford University Press.

Aligica, Paul Dragos, and Vlad Tarko. 2013. "Co-Production, Polycentricity, and Value Heterogeneity: The Ostroms' Public Choice Institutionalism Revisited." *American Political Science Review* 107 (4): 726–41.

Anderies, John M., Marco A. Janssen, and Elinor Ostrom. 2004. "A Framework to Analyze the Robustness of Social-Ecological Systems from an Institutional Perspective." *Ecology and Society* 9 (1): 18.

Cartwright, Nancy. 1983. *How the Laws of Physics Lie*. Oxford, UK: Oxford University Press.

Clarke, Kevin A., and David M. Primo. 2012. *A Model Discipline: Political Science and the Logic of Representations*. Oxford, UK: Oxford University Press.

Crawford, Sue E. S., and Elinor Ostrom. 1995. "A Grammar of Institutions." *American Political Science Review* 89 (3): 582–600.

Giere, Ronald. 1999. *Science Without Laws*. Chicago: The University of Chicago Press.

———. 2006. *Scientific Perspectivism*. Chicago: The University of Chicago Press.

Hempel, Carl G., and Paul Oppenheim. 1948. "Studies in the Logic of Explanation." *Philosophy of Science* 15: 135–75.

Janssen, Marco A., and Elinor Ostrom. 2006. "Empirically based, agent-based models." *Ecology and Society* 11 (2): 37.

Kuhn, Thomas. 1970. *The Structure of Scientific Revolutions*, 2nd ed. Chicago: The University of Chicago Press.

McGinnis, Michael D., and Elinor Ostrom. 2014. "Social-Ecological System Framework: Initial Changes and Continuing Challenges." *Ecology and Society* 19 (2): 30.

Morgan, Mary S., and Margaret Morrison, eds. 1999. *Models as Mediators: Perspectives on Natural and Social Science*. Cambridge, UK: Cambridge University Press.

Morgan, Mary S. 2012. *The World in the Model: How Economists Work and Think*. Cambridge, UK: Cambridge University Press.

Morrison, Margaret. 2015. *Reconstructing Reality: Models, Mathematics, and Simulations*. Oxford, UK: Oxford University Press.

Ostrom, Elinor. 1982. "Beyond Positivism." In *Strategies of Political Inquiry*, edited by Elinor Ostrom, 11–28. Beverly Hills, CA: Sage Publications.

———. 1990. *Governing the Commons: The Evolution of Institutions for Collective Action*. Cambridge, UK: Cambridge University Press.

———. 1998. "A Behavioral Approach to the Rational Choice Theory of Collective Action: Presidential Address, American Political Science Association, 1997." *American Political Science Review* 92 (1): 1–22.

———. 2005a. *Understanding Institutional Diversity*. Princeton, NJ: Princeton University Press.

———. 2005b. "Doing Institutional Analysis: Digging Deeper than Markets and Hierarchies." In *Handbook of New Institutional Economics*, edited by Claude Menard and Mary M. Shirley, 819–48. Dordrecht, Holland: Springer.

———. 2006. "Converting Threats into Opportunities." *PS: Political Science & Politics* 39 (1): 3–12.

———. 2007. "Institutional Rational Choice: An Assessment of the Institutional Analysis and Development Framework." In *Theories of the Policy Process*, 2nd ed., edited by Paul A. Sabatier. Boulder, CO: Westview Press.

———. 2009a. "Engaging with Impossibilities and Possibilities." In *Arguments for a Better World: Essays in Honor of Amartya Sen, Vol. II: Society, Institutions, and Development*, edited by Kaushik Basu and Ravi Kanbur, 522–41. Oxford, UK: Oxford University Press.

———. 2009b. "A General Framework for Analyzing Sustainability of Social-Ecological Systems." *Science* 325 (5939): 419–22.

———. 2010a. "Analyzing Collective Action." *Agricultural Economics* 41 (1): 155–66.

———. 2010b. "Beyond Markets and States: Polycentric Governance of Complex Economic Systems." *American Economic Review* 100 (3): 641–72.

———. 2011. "Background on the Institutional Analysis and Development Framework." *Policy Studies Journal* 39 (1): 7–27.

———. 2012. "Coevolving Relationships between Political Science and Economics." *Rationality, Markets and Morals* 3 (54): 51–65.

———. 2014. "Do Institutions for Collective Action Evolve?" *Journal of Bioeconomy* 16 (1): 3–30.

———. 2016. "The Comparative Study of Public Economies." *American Economist* 61 (1): 91–107.

Ostrom, Elinor, and Michael Cox. 2010. "Moving Beyond Panaceas: A Multi-Tiered Diagnostic Approach for Social-Ecological Analysis." *Environmental Conservation* 37 (4): 451–463.

Ostrom, Elinor, Roy Gardner, and James Walker. 1994. *Rules, Games, and Common-Pool Resources*. Ann Arbor: University of Michigan Press.

Ostrom, Vincent. 1997. *The Meaning of Democracy and the Vulnerability of Democracies*. Ann Arbor: University of Michigan Press.

Poteete, Amy R., Marco A. Janssen, and Elinor Ostrom. 2010. *Working Together: Collective Action, the Commons, and Multiple Methods in Practice*. Princeton, NJ: Princeton University Press.

Putnam, Hilary. 1975. *Philosophical Papers, Volume I: Mathematics, Matter and Method*. Cambridge, UK: Cambridge University Press.

———. 1998. "Pragmatism and Realism." In *The Revival of Pragmatism: New Essays on Social Thought, Law, and Culture*, edited by Morris Dickstein, 37–53. Durham, NC: Duke University Press.

Rawls, John. 1971. *A Theory of Justice*. Cambridge, MA: Harvard University Press.

———. 1999. *The Law of Peoples*. Cambridge, MA: Harvard University Press.

Schwab, D., and Elinor Ostrom. 2008. "The Vital Role of Norms and Rules in Maintaining Open Public and Private Economies." In *Moral Markets: The Critical Role of Values in the Economy*, edited by P. J. Zak, 204–27. Princeton, NJ: Princeton University Press.

Sen, Amartya. 1977. "Rational Fools: A Critique of the Behavioral Foundations of Economic Theory." *Philosophy and Public Affairs* 6 (4): 317–44.

———. 1999. "The Possibility of Social Choice." *American Economic Review* 89 (3): 349–78.

———. 2009. *The Idea of Justice*. Cambridge, MA: Harvard University Press.

Sneed, John D. 1971. *The Logical Structure of Mathematical Physics*. Dordrecht, Holland: D. Reidel Publishing Co.

Suppe, Frederick, ed. 1974. *The Structure of Scientific Theories*. Urbana: University of Illinois Press.

———. 2000. "Understanding Scientific Theories: An Assessment of Developments, 1969–1998." *Philosophy of Science*, 67, Supplement. Proceedings of the 1998 Biennial Meetings of the Philosophy of Science Association. Part II: Symposia Papers: S102–S115.

Suppes, Patrick. 1962. "Models of Data." In *Logic, Methodology, and Philosophy of Science: Proceedings of the 1960 International Congress*, edited by Ernest Nagel, Patrick Suppes, and Alfred Tarski, 252–61. Stanford, CA: Stanford University Press.

van Fraassen, Bas C. 1980. *The Scientific Image*. Oxford, UK: Oxford University Press.

Walker, James, Roy Gardner, Andrew Herr, and Elinor Ostrom. 2000. "Collective Choice in the Commons: Experimental Results on Proposed Allocation Rules and Votes." *Economic Journal* 110 (140): 212–34.

Wilson, Sloan D., Elinor Ostrom, and Michael Cox. 2013. "Generalizing the Core Design Principles for the Efficacy of Groups." *Journal of Economic Behavior & Organization* 90S (June): S21–S32.

Worrall, John. 1996. "Structural Realism: The Best of Both Worlds?" In *The Philosophy of Science*, edited by David Papineau, 139–65. Oxford, UK: Oxford University Press.

PUBLIC ADMINISTRATION TENSIONS

CHAPTER THREE

"WHAT SHOULD WE DO?"

THE BLOOMINGTON SCHOOL AND THE CITIZEN'S CORE QUESTION

PETER LEVINE

F or citizens, Elinor Ostrom's thought offers powerful resources. I take a "citizen" to be someone who seriously asks the question, "What should we do?" The subject of this question is plural for two reasons: because any individual has too little influence over the world to take effective action alone, and because every human being is too biased and cognitively limited to reason well alone about what is right to do. We must reason and act with others.

The question is not "what should be done?" That is often too easy. What should be done about climate change? Carbon should be taxed everywhere to reduce consumption. That may (or may not) be right, but it is also empty, because you and I cannot tax carbon. We might as well say that "consuming less carbon" is what *should be done*. The hard question is what *we* should do, especially if we are not satisfied with small-scale change but want to have tangible leverage over larger systems.

The question is what we *should* do, because we have a fundamental responsibility to do what is right—not merely what we want or have learned to value from our contingent backgrounds. We are obligated to deliberate with others about the differences between good and bad, right and wrong, fair and unfair. And the question is what we should *do* because it is not satisfactory merely to form or express opinions; we are obliged to act. (Nonaction is just a form of action—sometimes an effective one—for which we are also responsible.) Besides, it is only by acting and reflecting on our actions that we seriously learn.

For citizens (so defined), Ostrom offers a helpful overall model. Human beings belong simultaneously to groups of many sizes and formats that operate by rules of various types. We not only participate in these groups but also can change their rules or start new groups. Certain principles and practices tend to make groups work better. When these principles are applied, groups become better forums for asking, "What should we do?"

Usefully for citizens, Ostrom shifts the focus of political theory away from governments—which are simply assemblages of organizations with various rules that interact with other organizations with rules of their own—and turns our attention back to ourselves: the "we" who must decide what to do. Also usefully for citizens, Ostrom shifts the attention from end states, fully specified ideals of a good society, toward the groups in which we actually participate, asking how we should structure these groups so that they bring out the best in their members and increase the odds that *we* will move society in better directions.

However, Ostrom's theory will not suffice for citizens. Her design principles can easily conflict in practice; they are in tension. We need normative standards to select among the design principles, and she is largely silent about such standards. Also, she emphasizes a certain category of problems that confront members of groups: how to coordinate individuals' behavior so as to create and preserve resources for the group itself. Those are inescapable problems, but they are not the only challenges we face as citizens. We must also confront uncertainties or disagreements about what is right: about the means and ends that we *should* choose. For guidance on those questions, we need a theory of deliberation. Finally, we must relate appropriately to people not in our own groups. That problem is especially challenging when the normative debate is about the definition of the "we." For example, the Indian independence movement wanted Indians not to be part of the collective of the British Empire, and the American civil rights movement demanded that African Americans become full members of the collective of the United States.[1] For situations like these, Elinor Ostrom is not particularly illuminating; her views should be combined and synthesized with others.

In 2007, Ostrom, two future presidents of the American Political Science Association (Jane Mansbridge and Rogers Smith), Harry Boyte, Stephen Elkin, Karol Soltan, and I wrote a manifesto for "Civic Studies" titled "The New Civic Politics: Civic Theory and Practice for the Future" (Boyte et al. 2008). To develop Civic Studies as a nascent discipline, Soltan and I have since taught 14 Summer Institutes of Civic Studies: 10 at Tufts, two in Ukraine, and two in Germany. These institutes have drawn about 220 advanced graduate students, seasoned civic activists, and professors from at least 17 countries. The syllabus has evolved, but in reflecting on a decade of readings and discussions, I have come to see three main pillars of Civic Studies. Elinor and Vincent Ostrom and the Bloomington School address problems of *collective action*, Jürgen Habermas and his generation of the Frankfurt School address problems of *discourse about values*, and Mohandas K. Gandhi and Martin Luther King Jr. address problems of *inclusion and exclusion based on identities*, such as race and nationality. In this chapter, I place the Bloomington School in that context, exploring both its unique contributions and its limitations.

A FOCUS ON MEANS, NOT ENDS

To help explain the Bloomington School's distinctive approach, Aligica cites the distinction between "end state social theories" and "process theories." He observes, "While a large part of theorizing in political economy is more or less explicitly 'end state' oriented, the Ostrom's research agenda seems to be closer to the 'process' perspective" (Aligica 2014, 28). That could imply a purely empirical, social-scientific "focus on the way ends states emerge," but Aligica adds that "the Ostrom brand of institutionalism has a robust normative component." I have argued elsewhere that the Ostroms' normative stance is often implicit and elusive (Aligica 2014, 22; Levine 2011, 3–14). One reason is that the Bloomington School proposes principles for processes and not for end states. In that respect, it departs from the dominant mode of political philosophy in the English-speaking world since the 1960s. I believe this move is salutary.

Most recent Anglophone philosophy begins by defining justice, understood as an end state. Political *ethics* then involves a set of questions about whether various means (e.g., civil disobedience, misinformation, compromise, or violence) are acceptable—or necessary—when pursuing justice under various circumstances. However, a century ago, as Karuna Mantena notes, there was a more vibrant debate about processes or means (Mantena 2012b). The central question was not what constituted justice but whether and when to use electoral campaigns, disciplined parties with leadership cadres, unions and strikes, consumer movements and boycotts, assassinations, or revolutions, among other options. Mantena reads Gandhi as a participant in that debate who developed and defended nonviolence as a cluster of strategies. I read the Bloomington School as an heir to the same tradition.

Gandhi explicitly argued that the best way to think about politics was to determine the right means or strategies, not to pretend to define justice. "Means are after all everything," he wrote, in response to a group of Indian political leaders who had issued an "Appeal to the Nation" in 1924. These leaders had proposed a concrete ideal of justice: the immediate creation of a new, independent "Federated Republic of the United States of India." They argued that this end justified a wide range of strategies. They wanted to "delete the words 'by peaceful and legitimate means' from the Congress creed, so that men holding every shade of opinion may have no difficulty in joining" the independence struggle. That move would have expanded the range of means employed to achieve the end of home rule. Gandhi replied that these leaders had no right to define an abstract concept of justice, such as "independence," by themselves. The "only universal definition to give it is 'that status of India which her people desire at a given moment.' If I were asked what India desires at the present moment, I should say I do not know." Furthermore, the means used to pursue *swaraj* (independence in its deepest sense) had to be good ones. "As the means so the end. Violent means will give violent swaraj. That would be a menace to the world and to India herself" (Gandhi 1999a).[2]

Drawing on Mantena, I would suggest the following reasons to focus on means rather than ends. Human beings are cognitively limited and cannot see justice far beyond our own present circumstances. Human beings are motivationally flawed and highly susceptible to various distorting and destructive impulses (Aligica 2017, 202–17). Therefore, we must choose modes of politics that channel our impulses in beneficial rather than harmful directions. Forming too sharp a definition of justice can simply excuse bad behavior. Consequences are always difficult to predict and control, and trying to pursue elaborate ends is foolish. We disagree with each other, and what we decide about justice right now is contingent on how we are organized, so it is crucial to get the organization right. Finally, how we participate in politics helps to constitute the world. By acting, we don't merely bring about a result (usually an unpredictable one); we immediately create a new reality just by our action.

For example, one of Gandhi's strategies was the *khadi* campaign: a mass effort to boycott European cloth, wear only homespun Indian *khadi* cloth, and enlist everyone—of all classes—in personally spinning and weaving their own clothes. The *khadi* campaign is widely understood as a means to one of the following ends: political independence from Britain through economic pressure, rural economic development, or spiritual education for those who spun (Mantena 2012b, 9–12).

Gandhi thought of it differently. It was impossible to know whether *khadi* would affect British policy, but an India full of people who wove their own clothes in the cause of independence would immediately be a different place. It would be more decentralized, equitable, ruminative, united, and free. Even if it worked and the British went home, it would be important to keep weaving *khadi* in their absence (Gandhi 1921, 118). "Khadi was educational: Before civil disobedience can be practiced on a vast scale, people must learn the art of civil or voluntary obedience" (Gandhi 1999c, 316). Physical production was essential to education because "awareness is possible only through public work and not through talks" (Gandhi 1999b, 262–63).[3] Apart from its educational outcomes, the *khadi* campaign was also important because it represented an institution that the people had "built up for themselves" (Gandhi 1999c, 317).[4] According to the Bloomington School, managing a common-pool resource requires a principle of participation: the users should create the rules and practices that govern the resource (Ostrom [1990] 2015, 90; 2010, 653). That was the case with the *khadi* campaign.

For Gandhi, "What is justice?" was the wrong question: our focus should be on forming groups of people who interact in ways that bring out the best in them. He saw a nation of home-weavers as such a group. We could certainly debate his specific vision of a *khadi* campaign, but the same general approach can take many forms. For example, Jürgen Habermas represents a dramatically different cultural context and political sensibility from Gandhi's, but he also rejects instrumental, means/ends reasoning in favor of creating groups of people who endlessly *make* justice by interacting. It's just that Habermas's interactive groups are highly critical, explicit, and discursive, whereas Gandhi's weavers may be literally silent. And the common-pool resource management systems studied by the Bloomington School vary enormously in their cultural contexts and purposes, but all are valuable as processes rather than ends.

SEEING LIKE CITIZENS, NOT STATES

Not only has mainstream political philosophy focused on ideal outcomes, but also it has put the *state* at the center of the analysis. The most common question for philosophers is not "What should we do?" but "What kind of government should we have?"

On the first page of the first chapter of the single most influential modern work of political philosophy written in English, *The Theory of Justice*, John Rawls writes, "Justice is the first virtue of social institutions." He presumes that philosophy ought to reveal what makes institutions just, and then individuals should comply with the laws of just societies and strive to reform or revolutionize unjust ones. Rawls explains that defining ideal legal, economic, and social institutions is necessary before we can know how to act when institutions are *not* fully just: in other words, before we can address such topics as charity for the oppressed, civil disobedience, or revolution. Nonideal theory is an offshoot of ideal theory (Rawls 1999a). Rawls later writes, "until the ideal is identified . . . nonideal theory lacks an objective, an aim, by reference to which its queries can be answered" (Rawls 1999b).

Philip Pettit defines *republicanism* as "a consequentialist doctrine which assigns to government, in particular to governmental authorities, the task of promoting freedom as non-domination." He explains that his "interest in a republican conception of liberty comes of the hope that it can persuasively articulate what a state ought to try to achieve, and what form it ought to assume, in the modern world." He acknowledges that "public life" must have an appropriate character—citizens must value and defend liberty. But that implies for him that "the state should concern itself with public life in order to make sure that people enjoy the benefits of non-domination." The state is the responsible agent even when citizens actually deliver justice through their actions and opinions (Pettit 2000, 207, 129, 166).

In an influential presentation of the *Capabilities Approach*, Martha Nussbaum writes, "Of course governments may delegate . . . to private entities, but in the end it is government, meaning the society's basic political structure, that bears the ultimate responsibilities for securing capabilities. . . . The Capabilities Approach . . . insists that all entitlements involve an affirmative task for government: it must actively support people's capabilities, not just fail to set up obstacles. . . . Fundamental rights are only words unless and until they are made real by government action" (Nussbaum 2011, 65).

Even a position that calls for substantially reducing the power of the state—*libertarianism*—is still state-centric in a similar way. In *Capitalism and Freedom*, Milton Friedman writes, "The free man will ask neither what his country can do for him nor what he can do for his country. He will ask rather 'What can I and my compatriots do through government' to help us discharge our individual responsibilities, to achieve our several goals and purposes, and above all, to protect our freedom? And he will accompany this question with another: How can we keep the government we create from becoming a Frankenstein that will destroy the very freedom we establish it to protect?" (Friedman 1962, 2).

These authors disagree about what the government should do and what powers it should have. Friedman wants as little government as necessary to protect a certain kind of freedom. Nussbaum and Rawls would assign the state the powers it needs to guarantee a range of social outcomes. Pettit starts with a certain conception of freedom and concludes with an argument for an assertive state. But all agree that justice means getting the role of the government right.

They also share the assumption that each political community maps onto a single state that has one sovereign government. In 1961, Vincent Ostrom, Charles M. Tiebout, and Robert Warren proposed an alternative "polycentric" view, according to which we belong at once to many overlapping *publics* of various scales, each constituted by its own set of public goods (Ostrom, Tiebout, and Warren 1961, 832–33). Polycentrism seems much more plausible as an account of the way the world functions.

Another objection is that no government alone can determine whether people experience justice or injustice. Amartya Sen begins *The Idea of Justice* with a quotation from *Great Expectations* ("In the little world in which children have their existence, nothing is so finely felt and perceived as injustice") to support the point that nonstate actors—in Pip's case, an older sister—can be just or unjust in ways that no state would be able to determine (Sen 2011, vii).

I would add a third objection. The books quoted above are all about justice, yet their authors and readers are not governments. These books are written by people for people. People can adopt views of what governments should do, and sometimes people influence governments. But individual people—even dictators—cannot directly make governments either just or unjust. Pettit at one point distinguishes the objectives of "the authorities"—people who might abuse power in a republican system—from what "we, as system designers" seek. He imagines his readers to be system designers, but we are *not* that. We are participants in existing systems, capable of influencing them (Pettit 2000, 207).

From our perspective as political actors, governments enter the picture, as do families, markets, customs, religions, ecosystems, laws of nature, and many other tools and constraints. The question for us is not how each of these things should ideally work (if so, we should choose laws of nature that guarantee us all perfect happiness forever), but rather how we should deal with the constraints and opportunities that confront us.

We do have governments. Some of us live in Denmark; others in North Korea or Burkina Faso. All the political philosophers cited above would agree that Denmark's government is better than North Korea's, but that conclusion has limited value for residents of either country. Further, citizens of Denmark can fine-tune the justice of their national policies by supporting the political parties that best reflect their views. In North Korea (because of tyranny) and in Burkina Faso (because of poverty), that approach to improving the world isn't really available.

I would venture an analogy to a family of theological views. For many theists, God is the Unmoved Mover, ultimately responsible for everything but not subject to being changed. Our stance toward God should involve such virtues as hope and faith. We can pray for certain outcomes, and we can be confident that divine choices will be just. We can ask what God is likely to do, given that God is just. We cannot, however, choose how God will act.

Likewise, in all the political philosophies cited above, the state is the unmoved mover of a system of justice. These theories suppose that the question of justice is, What is the ideal state? That resembles the theological question, What are the attributes of God? It is a matter for analysis and inquiry, but not a choice.

Unlike God, the modern Danish state didn't arise spontaneously; Danes made it and sustain it. They have also made the Danish language and economy and the physical layout of Danish towns and the countryside. How did a strategy for influencing the world become available in Denmark that is absent in North Korea? Because of the past behavior of people, both inside these countries and beyond. But the strategies and ethics of citizens' action are sidelined in all the political philosophies that focus on the state—even Friedman's libertarianism. He wants the state to do little, and private actors to do what they want; but that's still not a theory of how we can accomplish justice. Again, if we are Danes who agree with Friedman, we can vote for classical-liberal candidates; but if we are North Koreans, Friedman's ideals are empty.

Perhaps the reason that most political philosophers focus on the state rather than on people as citizens is that the actions of citizens appear to be theoretically uninteresting. Action is a matter of praxis, and the only question is empirical: Given the actual circumstances, what will work to move the society toward justice? That's a question for strategists and empirical students of activism, lobbying, elections, social movements, revolutions, and so on, but not for political philosophers (or so they believe).

I disagree. Groups must deliberate about means and ends, must coordinate their members' actions, and must relate to outsiders. These activities generate problems that are just as conceptually and ethically complex as how to design a government. But they are more pressing for *us*, because we can work in groups, and we cannot implement our ideas of a good state.

The Bloomington School's critique of government-centered theory has important educational implications. Elinor Ostrom (1998, 18) concluded her presidential address to the American Political Science Association with a call for a new kind of civic education:

> All too many of our textbooks focus exclusively on leaders and, worse, only national-level leaders. Students completing an introductory course on American government, or political science more generally, will not learn that they play an essential role in sustaining democracy. Citizen participation is presented as contacting leaders, organizing interest groups and parties, and voting. That citizens need additional skills and knowledge to resolve the social dilemmas they face is left unaddressed. Their moral decisions are not discussed. . . . It is ordinary persons and citizens who craft and sustain the workability of the institutions of everyday life. We owe an obligation to the next generation to carry forward the best of our knowledge about how individuals solve the multiplicity of social dilemmas—large and small—that they face.

THE BLOOMINGTON SCHOOL AND POLICY ANALYSIS

Elinor Ostrom suggests not only a critique of much political theory but also an alternative to a mainstream form of policy analysis. I have in mind a simple

FIGURE 3.1: INSTITUTIONAL ANALYSIS AND DEVELOPMENT (IAD) FRAMEWORK

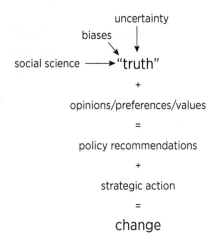

(perhaps *over*-simple or stereotyped) model of how policy analysis is often taught: see figure 3.1. It will suffice to make a point.

In this model, social science aims at truth, truth about how the world works. But from the very first day of a class on social science, a responsible teacher will note that any social science is beset by biases. Also, our understanding of the world is inevitably uncertain. Therefore, "truth" deserves quotation marks. It is always problematic. Still, we use a large array of sophisticated tools to reduce both bias and uncertainty and to cumulatively approximate truth.

The truth about the world does not tell anyone what to do, because facts are not judgments or prescriptions. To move toward policy advice, we need something else: opinions, preferences, or values about what should be. Those cannot come from social science itself. They may come from public opinion, or from policymakers, or perhaps from a different discipline, such as philosophy. Wherever they come from, they are added to facts to produce policy recommendations.

But policy recommendations do not jump off the shelf to implement themselves. Someone must take strategic action to implement any recommendation. That someone is usually quite separate from the social scientist who originally studied the truth about the social world. It takes policy recommendations plus strategic action to generate change.

There are many problems with the model depicted in figure 3.1, and I'll just hint at a few major ones.

Norms or moral commitments are not mere biases. If I say, "education is good," I am not expressing an opinion that might bias my analysis. I am stating a truth, albeit one that needs more detail. (What kind of education is good? For whom? Why?) How to ground or justify moral claims is a complex question, but it is nihilistic to treat facts as objective and all moral claims as subjective in the sense of arbitrary. There are better and worse moral claims.

Data are, and should be, imbued with norms. When we measure an educational system with graduation rates or test scores, we are claiming that these outcomes are valuable. There is no such thing as a value-neutral test, nor should there be.

Empirical information also influences norms. After all, why *do* I think education is good? In part because we have more than a century's experience with near-universal schooling. That experience influences our normative judgment that schooling should be universal.

Another reason for the norm in favor of education is that we have a strategy for making schooling universal. We know how to pass laws that require enrollment and how to fund a system of public education. "Everyone should be educated" is not an empty slogan or a utopian ideal that might have terrible unanticipated consequences when put into action. It is a policy framework that has had decent results in practice, although it needs constant review and improvement. In contrast, the ideal that every human being should have highly rewarding *work* may be appealing in the abstract but it is not clear what it means for policy. In general, our norms are, and ought to be, influenced by what we know about how to implement them.

And why do we have data on students' performance and graduation but not on many other topics that might be equally important, such as their happiness? Because people have organized to compel institutions to collect certain kinds of data, and not other kinds. In that sense, strategy influences the empirical evidence that we have.

In short, strategy, empirical evidence, and normative argument are much more deeply intertwined than the model in figure 3.1 suggests. A policy analyst is not fundamentally different from any other citizen. We must all ask the question "What should we do?" in ways that are influenced all the way down by facts, strategic arguments, and norms. The Institutional Analysis and Development (IAD) and Social-Ecological System (SES) frameworks of the

Bloomington School help to shift in that direction by bringing "evaluative criteria" into the same model with the actions the group takes, its rules, the outcomes, and the context. But again, the Bloomington School focuses on a certain set of challenges faced by groups, not on the full range of problems. And it is vague about the "evaluative criteria."

ADDING TWO OTHER TRADITIONS

An ethical individual asks, "What should I do?" But because none of us can accomplish much alone, or even know what is right without discussing with others, we need groups in which we can ask, "What should *we* do?" In general, groups face three categories of problems.

Problems of discourse arise when we discuss what we should value (or accept) rather than criticize and reject. We must discuss values to gain the benefit of multiple perspectives, but discourse is prone to such threats as propaganda, ideology, rhetorical manipulation, and polarization.

Problems of collective action arise even when we agree on what to value, because it is difficult to coordinate individual behavior and avoid such threats as free-riding, externalities, and the Iron Law of Oligarchy.

Problems of identity and exclusion arise when there is no "we," when *we* are *them* to someone else. In some versions of this problem, there is an existing "we" from which some people have a legitimate desire to exit. They may be, for example, subjects of a mighty empire who want to exercise self-rule (*swaraj*) in their own republic. Or they may be treated as outsiders or quasi outsiders even though they have a legitimate claim to full inclusion.

THREE TRADITIONS

These problems are sufficiently complex that no one can solve them alone. Answers come from robust traditions that fruitfully combine theory with practice.

Table 3.1 compares the three traditions mentioned earlier: (a) the Bloomington School of Vincent and Elinor Ostrom; (b) Jürgen Habermas, his colleagues in the post–World War II Frankfurt School, and practical experiments

TABLE 3.1: A COMPARISON OF THREE TRADITIONS

	The Bloomington School of Political Economy (Elinor Ostrom et al.)	The Frankfurt School in Its Second Generation (Jürgen Habermas et al.)	Nonviolent Social Movements (Gandhi/King)
Fundamental problem	People fail to achieve what would be good for them collectively.	People manipulate other people by influencing their opinions and goals.	People fail to view others (or themselves) as fully human.
Characteristic starting point	People know what they want but can't get it.	People don't know what they want or want the wrong things.	Some people won't recognize other people as fellow citizens.
Prominent example of failure	We destroy an environmental asset by failing to work together.	Government or corporate propaganda distorts our authentic values.	One national or ethnic group exploits another.
Essential behavior of a citizen	Working together to make or preserve something	Talking and listening about controversial values	Using nonviolent sacrifice to compel change
Keyword	Collaboration	Deliberation	Relationships
Instead of *homo economicus* (the individual who maximizes material self-interest), we need . . .	*Homo faber* (the person as a maker)	*Homo sapiens* (the person as a reasoner) or *homo politicus* (the participant in public assemblies)	A *satyagrahi* (the person as a bearer of soul force)
Role of the state	A set of nested and overlapping associations, not fundamentally different from other associations (firms, nonprofits, etc.)	Citizens form public opinion, which should guide the state, which makes law. The state should be radically distinct from other sectors.	A target of demands
Modernity is . . .	A threat to local and traditional ways of cooperating, but we can use science to assist people in solving their own problems	A process of enlightenment that liberates people, but it goes wrong when states and markets "colonize" the private domain	For Gandhi: An imperialist imposition, undermining *swaraj*

(*continued*)

TABLE 3.1: A COMPARISON OF THREE TRADITIONS (*CONTINUED*)

	The Bloomington School of Political Economy (Elinor Ostrom et al.)	The Frankfurt School in Its Second Generation (Jürgen Habermas et al.)	Nonviolent Social Movements (Gandhi/King)
How facts and values are combined	Not explicitly. Implicitly by using research on collective action to liberate people for reflective self-government	By proposing counterfactual ideals such as "the ideal speech situation" and diagnosing the reasons these are not met	Through "experiments in living" In a prophetic mode
Main interdisciplinary combination	Game theory plus observations of indigenous problem-solving	Normative philosophy (mainly achieved through critical readings of past philosophers) plus system-level sociology	Critical theology plus military strategy

with deliberative democracy; and (c) the nonviolent social movement theories of Gandhi and Martin Luther King Jr.

Each tradition focuses on a different core problem. For the Bloomington School, the problem is a failure to accomplish ends that everyone agrees with. Often, this failure involves a common resource, such as an environmental asset, that is valued by all—the problem is that individuals degrade it. For Habermas, the problem involves not knowing what to value, or disagreeing about goods and ends, or choosing goals that are bad (in the extreme, fascist goals). And for the nonviolent tradition of Gandhi and King, the problem is a lack of a "we" in the first place. Some people exclude other people from participation—for instance, on the basis of race—or demand that other people remain in a "we" that they would prefer to exit.

These differences mean that each tradition detects a different characteristic symptom of social dysfunction: a degraded public resource for the Bloomington School, the influence of ideological propaganda for the Frankfurt School, and a closed door or wall or other barrier for the nonviolent tradition.

Each looks closely at relatively pure and idealized cases that may generate insights about solutions. For the Bloomington School, these "petri dishes" are common-pool resource management systems, such as collective arrangements for managing fisheries or forests, that have arisen around the world (Ostrom et al. 2002, 5). For advocates of deliberative democracy who are influenced by

Habermas, the petri dishes are deliberative forums, intentionally organized to convene citizens for discussion. Such forums range from participatory budgeting processes to formal parliaments. For the nonviolence tradition, the petri dishes are social movement campaigns composed of actions like marches, sit-ins, and boycotts.

The core act of a citizen in the Bloomington School is collaboration, whose etymology is *working together*. Some common-pool resource management regimes require very little talk. They almost always require work: actually restoring a wetland or editing a Wikipedia page.

The core civic act for the second-generation Frankfurt School is deliberation: reasoning with others about good means and ends.

And the core civic act for Gandhi and King is sacrifice: explicitly and publicly renouncing something (money, time, one's freedom or bodily safety) to demonstrate commitment. The words *sacrifice* and *suffering* create a leitmotif in King's *Stride Toward Freedom*, his account of the Montgomery Bus Boycott. Similarly, Gandhi defines "soul-force" (*satyagraha*) as "sacrifice of self" (Gandhi 1921, 90). Sacrifice rarely changes the mind of the direct target but often converts bystanders to support the cause.

Despite the differences among these approaches, they share three fundamental commitments. All are devoted to expanding human agency and responsibility. The question is not whether agency or structure causes social outcomes. The question is how to enhance whatever agency we may have.

All must therefore deny determinism. Elinor Ostrom argues against Garret Hardin that the commons is not a tragedy, an inexorable defeat. Nor is it a comedy, an automatic success. It is a drama whose outcome depends on us. Ostrom writes, "As long as people are described as prisoners, policy prescriptions will address this metaphor. I would rather address the question how to enhance the capabilities of those involved to change the constraining rules of the game to lead to outcomes other than remorseless tragedy" (Ostrom [1990] 2015, 54–57). First-person sentences are relatively rare in Ostrom's formal writing, but by saying what she would "rather address," she expresses a personal value commitment. She wants people to be able to solve their own problems collaboratively, because that is a form of liberation from constraint. It is dignified and creative. She seeks to enhance their capacities for self-governance.

Likewise, Habermas argues against his Marxist forebears in the Frankfurt School that democratic deliberation is not impossible in a capitalist society. Nor is deliberation inevitable in a society with a liberal democratic constitution, because it can be ruined by powerful actors or by public apathy. It is a drama whose outcome is up to us. Finally, nothing is more characteristic of a social movement leader like Gandhi and King than their powerful rhetoric against determinism and complacency. "Yes, we can!" is their basic message to their followers.

SYNTHESIS

At this point, we can begin to put the three traditions together, using each to compensate for the limitations of the others. We might begin with a classic situation for the Bloomington School: a group of people is trying to manage a common-pool resource, which may be as traditional and tangible as a fishery or as current and abstract as protocols for the internet. They should consider the list of design principles enumerated by Elinor Ostrom and her colleagues, including broad participation, clear boundaries, graduated sanctions, shared monitoring, rules congruent with the context, and efficient mechanisms for conflict resolution (Ostrom, [1990] 2015, 90; 2010, 653).

However, these principles may conflict in practice or may conflict with other valid principles not on Ostrom's list. For example, groups function better when they distinguish sharply between insiders and outsiders. But setting *clear boundaries* can curtail *participation* by blocking a discussion of who should be included in the group. Or clear boundaries may settle matters that members *should* discuss (whether they want to or not), such as whether they are mistreating outsiders by setting unjustifiable limits.

I often teach these tensions with the text of the biblical Book of Nehemiah, which is about building a complete city wall to reconstruct Jerusalem after its destruction many years earlier. The prophet Nehemiah applies many of the design principles that Ostrom advocated more than two millennia later. He persuades his people to build the common asset of the wall and then encourages individuals to build their own houses within it. He has the Law publicly narrated so that everyone remembers the rules. He conspicuously applies the Law to himself, "not eat[ing] the bread of the governor" (5:14) but working with his bare hands. He sets up processes of monitoring individuals' labor.

But the wall also excludes outsiders, named in the King James Version as a Horonite, a servant, an Ammonite, and an Arabian (2:19). A running theme of the whole book is the moral and cultural distinction between the Jews and these "heathens" who are left outside the wall, laughing at first and crestfallen at the end. The solidarity of Jerusalem depends on exclusion.

Justice would not demand that all walls and other boundaries come down (they may be essential for coordination) but that people critically discuss whether a particular wall is just. And the Horonite, the servant, the Ammonite, and the Arabian may have a right to participate in the discussion about a wall built to keep them out.

Thus, inspired by Habermas, we will elevate one design principle above the rest—participation—and will define it to be basically synonymous with public deliberation. People should deliberate about which of the other principles to employ, and how. The reason is that deliberation is our best mechanism for deciding what is right and wrong. It is also because talking with and listening to other people about public matters is an important aspect of the good life for human beings; it enriches our inner lives. While deliberating, people should strive for an ideal speech situation, one that is devoid of coercion and constraint, so that the only power is the power of the best argument.

Now the theory is beginning to sound fully Habermasian, but the Bloomington School puts deliberation in an essential context. After all, it is easier not to attend a discussion in the first place and let others do the work of governance. Thus, the very existence of a discussion implies at least a partial prior solution to a free-rider problem. What's more, the fact that the group has something to manage implies that its members have already done some work together. Nehemiah (9:24–25) reminds the Jerusalemites how they came to possess the property on which they construct their city:

> So the children went in and possessed the land, and [the Lord] subduedst before them the inhabitants of the land, the Canaanites, and gavest them into their hands, with their kings, and the people of the land, that they might do with them as they would. And they took strong cities, and a fat land, and possessed houses full of all goods, wells digged, vineyards, and oliveyards, and fruit trees in abundance: so they did eat, and were filled, and became fat, and delighted themselves in thy great goodness.

To have a community that could discuss whether to build a wall, the Israelites first took others' strong cities and fat lands in war. It was a notably coercive start (and accomplished by divine will). The general point, however, is that any group that is in a position to govern a resource has typically managed to coordinate its members' behavior *already*. Discussion rarely precedes governance; it is more typically a moment in an ongoing process of governance. Often a small group of founders chooses the rules-in-use that create a group in which deliberation can occur.

Moreover, the norms that allow groups to approach an ideal speech situation—norms like civility, reasonable trust, and openness—are fragile common resources that they must build and sustain. Almost all real discussions are imperfect, by these criteria: some people are missing because they chose to free ride, some participants undermine civility and trust in the way they talk, and time usually runs out before consensus can be reached, necessitating a vote. Thus, the degree to which groups meet the Habermasian ideal of reasonable discourse depends on how well they have already addressed core collective action problems.

And not everything can be thrown open to discussion. The Bloomington School advises that boundaries must be clear and rules must be congruent with local circumstances and traditions if people are to coordinate. In theory, boundaries and traditions could be freely discussed. Citizens could deliberate about who should be included in the group and what norms they should hold dear. But because a discussion already requires a reasonably functional group, and forming a group requires boundaries and congruence with local traditions, it is not literally possible to start from a neutral place. Instead, a group with some kind of boundary and set of traditions can consider modifying them in the interests of justice or practicality. They can rebuild their ship at sea, but they cannot start from scratch. The group comes first; then the discussion.

Although moments of explicit deliberation have special normative value, they need not be frequent, and discourse should not be allowed to overshadow other kinds of contribution to the commons. People also contribute with their emotions, their labor, and their bodies.

In this combination of Habermas plus Ostrom, we have the nucleus of a satisfactory theory, but it doesn't tell us what to do when some *other* group feels itself fundamentally different and has no interest in joining the deliberation or sharing resources fairly. It is when you stand like Sanballat the Horonite or Geshem the Arabian *outside* of Jerusalem's walls that you need the distinctive contributions of nonviolent theory. Nonviolent social movements can force changes in the underlying rules and norms that govern a situation. They can compel people to deliberate and to cooperate. They can make the oppressed efficacious, bystanders supportive, and oppression yield.

However, nonviolent social movements need insights from the schools of Habermas and of Ostrom, for three important reasons. First, not every nonviolent social movement has desirable or worthy ends. The only way for human beings to test and reconsider whether their own values are appropriate is to deliberate with people who do not agree with them (see Habermas). Second, a successful social movement requires people to coordinate their sacrifices, and that happens only when they already belong to, or can create, functional self-governing entities (see Ostrom). Finally, a social movement cannot *move* forever. It must pursue a relatively stable or even permanent outcome as its objective. Participants in the civil rights movement did not imagine that the Civil Rights Act of 1964 would remove racism from the United States, but they pursued that legislation as a meaningful target during the early 1960s. The Civil Rights Act was an appropriate goal because it incorporated good institutional design (see Ostrom) and would require ongoing deliberation (see Habermas). With this kind of example, the three strands truly come together.

NOTES

1. See McGinnis, (chap. 1, 43): "I argue that when Ostrom was working her way toward her famous list of design principles for sustainable community-based management of natural resources, she concentrated her attention on four critical, or focal, action situations in her case studies: (a) appropriation, (b) provision, (c) rulemaking, and (d) monitoring and sanctioning. Other related action situations were treated more superficially, such as the processes through which new organizations are constructed (or constitution-making; see Ostrom 1989), dispute resolution, evaluative processes, and the slow accumulation of indigenous knowledge." In this chapter, I argue that we need a theory like Habermas's for "evaluative processes" and a theory like Gandhi's or King's for "constitutive processes" and "dispute resolution."

2. I owe the reference to Mantena (2012a, 457). See also Gandhi (1921, 81): "The means may be likened to a seed, the end to a tree; and there is just the same inviolable connection between the means and the end as there is between the seed and the tree."

3. I owe the reference to Mantena (2012b, 11).

4. I owe the reference to Mantena (2012b, 9).

REFERENCES

Aligica, Paul Dragos. 2014. *Institutional Diversity and Political Economy: The Ostroms and Beyond.* New York: Oxford University Press.

———. 2017. "Civic Competence, Self-Governance and the New Epistocratic Paternalism: An Ostromanian Perspective." *Good Society* 26 (2-3): 202-17.

Boyte, Harry, Stephen Elkin, Peter Levine, Jane Mansbridge, Elinor Ostrom, Karol Soltan, and Rogers Smith. 2008. "A New Civic Politics." *Framing Statement of Civic Studies,* Jonathan M. Tisch College of Civic Life, Tufts University, Medford, MA.

Friedman, Milton. 1962. *Capitalism and Freedom.* Chicago: University of Chicago Press.

Gandhi, Mahatma. 1921. *Hind Swaraj, or Indian Home Rule.* Ahmedabad, India: Navajivan Publishing House.

———. 1999a. "Volume Twenty-Eight: May 22, 1924–August 15, 1924." In *The Collected Works of Mahatma Gandhi,* by Mahatma Gandhi, 307-10. New Delhi: Publications Division, Government of India. .

———. 1999b. "Volume Thirty-Two: Personal Note 1925." In *The Collected Works of Mahatma Gandhi,* by Mahatma Gandhi, 262-63. New Delhi: Publications Division, Government of India.

———. 1999c. "Volume Sixty-Five: Interview with Nirmal Kumar Bose, November 9-10, 1934." In *The Collected Works of Mahatma Gandhi,* by Mahatma Gandhi, 316-17. New Delhi: Publications Division, Government of India.

Levine, Peter. 2011. "Seeing Like a Citizen: The Contributions of Elinor Ostrom to 'Civic Studies.'" *Good Society* 20 (1): 3-14.

Mantena, Karuna. 2012a. "Another Realism, the Politics of Gandhian Nonviolence." *American Political Science Review* 106 (2): 457.

———. 2012b. "Gandhi and the Means-Ends Question in Politics." *Occasional Papers of the School of Social Sciences* 46: 1-25.

Nussbaum, Martha. 2011. *Creating Capabilities: The Human Development Approach.* Cambridge, MA: Belknap Press.

Ostrom, Elinor. 1989. "Microconstitutional Change in Multiconstitutional Political Systems." *Rationality and Society* 1: 11-50.

———. 1998. "A Behavioral Approach to the Rational Choice Theory of Collective Action: Presidential Address, American Political Science Association, 1997." *American Political Science Review* 92 (1): 18.

———. (1990) 2015. *Governing the Commons: The Evolution of Institutions for Collective Action.* Cambridge, UK: Cambridge University Press.

————. 2010. "Beyond Markets and States: Polycentric Governance of Complex Economic Systems." *American Economic Review* 100 (3): 653.

Ostrom, Elinor, Thomas Dietz, Nives Dolsak, Paul C. Stern, Susan Stonich, and Elke U. Weber, eds. 2002. *The Drama of the Commons: Committee on the Human Dimensions of Global Change.* Washington, DC: National Academy Press.

Ostrom, Vincent, Charles M. Tiebout, and Robert Warren. 1961. "The Organization of Government in Metropolitan Areas: A Theoretical Inquiry." *American Political Science Review* 55 (4): 832–33.

Pettit, Philip. 2000. *A Theory of Freedom and Government.* Oxford, UK: Oxford University Press.

Rawls, John. 1999a. *A Theory of Justice.* Cambridge, MA: Harvard University Press.

————. 1999b. *The Law of Peoples.* Cambridge, MA: Harvard University Press.

Sen, Amartya. 2011. *The Idea of Justice.* Cambridge, MA: Harvard University Press.

CHAPTER FOUR

SOCIAL RECONTRACTING

ADAM MARTIN

E linor Ostrom's work is situated in the centuries-long literature on self-governance. Why does self-governance matter? Philosophers and political theorists have offered a variety of answers. Some appeal to deontological considerations such as the importance of consent, natural or human rights, the obligations of justice, or freedom from domination. Others offer consequentialist arguments in favor of self-governance, including the desire to avoid exploitation by the powerful, to preserve liberty, or simply to minimize the risk of violent conflict by allowing for peaceful changes in governance.

But what does self-governance mean? Any ideal of self-governance must ultimately be cashed out in some set of institutional details that approximate or effectuate that ideal. Most obviously, many thinkers lean on voting rights as the centerpiece of self-governing political institutions. But few imagine that voting rights are sufficient. Other political liberties such as freedom of speech and the right to peaceably assemble typically receive some lip service. And some theorists push even further, arguing that genuine, earnest political deliberation is a necessary constituent of self-governance.

Elinor Ostrom—while not rejecting all those other ideas outright— calls our attention to alternative answers to these two questions about self- governance. First, Ostrom identifies adaptability as a beneficial consequence of self-governance. Having emerged as a scholar alongside the public choice tradition, Ostrom is keenly aware of the many ways in which governance could go awry. And the distinctive concerns of the Bloomington approach within public choice that she represents is recognition of the variety and complexity of collective action problems. It is easy for good governance to break down. Effective self-governance matters—among other reasons—because it allows for more fine-tuned and rapid adjustment to varied and changing situations. While it is difficult to maintain, self-governance proves more robust in the face of complex and changing social problems.

Second, Ostrom associates self-governance with polycentricity. Governance systems are polycentric when they have a variety of independent authorities. There is no center of power—not even a democratically constituted body—that is the provider of governance. Governance is spread across many jurisdictions, each defined by some combination of geography and function. These jurisdictions are also independent: they are not mere administrative arms of larger governance bodies in the way that a marketing department is an arm of a corporation. And jurisdictions overlap. Individuals and communities are not beholden to a singular sovereign but rather can appeal to a variety of governance providers. Polycentricity maps onto self-governance because individuals are part of many communities of shared interests, and these communities do not perfectly coincide. Life involves a wide array of specialized activities. So does self-governance.

This chapter proceeds as follows. The first section summarizes Ostrom's case in favor of polycentric governance, focusing on three aspects in particular. First, I argue that Ostrom's understanding of a self-governing system can be accurately framed as a process of piecemeal, bottom-up social contracting. Second, I connect her arguments for this sort of polycentric, bottom-up system to her empirical projects. Third, I explain her arguments for "contracting up," part of that process by which lower-level jurisdictions create formal governance structures to deal with interjurisdictional spillovers and achieve other goals such as redistribution. The second section introduces and explores the problem of social recontracting. The Ostroms' work calls attention not only to what government ought to do but how government and other forms of governance ought to be organized (Ostrom and Ostrom 1977). The conditions that make governance arrangements effective can change. I argue that, if one accepts Ostrom's view of effective jurisdictional organization, one must also confront the problem of social recontracting: jurisdictions need periodic reorganization to remain robust and effective. The third section argues that public-sector institutions often make social recontracting difficult. In particular, I argue that there is an asymmetric difficulty in recontracting back down when higher-level governance structures are no longer beneficial. Contracting up may solve present problems but create future ones if vested political interests can block recontracting down. Finally, I conclude with some brief remarks about the analytical and ideological challenges to understanding and effectuating a regime that enables recontracting.

Two qualifications are in order. First, my argument is not meant to imply that thinkers should jettison Ostrom's approach. Rather, my goal is to point out ways in which it might be extended. That requires earnestly sizing up its current limitations. Moreover, I am not claiming that Ostrom was innocent of the concerns I raise. She was keenly aware of their root causes. If anything, I am advancing an Ostromian critique of Ostrom. Consistent with her own views, by focusing on some social problems, she necessarily neglected others, both analytically and empirically.

Second, though my primary focus in this essay is on the work of Elinor Ostrom, I occasionally make reference to the work of Vincent Ostrom and other Bloomington School scholars. This is unavoidable. Any serious engagement with Elinor's work must mention Vincent's, and vice versa (Tarko 2017, 3). Although they were, of course, distinctive scholars with their own contributions, their work is so complementary that treating either as a separate, freestanding theory would be both inaccurate and ultimately uncharitable.

POLYCENTRIC SOCIAL CONTRACTING

Ostrom's work can be understood as a grounded and far more realistic theory of self-governance than what emerges from most political philosophy. The Social Contract is often imagined as the civilizational equivalent of the Big Bang. It occurs in some primordial moment or eternal bargaining situation outside of time. Our understanding of the Contract might change in watershed "constitutional moments," but the Contract itself remains as a sort of Platonic form used to evaluate our institutions. Ostrom's view of self-governance, by contrast, is bottom-up. It involves an often slow, uneven, messy, widely dispersed, and imperfect series of bargains and political settlements that gradually evolves into a complex array of effective governance arrangements.

Only by understanding this messy process—when it goes right and when it goes wrong—can political science hope to improve it and better realize the potential for self-governance.

Ostrom began her exploration of this process by studying water governance in California. In her doctoral dissertation, Ostrom (1965) examines the evolution of collective action institutions dealing with salt water intrusion into groundwater reserves. She documents the process by which various governance arrangements succeeded and built upon one another in response to changing ecological conditions. Characteristically, she first analyzes *both* the formal and informal aspects of groundwater management before drawing conclusions about the efficacy of these arrangements, essentially arguing that they were effective but had not completely dispensed with the problem.

The next major chapter in the development of Ostrom's approach was the metropolitan reform debate (Aligica and Boettke 2009, chap. 1; Tarko 2017, chap. 1). On one side of this debate were metropolitan reformers who lamented the dizzying array of local jurisdictions—a "crazy quilt pattern"—responsible for metropolitan governance. They argued that centralized, rationalized, and professionalized governance providers could streamline redundancies, eliminate confusing webs of responsibility, leverage scarce expertise, and take advantage of economies of scale. Elinor Ostrom (1972) argues that these claims should be treated as testable propositions rather than articles of faith, comparing them to alternative propositions derived from public choice. The extensive studies carried out by the Bloomington group found mountains of evidence for the latter approach. On many measures of performance, smaller police departments perform better than larger ones (Ostrom 1976). But size was not the most important factor. The existence of a multiplicity of jurisdictions was robustly correlated with better service and citizens having a more favorable impression of local police (Ostrom and Parks 1987).

Ostrom's later, most famous work focuses on common-pool resource governance (Ostrom 1990; Tarko 2017, chap. 3–4). In this work, Ostrom criticizes "one size fits all" approaches from advocates of both markets and regulation. Again, compiling a mass of case studies, she finds that there are many examples of common property systems that are neither privatized nor regulated from the outside that avoid the tragedy of the commons. Moreover, these systems exhibit a staggering variety of rules. Rather than generating a list of definite prescriptions, Ostrom concludes that only some broad, abstract "design principles" can adequately characterize successful systems. These design principles include demarcating clear boundaries—who gets to use the resource and who doesn't—and collective decision rules for resource users themselves to determine appropriate limits on usage. Her findings consistently reinforce the effectiveness of a variety of specialized governance providers at responding to particular governance needs.

Many threads in this body of empirical work are woven into Ostrom's appreciation for polycentric governance arrangements. I focus on three here. First, polycentric systems offer citizens more opportunities to correct governance errors. Errors are inevitable, but institutions are not all equal in their ability to correct them. This is essentially an anti-monopoly argument. Distributed authority makes it more likely that errors will be detected, because different jurisdictions can adopt different practices. It also creates more avenues by which individuals and groups can seek to implement change. And even if some jurisdictions are unresponsive, the possibility of exit to other jurisdictions imposes at least some discipline on authorities.

> While all institutions are subject to takeover by opportunistic individuals and to the potential for perverse dynamics, a political system that has multiple centers of power at differing scales provides more opportunity for citizens and their officials to innovate and to intervene so as to correct maldistributions of authority and outcomes. Thus, polycentric systems are more likely than monocentric systems to provide incentives leading to self-organized, self-corrective institutional change. (Ostrom, quoted in Aligica and Boettke 2009, 23)

Second, governance problems are not uniform. In her early work, Ostrom's "objective was to identify and investigate specific urban problems rather than *the* urban problem" (Aligica and Boettke 2009, 11; emphasis in original). Speaking about her later work on common-pool resources, she states: "Given the wide variety of ecological problems that individuals face at different scales, an important design principle is getting the boundaries to roughly fit the ecological boundaries of the problem it is designed to address" (Ostrom 2005, 258). These lessons are general and important for policy analysis beyond Ostrom's areas of inquiry. Positive and negative externalities come in different sizes. Public service production involves many different tasks with different economies of scale. And environmental factors vary tremendously across different contexts. Governance problems differ in scale, nature, and scope, so jurisdictions should exhibit parallel diversity and complexity to effectively grapple with them (Ostrom et al. 1961, in McGinnis 1999, 33; Ostrom and Parks 1987, in McGinnis 1999, 294; Aligica and Boettke 2009, 13).

The final key argument underwriting Ostrom's enthusiasm for polycentric governance is coproduction (Ostrom and Ostrom 1977, in McGinnis 1999, 94–5; Aligica and Boettke 2009, 32–36). Public services are "coproduced" when their efficacy depends on the active participation of "consumers" of those services. For example, successful schooling depends on the involvement of both students and parents, not merely teachers and administrators. Public safety and environmental quality are also heavily influenced by ordinary citizens as much as by specialized producers. This creates another important source of variation in governance problems: the characteristics of the community itself. Different communities have different problems and different solutions available to them based on characteristics such as trust, the nature and quality of social capital among members, and the level of mobility. An optimal governance solution for one community might completely backfire in another.

These arguments combine into a powerful presumptive case against top-down solutions to pressing social problems. Ostrom is clear that, by default, jurisdictions should be as small as possible. She approvingly quotes Buchanan and Tullock (1962):

> A fundamental lesson that we all learned from Buchanan and Tullock is captured on page 114 of *Calculus of Consent* where they state: "both decentralization and size factors suggest that when possible, collective action should be organized in small rather than large political units. Organizations in large units may be justified only by the overwhelming importance of the externalities that remain after localized and decentralized collectivization." I wish I could get that quote put on a poster to be hung on a wall of every university I visit as well as integrated into the textbooks on public policy and urban governance! (Ostrom 2011, 370)

But however strong it is, this presumption can be overcome. Some spillovers are very large, and may require large-scale coordination to deal with. Ostrom argues that this exception may be especially necessary in emergency situations (Ostrom and Whitaker 1974). And though in principle Ostrom favors tying fiscal decisions to jurisdictions, she allows that some intergovernmental redistribution may be desirable (Tarko 2017, 38).

However, if the most efficient scale of production is small, but there are spillovers to other jurisdictions, the political economist as policy analyst would recommend that production be undertaken by small units and that larger units of government provide grants-in-aid to cover the marginal cost of the production that benefits the larger units. If the policy concern is primarily that of redistribution, the political economist is apt to recommend that grants-in-aid be provided by larger units of government to smaller units of government without concern for marginal cost. (E. Ostrom 1972, in McGinnis 1999, 147)

Ostrom allows that many such interjurisdictional spillovers may be solved by informal agreements between jurisdictions. Indeed, a recurring theme in her work is chastising other social scientists for privileging formal "rules in form" over effective "rules in use" (cf. Tarko 2017, 6). But she nevertheless argues that in some cases larger-scale governance problems require the formal constitution of higher-level jurisdictions. In "Neither Gargantua Nor the Land of the Lilliputs," Ostrom and Parks (1987) argue that at some scale the transaction costs of coordinating many smaller jurisdictions become too high. Similar to Oates (1972), they argue that what is required is neither a centralized state nor a large array of small jurisdictions, but rather a multilevel system of *both* small *and* large jurisdictions. Ideally, these higher- and lower-level governments could be complements (Ostrom, in Aligica and Boettke 2009, 152):

> With better knowledge about what enhances local self-governance, it is possible to design larger-scale institutional arrangements that generate accurate information, provide open and fair conflict-resolution mechanisms, share risk, and back up efforts at local and regional levels.

But while Ostrom emphasizes the benefits of local governance and dispersed authority, she does not claim that large-scale governments should be laissez faire (Ostrom, in Aligica and Boettke 2009, 153):

> Improving the abilities of those directly engaged in the particulars of their local conditions to organize themselves in deeply nested enterprises is potentially a more successful strategy for solving resource problems than attempting to implement idealized, theoretically optimal institutional arrangements. There is plenty that national government officials can do to

help a self-governing society. They can provide efficient, fair, and honest court systems, effective property right systems, and large-scale infrastructure projects—such as national highways—that cannot be provided locally.

When larger-scale governance is called for, Ostrom argues that it matters how it comes about. Ostrom and Parks speculate that

> starting from smaller units and building upward is more likely to lead to better solutions than trying to create effective smaller scale units within already constituted large units. . . . What is created by administrative decentralization can be as easily destroyed through administrative recentralization. (Ostrom and Parks 1987, in McGinnis 1999, 300)

Following Pennington (2013), I refer to this phenomenon as "contracting up." Ostrom does not trust larger-scale jurisdictions to credibly fragment, or "contract down." This is why one of the key conditions of polycentric governance is that jurisdictions be independently constituted. The benefit of contracting up is that it maintains smaller-scale accountability relations between citizens and local jurisdictions. I agree with Ostrom that contracting up is likely to lead to better outcomes than administrative decentralization. But however carefully smaller-scale jurisdictions band together, there are still risks from any form of centralization. I focus on one in particular in the next section.

THE RECONTRACTING PROBLEM

The Ostroms return on multiple occasions to the idea of a "public economy." (Aligica and Boettke 2009, 36–39). This phrase is meant to create distance from a Hobbesian notion that the state is a unitary, sovereign entity. When Elinor Ostrom positions what she studies as "between markets and states" (Ostrom 2010), she specifically objects not to the existence or relevance of government—her studies of municipal services clearly involve governments—but to this unitary mental model. In the real world that Ostrom explores, the provision of public services involves a multiplicity of agents and organizations. Some are governmental in our every sense. But these governmental agents interact with the agents of other jurisdictions on transactional terms. They also have dealings with private companies, organizations, and individuals acting on their own initiative. The Ostroms use the phrase "public economy" to denote this nexus of relationships.

"No single center of authority is responsible for coordinating all relationships in a public economy" (Ostrom and Ostrom 1977, in McGinnis 1999, 98). Like markets, the key principle that makes for a public economy is *mutual coordination*. A multiplicity of groups adjust their activities to one another. This distinguishes a public economy both from a Balkanized set of atomistic jurisdictions and from a singular, monopolistic sovereign. What makes them public economies is that they are not governed by the rules of private property, contract, and consent.

> Local public economies are not markets. Nor are they hierarchical in structure. Individuals are not able to engage in a wide diversity of independent *quid pro quo* relationships with any vendor they choose. Decisions are made for collectivities of individuals who are then held responsible to provide tax revenue and user charges to pay for the provision of public goods and services. Like markets, however, there are regular relationships among entities in a local public economy. (Ostrom and Ostrom, quoted in Aligica and Boettke 2009, 37)

If there are market-like relationships in a public economy, it is worth asking what theory of markets Ostrom calls on. Ostrom and Ostrom (1965, in McGinnis 1999, 108–10) argue that production technologies tend to drive market structure. Although they admit that the concept of an industry is "crude," they also take on the assumption that given production technologies will lead firms in an industry to have a certain scale. These passages sound very much like the orthodox Structure-Conduct-Performance approach to understanding markets. This approach can be useful for understanding "snapshot" differences between industries as defined by the analyst. But it has limitations, as the Ostroms themselves recognize (Ostrom and Ostrom 1965, in McGinnis 1999, 109):

> The concept of an industry is subject to a limitation that derives from the inability to specify precise boundaries to any particular industry. What was a relatively simple lumber industry at one period may become a relatively complex forest-products industry at another point in time. The precise boundaries between the oil industry, the automobile industry, and the electric power

industry may also be somewhat obscure. The absence of precision in being able to specify exact boundary conditions, however, does not constitute a serious impediment to the use of the concept of an industry for examining the regularities that occur in the behavior of the many organizations that perform closely interrelated activities in the production of similar goods or services.

This difficulty is precisely the problem I wish to highlight. A public economy is a nexus of relationships that require mutual adjustment. But adjustment is not a one-time process. The factors that affect the success of public enterprises change, just as those that affect markets do. Hayek (1945, 1948, [1968] 2014) criticizes the neoclassical models that form the basis of the economic models that the Ostroms seem to be referencing on precisely these grounds. Since the conditions relevant to economic decision-making are constantly changing, coordination is always a work in progress. Individual enterprises must continually adjust their behavior to recoordinate with customers and with other enterprises. A state of equilibrium—of *achieved* coordination—is at best an ephemeral, elusive target.

To be clear, I am not claiming that the Ostroms believe that coordination is a static, one-time problem. It only makes sense that they would appropriate the most widely known economic models to make their point, since they were often engaged with public policy scholars and practitioners entirely innocent of economic reasoning. Moreover, the standard equilibrium models do, in fact, illustrate the concept of interdependence among enterprises (Hayek 1976, chap. 10). But they also obscure the process of adjustment by which individuals and groups adapt their plans to changing conditions and to one another's adaptations (cf. Kirzner 1997).

Market institutions enable a number of responses to the need for ongoing recoordination. Consider firms. Firms exist because joint action is sometimes more profitable than individual action coordinated through spot markets. Firms must decide whether to perform some task internally or to contract that task out to an external party; to "make or buy." Economists have proposed different theories about where this boundary gets drawn (Coase 1937, Alchian and Demsetz 1972), but this puzzle is fundamental. Making or buying might be more profitable depending on a host of factors, including transaction costs, monitoring costs, and so on. But when these conditions change, so too do the boundaries of firms. Firms might splinter. They might integrate. Or they might go bankrupt. There is a market for corporate control to correct errors (Manne 1965). And there is free entry in most industries, allowing newcomers to challenge the existing ways business is done. We can describe these various adjustments as a process of *recontracting*. Firms are constantly reorganized as part of the ongoing market process adjusting to changing conditions.

The problem of social recontracting is how to make such adjustments in a public economy. Vincent Ostrom identifies a process of challenge and response as the key to understanding the successful or unsuccessful trajectory of a polycentric system (Aligica and Boettke 2009, 58). What if organizational responses to previous governance challenges impede our responses to new challenges? How should governance arrangements respond to changes in the extent of spillovers? Such changes can stem from a variety of sources:

▶ *Technological change*: The boundaries of an industry shift with technological and other changes (Aligica and Boettke 2009, 43). In a public economy, changes in technology can affect the extent of spillovers as well as the publicness (that is, the non-excludability) of public services. Foldvary and Klein (2003) collect a number of cases in which innovation eliminates some need for public provision. For example, with advanced communication technology, tolls can be collected automatically and instantaneously without slowing traffic with a tollbooth plaza, dramatically decreasing the costs of excluding nonpayers from roads. Meanwhile, hydraulic fracturing has potentially increased the scale of spillover effects from pumping crude oil as it opens up new reserves and extends the horizontal range of drilling. Some technological changes will increase the relevant jurisdictional size while others will decrease it.

▶ *Community change*: "An appropriately constituted collective consumption unit would include within its jurisdictional boundary the relevant beneficiaries who share a common interest in the joint good or service and would exclude those who do not benefit" (Ostrom and Ostrom 1977, in McGinnis 1999, 84). Over time, social groups change in often-unexpected ways. The composition of communities changes through migration, aging, and childrearing. These changes can affect the valuations of citizens for various public services, the nature of social capital possessed by community members, and what those members consider to be the relevant opportunity cost for providing public services. For example, demands for environmental tourism have changed drastically over time. The opportunity cost of using various natural resources in private or public industry has therefore shifted as well. And because competing demands on resources often originate from outside an existing community, existing jurisdictions often do not take account of their preferences. It is easy to say that all those affected by a decision should be taken into account, but "all-affected" is a moving target that jurisdictional organizations can hit or miss.

▸ *Ecological change*: As Ostrom was well aware—she discusses the challenges of governing an "ever-changing biological and socio-economic environment" (Ostrom, in Aligica and Boettke 2009, 156)—ecological conditions are not static either. Water sources merge, split, dry up, and emerge. Invasive species create new challenges that do not respect existing jurisdictional boundaries. Insects, bacteria, and other pests adapt to attempts to manage or eliminate them. The boundaries of an ecosystem probably do not change as quickly as technological or social spillovers, but they change nonetheless. For example, Ostrom, Tiebout, and Warren (1961, in McGinnis 1999, 47) note that, in California, state courts serve the primary role in settling disputes between jurisdictions. Libecap (2007) argues that, as the decades have progressed and water has become more scarce relative to demand, this use of litigation has turned Californian water governance into a winner-take-all game between environmentalists, local users, and municipalities.

Owing to these sorts of factors, Martin (2018) argues that effective jurisdictional boundaries need to be discovered through a rivalrous, competitive process. *Who* should be included in a jurisdiction and *what* authority should be vested in it depend on a multiplicity of changing factors. Given the limitations of human knowledge, a process of governance experimentation is a permanent rather than a one-time precondition for getting boundaries right. The same is true of the *internal* organization of jurisdictions. Different governance problems rely on different mixes of citizen voice, expert opinion, managerial coordination, and entrepreneurial leadership. Just as firms differ in the extent to which they are hierarchical and the relative role of makers versus managers, so too should jurisdictions.

One might respond that jurisdictions do not need reorganizing with such changes. And it is true that many changes can be dealt with at the level of policy without needing to tinker at the level of decision rules. But this argument by implication ultimately dismisses the entire thrust of Ostrom's body of research.

Research consistently shows that organizational patterns powerfully shape the efficacy of public services and governance provision. These patterns help deter mine how well incentives are aligned and how effectively knowledge is generated and used. All-purpose, unitary jurisdictions do not have to be reorganized, but they are also unlikely to perform at a high level in the first place.

THE INSTITUTIONAL CHALLENGES OF SOCIAL RECONTRACTING

Saying that boundaries and internal organization should change is one thing. And in markets, they change quite rapidly. That process of adjustment can be painful, but it is quite effective. Public enterprises, by contrast, lack several of the institutional mechanisms that mitigate the pain and increase the effectiveness of recontracting in the private sector. First, public enterprises often have soft budget constraints, especially if they draw on tax revenue severed from the quality of services they provide. This enables such enterprises to weather some changes in conditions more durably but can create a perverse incentive to put off needed changes. Second, many public enterprises lack obvious performance indicators; thus they lack access to signals that indicate adjustment is necessary. Profitability imposes at least some discipline on for-profit firms. Accounting profits are not perfect indicators of success, but private-sector entrepreneurs can at least calculate whether alternative lines of investment offer higher rates of return (Mises 1944). Ostrom also recognizes the importance and difficulty of gauging opportunity cost in the public sector (Ostrom and Ostrom 1977, in McGinnis 1999, 90). Third, freedom of entry and exit are often curtailed in a public economy. Vincent Ostrom (1972, 70) suggests the possibility that "general rules of law might provide for incorporation, annexation, merger, separation, and disincorporation." Aligica and Boettke (2009, 24) argue that freedom of entry and exit is vital for polycentric orders to emerge. The same condition holds if they are to endure. But as of yet such regularized procedures do not exist, and so real-world polycentric systems face the threat of ossification. This is not to say that restrictions on entry and exit are necessarily unjustified: some public services by their nature must be collectively consumed. Not all commons can be privatized (Martin 2018). But such restrictions eliminate one source of information about the necessity of adjustment. In particular, they limit the amount of experimentation in governance. Limited experimentation limits knowledge about alternative governance options, both at the level of policy and the level of organization.

These difficulties afflict all aspects of public administration. They are well explored in the broader political economy literature, especially that informed by Ostrom's work. My aim here is to point out a more specific difficulty: contracting up into larger-scale governance arrangements can impair future organizational adjustments. Ostrom recognizes that beneficial social contracting is tenuous business: "Self-governing, democratic systems are always fragile enterprises" (Ostrom, in Aligica and Boettke 2009, 159; cf. 56–57). My claim is that it is even more difficult to recontract back down when authority should be refragmented. There are a number of reasons to suspect that recontracting down is more difficult than contracting up. The most obvious is that larger-scale collective action is more costly. But there are a few more subtle reasons that I wish to explore here as well.

First, the more that jurisdictions contract up, the closer they approximate a "sovereign" that can be held accountable. The Ostroms' work can be read as a sustained attack on the mental and policy model of a sovereign state that exists as a singular, final authority over society. But as a jurisdiction gets larger, the probability that there is a counterweight to check its abuses becomes smaller. More powerful guardians are harder to guard against. Ostrom (2005, 258) argues that, ideally, all jurisdictions are checked *both* from above *and* below, but at some scale there is no bigger fish. The closer that governments approximate sovereignty, the more difficult it becomes for state agents to credibly commit to beneficial political settlements (Acemoglu 2003). Groups of public-sector employees can fight jurisdictional reorganization that threatens their own position (Ostrom and Ostrom 1977, in McGinnis 1999, 81).

Second, any social recontracting will create losers. Tollison and Wagner (1991) explore the difficulties of economic reform when existing interests stand to lose out. Acemoglu and Robinson (2000) point out that it is political losers—those who lose access to the levers of power—that typically create roadblocks to reform. This problem exists for any social recontracting, but is likely to be more acute for recontracting down. As jurisdictions grow larger, the ability to disperse costs becomes greater. Concentrated beneficiaries in a larger jurisdiction will thus, *ceteris paribus*, have more resources with which to fight reform efforts.

Third, interjurisdictional cooperation can become collusive. By making it cheaper to solve detrimental collective action problems, contracting up also creates the capacity to solve beneficial collective action problems. Greve (2012) documents the process by which the United States has evolved from a system of competitive federalism to a system of "cartel federalism." In a cartel federalist system, the power of the central government acts as an enabler of, rather than as a check against, state government power. Higher-level jurisdictions can enforce collusive agreements between lower-level jurisdictions that they might otherwise renege on. Lower-level authorities are often all too happy to have their hands tied from above, making them less responsive to local constituents.

Finally, larger-scale political organizations are often pressured into expanding their scope. A key lesson of Ostrom's work is that governments are usually most effective when constituted to solve particular problems. But once those higher-level organizations exist, lower-level jurisdictions and other parties often appeal to them to solve all sorts of different problems. The decision mechanisms appropriate for some problems are often inappropriate for others. Martin (2015) considers the case of the Agreement on Trade-Related Aspects of Intellectual Property Rights (TRIPS) adopted by the World Trade Organization in 1994. The World Trade Organization was not constituted to deal with intellectual property issues. Rather, the existence and clout of the organization was seized upon by a small group of US firms to restrict potential sources of competition. The result is a fragile system that does not take into account the needs of developing countries. Furthermore, the more functions a larger jurisdiction takes on, the less likely it is that there will be consensus to break it up.

My claim is not that contracting up is never justified but only that the argumentative burden for doing so is even higher than reading Ostrom would have us believe. The problem of recontracting creates an obvious institutional challenge: what institutional arrangements enable *organizational* responses—not merely policy changes—to changing conditions? Vincent Ostrom points out that, because human beings can learn, we cannot eliminate uncertainty (Aligica and Boettke 2009, 63). The challenge is to build institutions that correct errors, including in how the institutions are built. As the Ostroms rightly argue, thinking in terms of a market-state dichotomy may impede our ability to design such institutions.

CONCLUSION

Patterns of organization that can mobilize coercive sanctions are necessary for the operation of a public economy. . . . But recourse to coercive sanctions and governmental organization does not provide both the necessary and sufficient conditions for the delivery of public goods and services under relatively optimal conditions. Instruments of coercion can be used to deprive others and make them worse off rather than better off. Governmental institutions permit those who mobilize majority support to impose deprivations upon those in the minority. Governmental institutions can become instruments of tyranny when some dominate the allocation of goods in a society to the detriment of others. (Ostrom and Ostrom 1977, in McGinnis 1999, 81)

This chapter has tugged on three threads in Ostrom's work. First, polycentric systems are better suited to deal with complex, interrelated, and constantly changing governance problems. Second, sometimes interjurisdictional spillovers, economies of scale, or other policy goals such as redistribution commend contracting up, in which smaller-scale jurisdictions formally create a higher-level authority. Third, it is more difficult to decentralize authority than to centralize it. When all three of these threads are tugged on at the same time, the problem of social recontracting—especially recontracting back down— becomes apparent. My claim is not that tugging on these threads unravels the Ostrom's project, but only that a patch might be in order.

The Ostroms recognize that fragmentation may be harder than consolidation. But they typically deploy this argument in a conservative fashion. Do not centralize existing polycentric governance systems lightly, because it may be difficult to put the toothpaste back in the tube. Given the debates in which they were engaging, that admonition is wise. However, in making concessions that contracting up will sometimes be necessary to deal with interjurisdictional spillovers or pursue goals such as redistribution, the Ostroms do not explicitly confront the recontracting problem. Recognizing that problem will probably not lead us to reject all efforts to contract up, but it will probably make us even more cautious about centralization than the Ostroms are.

How to respond to the problem of social recontracting is an open question. As noted above, there is an institutional design challenge: how can we get the benefits of contracting up while also enabling contracting down? But there are other, related challenges as well.

First, there is an analytical challenge: what theory and evidence can be brought to bear to answer this question. Ostrom found existing economic theory lacking when trying to understand how communities responded to various collective action problems. One concern I have is that she might not have gone far enough. For example, as noted above, the Ostroms did not appear to take on a full-blooded market process approach when bringing economic tools into political science.

Part of the analytic approach is also in case selection. In the areas Ostrom focused on, the limitations of the Structure-Conduct-Performance approach were probably not binding. She was, after all, studying the decision about when to contract up and when to stay local. Similarly, when she studied common-pool resources, she focused on long-standing institutional arrangements that avoided the tragedy of the commons. Using more dynamic models would probably not reveal much more about these cases. What cases might illuminate how to recontract down or otherwise escape from already overly centralized forms of governance? One possible case is Montreal, which contracted up and subsequently partially back down in the early 2000s. Another is Manchester in the United Kingdom, where powers were reshuffled among existing jurisdictions rather than new jurisdictions being created.[1]

Second, there is an ideological challenge to recontracting. If we take the Ostroms' ideas seriously, it will sometimes require the dissolution of existing jurisdictions. This is a tough sell. The Ostroms were obviously aware of the importance of cultural attitudes in shaping governance (Tarko 2017, 133–35, 165–68). Effective governance jurisdictions command not only provisional assent but also intense, often emotional, loyalty. If I pledge allegiance to the flag, you know that it's not a piece of cloth, and it might not just be a set of principles.

Recontracting down would likely be seen as giving up on the need for governance rather than as an exercise in democratic citizenship. Nonetheless, I maintain that its necessity is implied by Ostrom's framework. "Competitive pressures are the key factors in maintaining the viability of a democratic system of public administration" (Ostrom and Ostrom 1977, in McGinnis 1999, 99). Indeed. But this idea is so far from most people's view of democracy that I am doubtful of its appeal. Arguing in favor of any view of democracy that emphasizes competition and polycentricity is swimming uphill against the pull of mass populism. Recontracting would, of course, be easier in some jurisdictions than others, especially those of a more pedestrian administrative variety. For example, breaking up a waste disposal district would be less contentious than breaking up New York City's boroughs. In the Montreal case mentioned above, a few years of consolidation were probably not enough for citizens to come to identify with the larger jurisdiction. But individuals do form strong emotional attachments to existing jurisdictional forms from the national level all the way down to the school board. In such cases, it will take much more than clever institutional design to effectively grapple with the problem of social recontracting.

NOTE

1. I am grateful to Eric Crampton for bringing to my attention these two cases.

REFERENCES

Acemoglu, Daron. 2003. "Why Not a Political Coase Theorem?" *Journal of Comparative Economics* 31: 620–52.

Acemoglu, Daron, and James A. Robinson. 2000. "Political Losers as a Barrier to Economic Development." *American Economic Review* 90 (2): 126–30.

Alchian, Armen, and Harold Demsetz. 1972. "Production, Information Costs, and Economic Organization." *American Economic Review* 62 (5): 777–95.

Aligica, Paul Dragos, and Peter J. Boettke. 2009. *Challenging Institutional Analysis and Development: The Bloomington School.* New York: Routledge.

Buchanan, James, and Gordon Tullock. 1962. *The Calculus of Consent: Logical Foundations of Constitutional Democracy.* Ann Arbor: University of Michigan Press.

Coase, Ronald. 1937. "The Nature of the Firm." *Economica* 4 (16): 386–405.

Foldvary, Fred E., and Daniel B. Klein. 2003. *The Half-Life of Public Policy Rationales: How New Technology Affects Old Policy Issues.* New York: New York University Press.

Greve, Michael. 2012. *The Upside-Down Constitution.* Cambridge, MA: Harvard University Press.

Hayek, F. A. 1945. "The Use of Knowledge in Society." *American Economic Review* 35 (7): 519–30.

———. 1948. "The Meaning of Competition." In *Individualism and Economic Order.* Chicago: University of Chicago Press.

———. (1968) 2014. "Competition as a Discovery Procedure." In *The Market and Other Orders,* ed. Bruce Caldwell. Chicago: University of Chicago Press.

———. 1976. *Law, Legislation, and Liberty Vol. 2: The Mirage of Social Justice.* Chicago: University of Chicago Press.

Kirzner, Israel M. 1997. "Entrepreneurial Discovery and the Competitive Market Process: An Austrian Approach." *Journal of Economic Literature* 35 (1): 60–85.

Libecap, Gary. 2007. *Owens Valley Revisited.* Stanford, CA: Stanford University Press.

Manne, Henry. 1965. "Mergers and the Market for Corporate Control." *Journal of Political Economy* 73 (2): 110–20.

Martin, Adam. 2015. "Degenerate Cosmopolitanism." *Social Philosophy and Policy* 32 (1): 74–100.

———. 2018. "The Limits of Liberalism: Good Boundaries Must Be Discovered." *Review of Austrian Economics* 31 (2): 265–76.

McGinnis, Michael D., ed. 1999. *Polycentricity and Local Public Economies: Readings from the Workshop in Political Theory and Policy Analysis.* Ann Arbor: University of Michigan Press.

Mises, Ludwig. 1944. *Bureaucracy.* New Haven, CT: Yale University Press.

Oates, Wallace. 1972. *Fiscal Federalism.* New York: Harcourt, Brace, Jovanovich.

Ostrom, Elinor. 1965. "Public Entrepreneurship: A Case Study in Ground Water Basin Management." PhD dissertation. Los Angeles: University of California, Los Angeles.

———. 1972. "Metropolitan Reform: Propositions Derived from Two Traditions." *Social Science Quarterly* 53 (3): 474–93. Reprinted in McGinnis 1999.

———. 1976. "Size and Performance in a Federal System." *Publius* 6 (2): 33–74. Reprinted in McGinnis 1999.

———. 1990. *Governing the Commons: The Evolution of Institutions for Collective Action.* Cambridge, UK: Cambridge University Press.

———. 2005. *Understanding Institutional Analysis and Diversity.* Princeton, NJ: Princeton University Press.

———. 2010. "Beyond Markets and States: Polycentric Governance of Complex Economic Systems." *American Economic Review* 100 (3): 641–72.

———. 2011. "Honoring James Buchanan." *Journal of Economic Behavior & Organization* 80 (2): 370–73.

Ostrom, Elinor, and Roger Parks. 1987. "Neither Gargantua nor the Land of the Lilliputs: Conjectures on Mixed Systems of Metropolitan Organization." Reprinted in McGinnis 1999.

Ostrom, Elinor, and G. P. Whitaker. 1974. "Community Control and Governmental Responsiveness: The Case of Police in Black Neighborhoods." Reprinted in McGinnis 1999.

Ostrom, Vincent. 1972. "Polycentricity." Reprinted in McGinnis 1999.

Ostrom, Vincent, and Elinor Ostrom. 1965. "A Behavioral Approach to the Study of Intergovernmental Relations." *Annals of the American Academy of Political and Social Science* 359 (1): 137–46. Reprinted in McGinnis 1999.

————. 1977. "Public Goods and Public Choices." In *Alternatives for Delivering Public Services: Toward Improved Performance,* edited by E.S. Savas. Boulder, CO: Westview, Press. Reprinted in McGinnis 1999.

Ostrom, Vincent, Charles Tiebout, and Robert Warren. 1961. "The Organization of Government in Metropolitan Areas." *American Political Science Review* 55 (4): 831–42. Reprinted in McGinnis 1999.

Pennington, Mark. 2013. "Elinor Ostrom and the Robust Political Economy of Common-Pool Resources." *Journal of Institutional Economics* 9 (4): 449–68.

Tarko, Vlad. 2017. *Elinor Ostrom: An Intellectual Biography.* London: Rowman & Littlefield.

Tollison, Robert D., and Richard E. Wagner. 1991. "Romance, Realism, and Economic Reform." *Kyklos* 44: 57–70.

CHAPTER FIVE

INSTITUTIONAL COMPLEXITY AND THE PUBLIC CHOICE ANALYSIS OF FEASIBLE POLICY CHANGES

VLAD TARKO

T he tension between the desire to reform institutions to achieve improved outcomes and the possibility of unintended consequences because of the complexity of institutional interactions has a long intellectual history. Often, the tension is marked by two extreme positions: either to deny the full complexity and nonlinearity of institutional reality to save the possibility of institutional design, or to deny the possibility of institutional design and fully embrace institutional and cultural evolution (even on normative grounds). The middle-ground position acknowledges institutional complexity while maintaining the possibility of institutional design and deliberate policy reforms. James Buchanan laid out the difficulty of holding this middle-ground position in his correspondence with Vincent Ostrom (Aligica 2018, 1106):

> There are two basic articles of faith in our position: (1) Institutions mat-
> ter; (2) Institutions can be constructed. We face opposition on both these
> counts. The reason George Stigler and the modern Chicago crowd object
> to so much of my own stuff is that they explicitly and implicitly deny the

former of these two articles. We face opposition from the "evolutionists" (Hayek, Oakeshott, Popper, etc.) on the second article of faith. . . . In a sense [we] argue for a different attitude toward politics, toward governance, what I have called a "constitutional attitude," based on the two articles of faith noted. This attitude is extremely important, . . . and here you face precisely the problem that I have faced and have not succeeded in resolving, namely, how can we talk about attitudes independently of precise normative content.

Elinor Ostrom has perhaps done more than any other institutional economist and political scientist to try to find a solution to this problem and place the middle-ground position on a more rigorous analytical and empirical footing. In this chapter, I argue that the Institutional Analysis and Development (IAD) framework (Ostrom 1990, 2005; McGinnis 2011; Tarko 2017), in conjunction with other statistical methods, provides a tentative solution to this tension. I argue that the relationship between statistical tools and the IAD framework is as follows: (a) statistical tools, such as factor analysis and cluster analysis, can provide a more rigorous grounding for mapping out the set of possible institutional (or policy) configurations, thus providing a better understanding of both the object of contention in institutional design and the scale of the combinatorial explosion problem; (b) the IAD framework provides a superior analysis of causality compared with statistical methods on their own, especially when its public choice intellectual background is fully used; and (c) the two provide complementary information about the relationship between institutions and outcomes, allowing analysts a better integration of theory and empirics and decreasing the ad hoc analytic narratives that need to be built.

Evaluating the performance of alternative institutional systems faces two main difficulties. First, the sheer number of rules is very large. Second, the effects of institutions usually occur as a consequence of their *interactions*. A given institution rarely has effects independent of the context provided by the other (informal and formal) rules. This situation means that we face a combinatorial explosion of possible institutional configurations. Outcomes are generated by possibly very complex configurations of interacting institutions, rather than each institutional factor having its own individual contribution toward the outcome. Elinor Ostrom has repeatedly highlighted this issue (Ostrom 2005, 2008, 2014; Poteete, Janssen, and Ostrom 2010;

Wilson, Ostrom, and Cox 2013). As she noted, "Given the nonlinearity and complexity of many action situations, it is challenging to predict the precise effect of a change in a particular rule" (Ostrom 2005, 239), and, furthermore, "given the logic of combinatorics, it is not possible to conduct a complete analysis of the expected performance of all the potential rule changes that could be made in an effort to improve outcomes" (Ostrom 2005, 243). As such, one is bound to ask whether institutional design or policy reform is even possible. Elinor Ostrom (2005, 244) noted that "human agents try to use reason and persuasion in their efforts to devise better rules, but the process of choice from the vast array of rules they might use always involves experimentation."

This issue raises serious methodological concerns about the econometric institutional literature, which operates almost entirely under the assumption that various measured institutional factors have unconditional effects (i.e., have independent contributions to the outcomes of interest). At best, interaction terms are sometimes added to regressions, but such possibilities are virtually never thoroughly explored and are added purely on the basis of intuitive hunches (Tarko 2015). As noted by Poteete, Janssen, and Elinor Ostrom (2010, 13), "The assumption that observations are independent . . . is called into question by globalization, diffusion effects, and actor-centered theories that emphasize strategic interactions," and it is often the case that "interaction effects, dummy variables, hierarchical models, and other similar statistical fixes do not accurately reflect the relationships posited in the underlying theories." Even so, the econometric analyses seem to occupy the methodological high ground. They set up and test falsifiable models, and a complexity-friendly approach needs to do more than just sing praises to unpredictability.

To illustrate the problem of institutional design, I'm going to focus on the choice of economic policies, as mapped out by the subcomponents of the Fraser Institute's Economic Freedom of the World index. How large is the space of possibilities? How can we try to take into account the interactions between different economic policies in determining different outcomes? How do we combine the statistical analysis with a public choice analysis of how various actors try to change policies in accordance with their interests? I will show how the statistical analysis can reveal the existence of some apparent institutional constraints—some institutional factors that tend to change in sync, rather than independently. Some of these institutional constraints are more mysterious than others, and this kind of analysis opens the door for possible political economy analyses. Economists should try to understand why such institutional constraints may be in place in terms of how different political actors interact. The IAD framework is useful for framing our political economy analysis. The framework (a) tells us how to simplify the analysis by defining "action arenas" triggered by certain events and involving a limited number of actors with specified institutional roles, and (b) gives us a checklist of the types of rules that we need to pay attention to.

IS INSTITUTIONAL DESIGN ABOUT INSTITUTIONS?

Before delving into the question of how to do institutional design in the face of complex nonlinearities, it is worth addressing the reason why skepticism sounds far-fetched. A large number of people currently are doing policy analysis and institutional (re)design. Newspapers are daily covering various policy debates, members of the general public of various ideological colors are often deeply emotionally invested in these debates, hundreds of think tanks analyze and advocate policies, firms pay millions of dollars on lobbying activities, and, of course, state and national legislatures and agencies are actively engaged in policy making. The skepticism about institutional design seems to claim that all those people are engaged in a bizarre form of mass delusion. The underlying complexity guarantees that they will constantly make errors, in the sense that they are advocating a variety of policies that will, because of unintended consequences, often lead to undesired results, and yet they persist. Emotional attachments to specific policy packages seem particularly misplaced.

There are two reasons that the previously mentioned activities may coexist with the deep impossibility of institutional design without implying a form of irrationality. First, in most policy debates the majority of conflicting parties may only be interested in the first-order effects. If complexity implies that higher-order effects are unpredictable, this interest in only first-order effects is entirely sensible. One should focus on what can be reliably changed. If second- and higher-order effects are swamped by uncertainties and can, more or less, go in any direction, it is, in some sense, sensible to ignore them, especially under time constraints. However, as famously argued by Hazlitt (1946), the hallmark of good economics is considering not just short-term effects but also long-term effects, and not just the effects on one group, but on all groups. In other words, the problem of institutional design manifests most starkly if we adopt the norms of good economics, but less so if one is driven by other (more self-interested) motivations. It may very well be the case that most people discussing policy are not following the norms of good economics, which is why the question about the possibility of institutional design may not appear as such a grave concern.

Second, as argued by Robin Hanson (2008), "politics isn't about policy." Politics is often about signaling allegiance to a group. As Simler and Hanson (2018, 298) put it:

> The fact that we use political beliefs to express loyalty, rather than to take action, also explains why we're emotionally attached to our beliefs, and why political discussions often generate more heat than light. When our beliefs are anchored not to reasons and evidence, but to social factors we don't share with our conversation partners (like loyalty to different political groups), disagreement is all but inevitable, and our arguments fall on deaf ears.

As such, expressing confidence in a position that is, in fact, deeply uncertain, or even knowingly false, can act as a signal for loyalty. For instance, Klein and Dompe's (2007) survey shows that some economists who believe that minimum wage laws in fact hurt the unskilled poor nonetheless support such laws because of the broader ideological signal they send. Such signaling may often be socially wasteful, but it does explain why it can still be rational to engage in policy making and policy advocacy even if one believes institutional design is impossible. But, for such signaling to work, one must also dismiss the doubts about the viability of institutional design. One cannot acknowledge that the emperor has no clothes while signaling loyalties by arguing about which of the emperor's clothes are the most beautiful.

The question about the *possibility* of institutional design might be misplaced. A better framing is to ask about the possible *deepness* of institutional design. Although it may be possible and relatively straightforward to do policy design, especially if one cares only about the first-order effects, it may be more difficult or even impossible to do constitutional design. In what follows, I am going to assume that we are adopting Hazlitt's norms of good economics and that, for the sake of our discussion, we care about institutions solely because of their outcomes, rather than as tools for signaling political loyalties.[1]

EVALUATING COMBINATORIAL COMPLEXITY

How many possible institutions are there? How large is the space of possibilities within which institutional design operates? The smaller this space of possibilities is, the easier the problem of institutional design becomes, and the easier it is to evaluate and compare the effects of different institutions.

For illustration purposes, consider the problem of determining the space of all possible economic policies. Fraser Institute's Economic Freedom of the World (EFW) project maps out 42 underlying policies (Gwartney, Lawson, and Hall 2017), which EFW aggregates into five basic components (table 5.1): (a) size of government; (b) legal system and protection of contracts and property; (c) freedom of movement for goods and capital; (d) sound money; and (e) regulation. Let us assume that these variables, which I call EFW5, provide a comprehensive picture of the space of possibilities, and that Fraser's aggregation into five components makes sense.

The choice of these variables is not an entirely harmless assumption, but I'm going to use them here for the sake of illustrating the problem of combinatorial complexity. One problem with the Fraser data is that some of the underlying variables in table 5.1 appear to describe *outcomes* rather than *policy choices*. This problem is important for the political economy analysis because it is important to distinguish between, for example, "a policy of judicial independence" and "having policies that result in an independent judiciary." The Fraser underlying variables mix these two perspectives. However, from the point of view of identifying the correlations between different areas of economic policy, that issue matters less.

Each of these variables can take a thousand values (from 0.00 to 10.00). The first question we need to ask is whether this degree of precision is justified. For instance, in 2015 Denmark had 0.01 points more economic freedom than Finland, and 0.02 more in 2017. To what extent is this a credible statement of *fact* about the difference between Denmark and Finland? To ask the question in a different way, could this result simply be an artifact of *measurement error* for some of the underlying variables? Unlike in the physical sciences, in which all reported measurements are required to be accompanied by margins of error, in the social sciences it is exceedingly common to provide only the "measurement." We do not, therefore, have an official account of the precision of these measurements. I think it is likely, however, that the claimed two-digit precision is false. On the

TABLE 5.1: THE COMPONENTS OF FRASER INSTITUTE'S ECONOMIC FREEDOM OF THE WORLD INDEX (1970–2015)

Variable	Obs.	Missing	Min	Max	Median	Mean	Std. dev.
Year	3,498	0	1970	2015	2004	2001	12.62
Economic Freedom	*2,841*	*657*	*1.97*	*9.19*	*6.65*	*6.498*	*1.142*
Size of Government	2,912	586	0.65	9.9	6.28	6.201	1.463
Government consumption	2,963	535	0	10	6.12	5.874	2.266
Transfers and subsidies	2,614	884	0	10	8.45	7.677	2.147
Government enterprises and investment	2,912	586	0	10	6	5.634	3.237
Top marginal income tax rate	2,517	981	0	10	7	6.532	2.821
Top marginal income and payroll tax rate	2,083	1,415	0	10	5	5.085	2.717
Top marginal tax rate	2,517	981	0	10	6	5.768	2.672
Legal System and Property Rights	2,809	689	0.96	9.28	5.24	5.252	1.803
Judicial independence	2,013	1,485	0.17	9.82	4.73	5.026	2.255
Impartial courts	2,385	1,113	0	9.69	4.38	4.708	1.771
Protection of property rights	2,032	1,466	0.87	9.61	5.29	5.481	1.875
Military interference in rule of law and politics	2,378	1,120	0	10	6.67	6.518	2.773
Integrity of the legal system	2,129	1,369	0	10	6.67	6.27	2.268
Legal enforcement of contracts	2,203	1,295	0	8.48	4.51	4.459	1.743
Regulatory restrictions on the sale of real property	2,182	1,316	0	9.98	7.5	7.01	2.047
Reliability of police	1,498	2,000	1.21	9.65	5.27	5.483	1.975
Business costs of crime	1,498	2,000	1.04	9.67	6.075	5.922	1.875
Gender adjustment	3,498	0	0	1	0.96	0.8736	0.1755
Sound Money	2,955	543	0	9.89	7.94	7.629	1.827
Money growth	2,918	580	0	10	8.695	8.216	1.775

(*continued*)

TABLE 5.1: THE COMPONENTS OF FRASER INSTITUTE'S ECONOMIC
FREEDOM OF THE WORLD INDEX (1970–2015) (*CONTINUED*)

Variable	Obs.	Missing	Min	Max	Median	Mean	Std. dev.
Standard deviation of inflation	2,957	541	0	9.95	8.85	7.98	2.256
Inflation most recent year	2,957	541	0	10	9.08	8.435	1.944
Freedom to own foreign-currency bank accounts	2,943	555	0	10	5	5.87	4.412
Freedom to Trade Internationally	**2,873**	**625**	**0**	**10**	**6.98**	**6.69**	**1.744**
Revenue from trade taxes (percent of trade sector)	2,707	791	0	10	8.73	7.664	2.495
Mean tariff rate	2,607	891	0	10	8.24	7.823	1.685
Standard deviation of tariff rates	2,314	1,184	0	10	6.28	5.933	2.194
Tariffs	2,878	620	0	10	7.47	7.054	1.842
Nontariff trade barriers	2,014	1,484	1.83	9.69	5.75	5.893	1.316
Compliance costs of importing and exporting	2,144	1,354	0	10	7.45	6.897	2.331
Regulatory trade barriers	2,160	1,338	0	9.76	6.57	6.332	1.688
Black market exchange rates	2,948	550	0	10	10	9.084	2.501
Foreign ownership investment restrictions	2,006	1,492	2.21	10	6.53	6.453	1.454
Capital controls	2,953	545	0	10	2.31	3.478	3.103
Freedom of foreigners to visit	1,636	1,862	0	10	5.97	4.958	3.347
Controls of the movement of capital and people	2,972	526	0	10	4.655	4.312	2.716
Regulation	**2,832**	**666**	**1**	**9.49**	**6.735**	**6.617**	**1.248**
Ownership of banks	2,742	756	0	10	8	6.721	3.384
Private-sector credit	2,877	621	0	10	8.59	8.015	2.12
Interest rate controls negative real interest rates	2,703	795	0	10	10	8.734	2.258

Variable	Obs.	Missing	Min	Max	Median	Mean	Std. dev.
Credit market regulations	2,945	553	0	10	8.27	7.705	2.15
Hiring regulations and minimum wage	2,247	1,251	0	10	6.67	6.304	2.733
Hiring and firing regulations	2,098	1,400	0.68	8.83	4.73	4.713	1.393
Centralized collective bargaining	2,234	1,264	1.83	10.04	6.66	6.391	1.447
Hours regulations	1,874	1,624	2	10	8	7.841	1.896
Mandated cost of worker dismissal	2,163	1,335	0	10	7.03	6.108	3.094
Conscription	2,911	587	0	10	10	6.008	4.35
Labor market regulations	2,401	1,097	1.48	9.73	6.17	6.157	1.523
Administrative requirements	1,959	1,539	0.53	8.54	3.73	3.888	1.328
Bureaucracy costs	2,063	1,435	0	10	5.4	5.351	2.215
Starting a business	2,256	1,242	0	9.98	8.85	8.307	1.577
Extra payments, bribes, favoritism	2,006	1,492	0.62	9.99	5.1	5.434	1.99
Licensing restrictions	1,731	1,767	0	10	7.66	7.268	1.998
Tax compliance	2,231	1,267	0	9.87	7.09	6.653	2.239
Business regulations	2,162	1,336	2.18	9.5	6.135	6.161	1.263

Note: Aggregated variables are in bold.
Source: Gwartney, Lawson, and Hall 2017.

basis of the list of ranked countries, we can perhaps justify the claim of a one-digit precision (table 5.2); for example, the fact that Romania has less economic freedom than the United States is probably not merely a measurement artifact.

If we assume a one-digit precision, each variable can take 100 distinct values. The five components thus define a space of $100^5 = 10$ billion possible institutional configurations. If we consider all 42 underlying variables, there are $100^{42} = 10^{84}$ possible institutional configurations. For comparison, there are only 10^{80} atoms in the observable universe. But this calculation, of course, is naïve, because economic policies are not chosen independently of one another. If a country chooses a particular policy in one area, it will probably also simultaneously choose many others in a predictable fashion. In other

TABLE 5.2: RANK OF COUNTRIES BY ECONOMIC FREEDOM (2017)

Rank	Country	Score	Rank	Country	Score
1	Hong Kong	8.97	11	Canada	7.94
2	Singapore	8.81	12	United States	7.94
3	New Zealand	8.48	13	Lithuania	7.92
4	Switzerland	8.44	14	Cyprus	7.79
5	Ireland	8.19	15	Chile	7.77
6	United Kingdom	8.05	15	Denmark	7.77
7	Mauritius	8.04	17	Finland	7.75
8	Georgia	8.01	17	Latvia	7.75
9	Australia	7.99	19	Netherlands	7.74
10	Estonia	7.95	20	Romania	7.72

Source: Gwartney, Lawson, and Hall 2017.

words, there are many constraints on institutional and policy choices. The exact number of *independent* economic policies (i.e., the nature of the constraints on such choices) is not known, but, in principle, the existence of such constraints can *dramatically* lower the true number of possibilities.

In order to guesstimate the true combinatorial range of possible institutional configurations, we need to use the observations of existing, real-world countries (from present and past), and perhaps also certain theoretical considerations (e.g., about historical path dependency) as tools for evaluating the degrees of freedom in institutional choices. As an illustration, suppose we have 100 measured characteristics, each of which could take only two values (true/false), but the first 50 characteristics always vary in sync with each other and the second 50 also always vary in sync. As such, we would have only two de facto characteristics, and the total number of possible constitutions would not be $2^{100} \approx 1.3 \times 10^{30}$, but would be only $2^2 = 4$. It is thus essential, when quantifying the true size of the combinatorial problem, to identify how correlated different institutional characteristics are.

Factor Analysis

One way to try to do this in practice is to perform a principal component analysis (or related factor analysis). This type of statistical analysis aims to find the smallest number of variables that can still account for the observed

TABLE 5.3: PRINCIPAL COMPONENT ANALYSIS ON EFW5 VARIABLES

	PC1	PC2	PC3	PC4	PC5
Standard deviation	1.73	1.03	0.67	0.55	0.42
Proportion of variance	0.60	0.21	0.09	0.06	0.04
Cumulative proportion	0.60	0.81	0.90	0.96	1.00

Source: Author's calculations based on data from Gwartney, Lawson, and Hall (2017).

TABLE 5.4: FACTOR ANALYSIS LOADINGS ON EFW5 VARIABLES

	Secure markets	Welfare state
Size of government		0.99
Legal system and property rights	0.79	−0.17
Sound money	0.81	
Freedom to trade internationally	0.93	
Regulation	0.75	

Source: Author's calculations based on data from Gwartney, Lawson, and Hall (2017).

diversity. This is done by defining a new set of variables as linear functions of the observed variables:

$$y_i = \sum_{k=1}^{N} \beta_{ik} x_k$$

The original set of measured variables, x_k, $k \in 1,2,...,N$ is reduced to the new set of variables y_i, $i \in 1,2,...,M, M < N$, where the y's are, by definition, independent of one another. The analysis determines the values of the loadings β_{ik}. The first component is defined such that it accounts for as much as possible of the observed variability, the second one accounts for as much as possible of the remaining unexplained variability, and so on.

Consider a principal component (PC) analysis on the across-years' averages of the five components of the EFW dataset (1970s to 2015). Table 5.3 shows the results. The first two components (PC1 and PC2) cover more than 80 percent of the observed variation. In other words, there are actually only two independent variables. A factor analysis leads to the same conclusion and reveals that the size-of-government variable is orthogonal to the other (table 5.4). We thus have one variable that is a combination of four of the Fraser components

FIGURE 5.1: FACTOR ANALYSIS ON EFW5

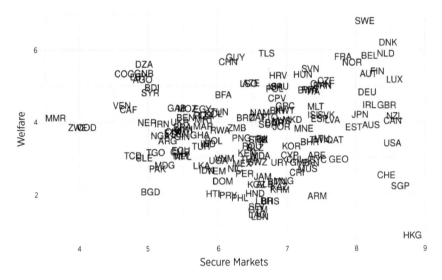

Note: Three-letter country codes are taken from the ISO 3166 standard published by the International Organization for Standardization.
Source: Author's calculations based on data from Gwartney, Lawson, and Hall (2017).

(see table 5.4 column heading, Secure markets), and another variable that corresponds to the size-of-government variable (which, in what follows, I've reverse coded and labeled "Welfare state").

Figure 5.1 shows the position of various countries within this universe of institutional possibilities. The position of each country is based on its average economic policies from the 1970s to the present. Assuming as before that each variable can take 100 distinct values, we have $100^2 = 10,000$ possible economic policies. This number is still much larger than the number of existing countries; however, it is much more manageable than the previous, naïve calculations.

Two Types of Constraints on Institutional Choices

The principal component and factor analysis are purely data-driven and theoretically agnostic methods. The downside of having a theory-free estimate is that such an estimate will only provide a lower bound for the true number of possible institutions. In other words, the data about observed (past and present) institutions will almost certainly overstate the constraints on policy choice, because some institutional configurations may not have been (yet) chosen—not because they are impossible, but simply because there has not been enough institutional experimentation to cover the entire space of true possibilities. The purely data-driven methods will, therefore, treat contingent circumstances (random reasons for why some institutional configurations have not yet been adopted) as if they are necessary hard constraints. Nevertheless, it is still useful to calculate this lower bound, because by itself it may still indicate a large degree of combinatorial complexity.

The result of this brief analysis suggests that there might exist political economy reasons behind the observed correlations. The observation is that if a country is weakening its property-rights protections, it is also likely to simultaneously have higher inflation, more protectionism, and more regulation. By contrast, observations about changes in a country's welfare state policies do not have predictive power about the other variables.

It is useful to bear in mind two possible reasons for the observed correlations: (a) Hard constraints: For example, Thomas Sargent's unpleasant arithmetic or the trilemma in international economics provides objective constraints upon the underlying policy variables. It is simply the case that the funds available for government spending must come from somewhere, and various other policies can affect revenues. (b) Ideated constraints: The results above sound suspiciously familiar in ideological terms. The horizontal axis in figure 5.1 corresponds to the mercantilism-liberalism opposition, while the vertical axis corresponds to the (neo)liberalism-social democracy opposition. In developed countries, basically all policy debates are about a move up or down the welfare state axis (i.e., "left" and "right," politically). One can wonder if the public sphere has intuitively zeroed in on the fundamental coordinates that map the space of institutional possibilities or, on the contrary, the coordinates are the *cause* of the result above (i.e., the observed correlations occur because everyone is thinking in terms of these same ideological positions and thus cannot conceive of other institutional alternatives).

Cluster Analysis

Another method we can use is the hierarchical cluster analysis of variables. This method calculates the correlations between all variables and builds a tree based on them—showing variables that are highly correlated closer to each other (close-by "twigs" on the tree). The result should be qualitatively equivalent to

FIGURE 5.2: CLUSTER ANALYSIS OF EFW5 VARIABLES

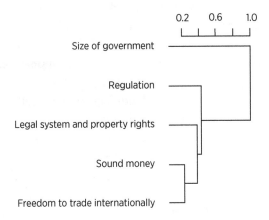

Note: Distances are based on the similarities between variables; smaller distances mean variables are more similar.
Source: Author's calculations based on data from Gwartney, Lawson, and Hall (2017).

the previous analysis. Indeed, as shown in figure 5.2, when we do the analysis on the EFW5 dataset, we obtain the same conclusion as before.

The results of a hierarchical cluster analysis on *all* the underlying EFW variables are shown in figure 5.3. As before, I considered the cross-time averages of each variable from 1970 to 2015, rather than picking just a year. As we can see, depending on the desired level of aggregation, we can combine variables to create two, three, or five larger aggregated variables,[2] but the *meaning* of the resulting variables is less clear than before. The five variables suggested by this analysis do not correspond to the five components proposed by Fraser. In other words, the underlying political economy that creates the constraints on policy making is far less obvious. In some sense, this is good news, because it means that these correlations are more likely to reflect objective constraints, rather than ideated ones created by our lack of institutional imagination.

Moreover, this tree opens up a number of political economy mysteries related to the fact that some of these underlying variables unexpectedly seem to go together. Are these spurious correlations, or do they reflect some deeper phenomena? For instance, why are business regulations most closely related to judicial independence, impartial courts, police reliability, property-rights protections, and bribes? Why are countries with higher labor regulations also more

FIGURE 5.3: CLUSTER ANALYSIS OF UNDERLYING EFW VARIABLES

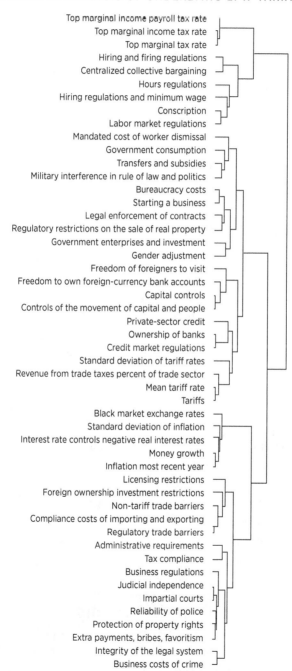

Source: Author's calculations based on data from Gwartney, Lawson, and Hall (2017).

likely to have a military draft? Why is the lack of women's rights most highly correlated with the government involvement in investments and ownership of enterprises? To reiterate, this clustering of variables generally indicates the existence of constraints on institutional choices and the fact that the possible institutional diversity is lower than one might naïvely think just by doing a combinatorial calculation based on the total number of measured indicators. This is what creates these potential political economy mysteries—Why are these constraints on institutional design in place? By comparison, the fact that all decisions regarding monetary policy go hand in hand—and the fact that all types of restrictions on trade (of goods, services, capital, and labor) happen in sync—and the fact that all marginal tax rates are decided together are all less mysterious.

Mapping the Diversity of Paths

Once we have reduced the number of variables to a few independent ones, we can also more easily map out the differences between countries in terms of their evolution in time. This is necessary for better understanding the underlying factors that may determine policy. If countries experience convergence, it is more likely that they are affected by the same kind of underlying factors. If, by contrast, we observe a diversity of paths, it is clear that different factors operate in different countries.

Let us consider here the variables "welfare state" and "secure markets" identified earlier. These variables allow us to map the different paths on a plane. Figure 5.4 shows the evolution in time of economic policies in a selection of developed countries, while figure 5.5 shows the time evolution of a selection of developing countries. We see that all countries tended to improve the security of markets, but there was some variation among developed countries in terms of increasing or decreasing their welfare states.

Figure 5.6 shows a more comprehensive picture of all the countries, by illustrating the change between the average before 1990 and the average after 2000. We see that the vast majority of countries increased market security and decreased their welfare states.

The empirical analysis above can be used to set the stage for the analysis of the underlying political economy mechanisms that generate the observed patterns. As pointed out by Wagner (1989, 2016), the regulatory and fiscal outcomes are all the product of the same political machinery. As such, if we observe that various variables tend to be correlated and move in sync with each other, especially if such correlations are not entirely obvious, we need to

FIGURE 5.4: THE ECONOMIC POLICY EVOLUTION OF SELECTED DEVELOPED COUNTRIES

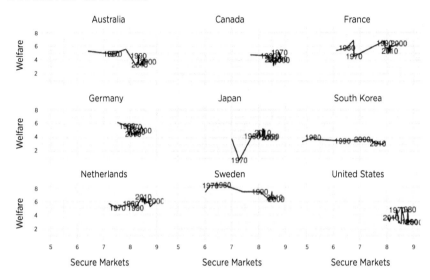

Source: Author's calculations based on data from Gwartney, Lawson, and Hall (2017).

FIGURE 5.5: THE ECONOMIC POLICY EVOLUTION OF SELECTED DEVELOPING COUNTRIES

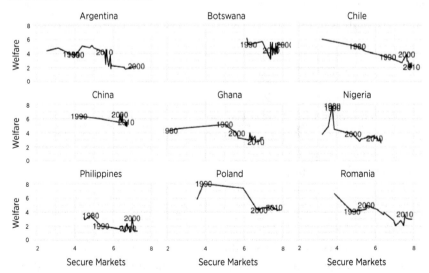

Source: Author's calculations based on data from Gwartney, Lawson, and Hall (2017).

FIGURE 5.6: CHANGES IN ECONOMIC POLICIES FROM BEFORE 1990 TO AFTER 2000

Change in Secure Markets from before 1990 to after 2000

Source: Author's calculations based on data from Gwartney, Lawson, and Hall (2017).

wonder if it is because of the underlying political machinery that generates the outcomes. Considering that the same government apparatus generates all policies, it is a mistake to treat them as if they occur independently of one another.

Evaluating Outcomes

A final way to assess the difficulty of institutional design is to see the extent to which countries with similar economic institutions end up with similar economic outcomes. Economic outcomes are not solely determined by formal policies. As such, institutional design is made more difficult if numerous other confounding factors affect outcomes.

One can think of institutional (and policy) design as moving a country from one category to another, in the hope of achieving the same outcomes as the countries already there. Thus, we need to see (a) how economic outcomes vary across the categories and (b) if these differences are statistically significant.

It is worth noting the distinction between institutional design in developing countries and institutional design in developed countries. This distinction mimics the distinction from growth theory between catch-up growth and growth on the frontier. In the same way that poorer countries can (in principle) adopt available technologies and engage in relatively rapid catch-up growth, thanks to improved productivity, they can also (in principle) adopt the institutions of rich countries.[3] By contrast, rich countries are on the frontier, both technologically and institutionally. If one wants to improve the institutions of rich countries, one, by definition, does not have empirical examples to follow. At best, we have uncertain extrapolations. The IAD framework becomes particularly important for institutional design on the frontier—because the arguments are mainly theoretical ones.

The analysis of institutional design is simpler for developing countries. Figure 5.7 shows the results across a wide range of different types of outcomes, and table 5.5 identifies the countries within each cluster (1 through 9) as a result of a hierarchical cluster analysis of all the countries. The height of the bars in figure 5.7 reflects the means within each cluster, and the error bars indicate the standard errors.

Unsurprisingly, most rich countries fall within the same cluster (cluster 4); that is, they are more institutionally similar to one another than to other countries. It is important to understand that Scandinavian social democracies are more institutionally similar to the "neoliberal" United States and Australia than any of them are to developing countries. We are used to emphasizing the differences along the "welfare state" axis in figure 5.1, although, in the context of development economics, it is mainly the other axis, "secure markets," that matters the most and that accounts for the large institutional gap between rich and poor countries. Nevertheless, cluster 9 (see table 5.5), which includes countries not commonly understood to be similar, raises the most interesting questions about possible noninstitutional factors that affect development.

In many, if not most, cases the differences in outcomes between clusters are indeed statistically significant. This observation means that, say, in the context of transition economies, it is meaningful to recommend "be more like Sweden or the United States," as long as one bears in mind that such a recommendation refers to the entire institutional package and it entails mostly improving protections of property rights and contracts and deregulating the economy.

It is also interesting to note the differences between various clusters of developing countries. The growth per capita graph (figure 5.7) shows

FIGURE 5.7: DIFFERENTIAL OUTCOMES ACROSS CLUSTERS

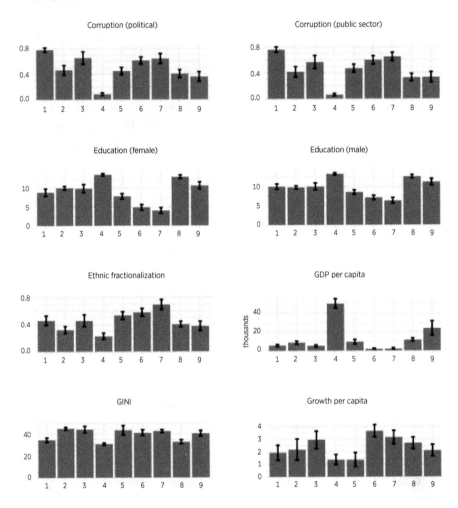

Note: GDP = gross domestic product; Gini = Gini coefficient, a measure of income inequality.
Source: Author's calculations based on data from Gwartney, Lawson, and Hall (2017).

that there are very large differences between developing countries because
of their economic policies. As noted by Olson (1996), the fact that not all
poor countries converge with rich ones, although that would be the naïve
expectation of the Solow model, is one of the key pieces of evidence we have
that institutions matter. The previous cluster analysis allows a more detailed
picture of this key fact.

TABLE 5.5: COMPOSITION OF CLUSTERS

Cluster	Countries
1	Albania, Algeria, Angola, Azerbaijan, China, Egypt, Iran, Kazakhstan, Madagascar, Russia, Syria, Tajikistan, Thailand
2	Argentina, Costa Rica, Dominican Republic, El Salvador, Honduras, Panama, Peru, Philippines, Seychelles, Uruguay
3	Armenia, Bolivia, Ecuador, Georgia, Guatemala, Paraguay, Venezuela
4	Australia, Austria, Belgium, Canada, Croatia, Denmark, Finland, France, Iceland, Ireland, Italy, Japan, Luxembourg, Netherlands, New Zealand, Norway, Portugal, Slovenia, Spain, Sweden, United States
5	Bahrain, Botswana, Burkina Faso, Burundi, The Gambia, Jamaica, Jordan, Kenya, Lesotho, Malta, Mauritius, Namibia, Nicaragua, Oman, South Africa, Suriname, Swaziland, Trinidad and Tobago, Uganda, United Arab Emirates
6	Bangladesh, Bhutan, Ethiopia, Ghana, India, Malawi, Malaysia, Nepal, Nigeria, Pakistan, Rwanda, Sierra Leone, Sri Lanka, Zambia, Zimbabwe
7	Benin, Cameroon, Chad, Democratic Republic of Congo, Côte d'Ivoire, Gabon, Mali, Morocco, Senegal, Tanzania, Tunisia
8	Bosnia and Herzegovina, Brazil, Bulgaria, Czech Republic, Estonia, Hungary, Latvia, Lithuania, Macedonia, Moldova, Poland, Romania, Slovak Republic, Ukraine
9	Chile, Colombia, Cyprus, Greece, Indonesia, Mexico, Mozambique, Singapore, South Korea, Switzerland, Taiwan, Turkey

Source: Author's calculations based on data from Gwartney, Lawson, and Hall (2017).

USING THE IAD FRAMEWORK FOR PUBLIC CHOICE ANALYSIS

The standard public choice analysis looks at the effect on policy outcomes of various types of actors: politicians, lobbying firms and organizations, voters, and the public administration bureaucracy. These types of actors interact in many different complex ways (figure 5.8). The IAD framework may allow us to bring more order to this complexity.

The IAD framework (figure 5.9) requires us, first, to identify the *action arena*, that is, the set of all possible institutions, actors, and events relevant to our outcomes of interest. Second, within the action arena, we need to identify specific *action situations* triggered by events, involving a small subset of the actors and governed by a small subset of the institutions. Third, we need to analyze the *patterns of interaction* within each action situation using the appropriate analytic tools, given the complexity of these patterns of interaction.

FIGURE 5.8: PUBLIC CHOICE ANALYSIS FRAMEWORK

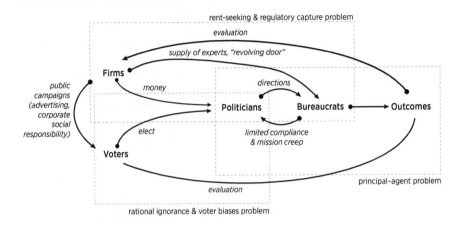

FIGURE 5.9: THE IAD FRAMEWORK

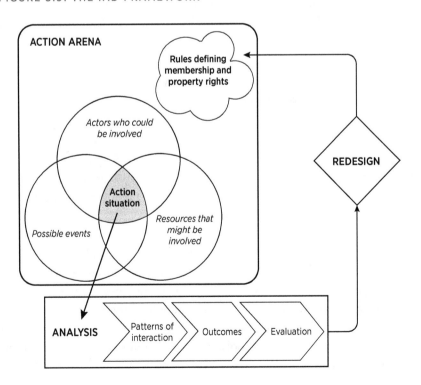

The action arena attempts to map out the set of all possibilities, acknowledging the complexity and nonlinearities, without any attempt to actually analyze the institutions-outcomes relation. The action situation attempts to restrict our focus to a context that is simple enough to analyze, and the patterns of interaction reflect our theoretical and empirical knowledge about the complexity of the situation on which we are focusing. This also means that we have three possible types of *sources of error:* (a) we may have misidentified the patterns of interaction; (b) we may have left out of the action situation some relevant institutions, actors, or events; or (c) we may have set up the universe of possibilities wrong by missing some institutions, actors, or events. By allowing us to map possible types of errors, the IAD framework helps us try to regain the methodological high ground by making it possible to put forth testable hypotheses within a complexity framework.

A key element for using this framework is identifying the relevant institutions and their possible configurations. As illustrated in figure 5.9, these possible institutional configurations are the object of contention in institutional design. Different actors with the capacity to change the rules may disagree with one another because of having either (a) different goals and values or (b) different opinions about what's possible and about the relationship between institutions and outcomes. The question about the possibility of institutional design also depends on how large the space of possible institutional configurations is. If nonlinear complexities make the analysis of the relationship between institutions and outcomes difficult (by undermining the value of simple extrapolations), the number of institutional configurations may ultimately make institutional design impossible.

The previous empirical analysis gives us useful insights into the nature of the institutional combinatorial complexity. These analyses can provide an *input* to the IAD framework. First, they can provide some indication about the overarching rules constraining the actors involved in policy making. Second, the dimension-reduction methods described earlier help us identify the object of contention in institutional design—they help us identify the apparent range of possible policy choices and curtail the combinatorial explosion problem (and the related epistemic difficulty) by reducing the number of relevant variables. As mentioned, one must be careful not to believe too strongly that these empirically revealed constraints are objective and immutable. Some of them might not be, because they may only reflect past experience rather than future possibility. But even so, the analysis might be significantly simplified, and, moreover, this simplification now has a justification beyond mere intuitive hunches.

In a nutshell, I have found that beyond the large diversity of possible policy changes, they mostly fit into two distinct, intuitive categories—on one hand, establishing more robust free markets (which involves everything from more secure property rights to deregulation and sound money), and, on the other hand, welfare policies (involving transfers). These two categories correspond to two distinct types of political debates that occur in all countries. Ideologically, these two categories often seem to go together, but the empirical analysis shows that it is *not* actually the case; regardless of what one's ideological intuitions might indicate, the two types of policies are, in fact, changed independently of one another. Explaining this fact opens the door to understanding some interesting political economy phenomena. For example, despite an ideological commitment to both more regulation and more welfare, social democratic governments in Europe have found themselves in the position of having to choose one or the other because of fiscal constraints. This situation is what led countries like France and Sweden to *deregulate* their economies to be able to obtain more revenues (by enabling higher growth), which would support their welfare states (Vogel 1996; Tarko and Farrant 2019).

The next step is to build a model of the possible action situations: identify the relevant actors and the possible events, and map out rules for their interactions. These are the basic building blocks for creating an *analytic narrative* (Bates et al. 1998; Parikh 2000; Carpenter 2000; Aligica 2003; Tilly 2006; Capoccia and Kelemen 2007). But the major danger in building such narratives is that of involuntarily rationalizing mere ad hoceries (Elster 2000; see also the response of Bates et al. 2000). In my view, part of the usefulness of the IAD framework is to curtail this danger by providing a *general template* of what to include in the narrative, in particular for the types of rules to look for (figure 5.10) (Crawford and Ostrom 1995; Ostrom 2010):

▸ *Boundary rules* specify under what conditions a person can occupy a given position—for example, who is eligible for various types of positions.
▸ *Position rules* specify the set of positions and how many actors hold each one.

FIGURE 5.10: THE IAD FRAMEWORK: INSIDE AN ACTION SITUATION

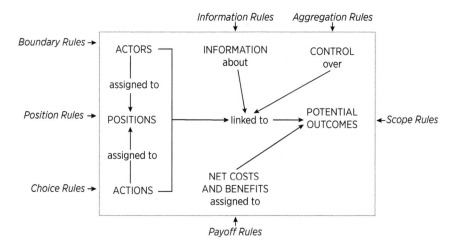

▸ *Choice rules* specify the rights and obligations assigned to an actor in each given position and the conditions under which the actor is allowed to get involved.

▸ *Information rules* specify what information must, may, or must not be shared and in what fashion.

▸ *Scope rules* restrict actions conditional on current observed outcomes.

▸ *Aggregation rules* specify the level of consent required to take various collective decisions (e.g., majority or unanimity rules).

▸ *Payoff rules* specify how benefits and costs are distributed to actors in various positions.

The usual alternative to analytic narratives is to try to solve the causality problem purely by means of statistical methods. The best-case scenario is if one has managed to create an actual randomized experiment, although even that is fraught with difficulties. It is beyond the scope of this chapter to provide a full critique, but it is enough to say that in the vast majority of cases in which instrumental variables are used, the instrumental variables do not actually fit the theoretical conditions of a valid instrument, and far too many "natural experiments" do not truly merit that label.

In the case of the running example in this chapter, the main actors influencing economic policy, as identified by public choice theory, are not only

politicians but also rent-seeking firms and civil society pressure groups lobbying for specific policies, and also the public administration bureaucracy,
which is only weakly controlled by elected politicians because of pervasive
principal–agent problems and which often engages in "mission creep" (for
an overview, see Aligica and Tarko 2014b, chap. 3). A full analysis along the
IAD lines would involve mapping out the interactions between these groups
and identifying the rules that govern these interactions (based on the above
list of different types of rules). Such an analysis can provide thick case studies to accompany the statistical overviews. If the statistical analysis suggests
some correlations but the thick case studies cannot identify any causal paths to
account for these correlations, we must conclude that they are spurious.

Consider the actors and their interactions described in figure 5.8, and let
us classify how the relevant rules apply to each actor:

Politicians

▸ *Boundary rules* specify the conditions under which someone can be a
  political candidate and obtain a political position. These include the rules
  that specify the nature of the electoral system and the organizational rules
  within political parties.
▸ *Position rules* specify the structure of the political system and the checks
  and balances between different positions.
▸ *Choice rules* specify the rights and obligations associated with different
  political positions.
▸ *Information rules* specify disclosure and transparency laws (e.g., campaign
  finance transparency), as well as the laws specifying the access to different
  types of information (e.g., what kind of information members of parlia-
  ment have compared with the president).
▸ *Scope rules* specify the powers associated with specific positions and the
  conditions under which specific powers can be used (e.g., under what
  conditions emergency powers can be granted to some political actors).
▸ *Aggregation rules* specify the level of consent required to take different
  types of political decisions (e.g., the level of consent required to change
  the constitution, filibuster rules, etc.).
▸ *Payoff rules* specify the benefits granted to people in various political positions (from their salaries to their informal benefits obtained from lobbying firms, etc.).

Voters

▶ *Boundary rules* specify the eligibility to vote in different types of elections (e.g., local elections versus general elections).

▶ *Position rules* specify the conditions under which one is granted citizenship and voting rights (e.g., how criminal convictions affect voting rights).

▶ *Choice rules* specify the rights and obligations that members of the political unit have. These include not only rules about voting but also rules about petitions and triggering popular referenda.

▶ *Information rules* reflect the nature of freedom of the press, both in terms of the formal laws and constitutional provisions and in terms of the actual organization of the media.

▶ *Scope rules* define the events that enable voters to vote, protest, or act in other ways.

▶ *Aggregation rules* specify the level of consent required in different elections (e.g., for normal legislative elections, for a referendum to pass, etc.).

▶ *Payoff rules* specify benefits and costs associated with various forms of political inclusion (e.g., the relative benefits from being a citizen, a permanent resident, a tourist, etc.).

Firms

▶ *Boundary rules* specify under what conditions a firm can lobby various levels of government or the public administration. More open-lobbying rules may increase the amount of rent-seeking waste, but overly restricted lobbying rules create a rigid crony capitalist system (Aligica and Tarko 2014a).

▶ *Position rules* specify various types of public-private partnerships (PPP) and the roles granted to various firms.

▶ *Choice rules* specify the rights and obligations that firms in PPP have, as well as the rights to lobby.

▶ *Information rules* specify how transparent the lobbying and PPP need to be.

▶ *Scope rules* restrict firm activities (e.g., based on licenses and other regulations).

▶ *Aggregation rules* specify the structure of industry as it relates to politics (e.g., the extent to which firms within a given industry need to cooperate to successfully lobby for certain rules).

▶ *Payoff rules* depend on the structure of the rent-seeking system, determining the benefits accruing to firms as a result of their lobbying activities and the risks involved (e.g., the costs associated with unsuccessful lobbying or with the lack of credible commitment that the government will indeed enforce certain restrictions).

Public Administration Bureaucracies

▸ *Boundary rules* specify the area of activity for the given bureaucracy and are subject to expansion under mission creep.
▸ *Position rules* specify the positions within the bureaucracy and define the internal organization of the bureaucracy.
▸ *Choice rules* specify the rights and obligations that each person working within the public administration has, as well as the rights and obligations that various public administration units have.
▸ *Information rules* specify the information available to the bureaucracy and the transparency rules that the bureaucracy must obey (the type of information that must be revealed to the general public, to various political actors, and to other bureaucracies).
▸ *Scope rules* specify the conditions under which a bureaucracy is allowed to act or the areas of activity that the bureaucracy can regulate.
▸ *Aggregation rules* specify the extent to which a bureaucracy can act on its own or needs the cooperation of other agencies.
▸ *Payoff rules* specify the benefits received by members of the bureaucracy and their budgetary constraints.

As should be obvious, these rules setting up the broad action arena from figure 5.8 can interact in numerous highly complex ways. The basic idea behind the IAD framework is to reduce this complexity by identifying specific action situations, involving fewer actors and fewer rules, triggered by specific events. For example, the lobbying activity for some specific rule, triggered by some economic event, can be the action situation that is our object of analysis.

Last, but not least, the evaluation stage in the IAD framework is more subjective than the statistical evaluation of outcomes described earlier. Different actors will evaluate the same social-economic-political outcome differently, depending on their own values and interests. The political economy analysis based on the IAD framework is, thus, less paternalistic and does not pretend that third parties can evaluate the outcomes in a disinterested fashion. Instead, the focus is on how different actors differ in their evaluations and push for different types of institutional and policy changes. The focus is, therefore, on the possible conflicts of interests between different actors and on the possible Coasean bargaining that may be possible between them. The statistical evaluation of outcomes is still useful for understanding such disputes because it often allows us to highlight tradeoffs between different desirable outcomes, and different actors may want to make these tradeoffs differently.

CONCLUSION

This chapter shows that we economists are indeed not entirely helpless in the face of the problem of combinatorial complexity. The first step toward addressing this difficulty is to try to reduce the number of variables while still accounting for the observed variability. This step can be achieved with methods like principal component analysis, factor analysis, and clustering of variables.

Second, once a more manageable picture emerges of the universe of possible institutional changes, we can adopt several complementary approaches. We can build analytic narratives based on the template provided by the IAD framework and on public choice insights. This step can also be useful for identifying possible errors in the previous reduction of variables, by identifying ways in which the actors involved could perhaps undermine apparent institutional constraints. Furthermore, such analytic narratives are crucial for the problem of institutional design on the frontier—when one aims at improving institutions beyond any empirical example available so far.

Alternatively, we can use cluster analysis as a way of analyzing institutional configurations as complex packages rather than attempting to identify the effects of changing rules one at a time. Cluster analysis also allows us to compare different types of institutional packages. Another approach, not discussed in this chapter, is Charles Ragin's comparative method (Ragin 1987, 1994, 2000; also see Aligica and Tarko 2014b, chap. 5), which allows us to identify alternative possible paths toward a specified outcome of interest. Other clustering methods can also be used.

Third, once we have identified clusters of countries, on the basis of their institutional similarities, we can proceed to analyze differences in means across clusters. If these differences in means are large and statistically significant, it gives us more confidence in the possibility of institutional design.

Large differences in outcomes across institutionally defined clusters mean that changes from one institutional configuration to another indeed matter. They provide a guide for deliberately improving the institutional framework by learning from the example of other countries. Conversely, the strange composition of a given cluster, as well as small and statistically insignificant differences in outcomes across clusters, indicate that other, noninstitutional factors are probably in play. By exploring such examples, we might be able to put forward alternative hypotheses about the relevant factors.

These analytic methods show that—even if we take at face value Elinor Ostrom's warning about the complications arising from nonlinear interactions of factors and the combinatorial explosion of possibilities that ensues—we can still have some form of policy analysis and institutional design. However, we should *not* dismiss these warnings out of a misplaced mathematical convenience. These warnings arise out of a profound understanding of how social systems work, and they should inspire curiosity and ingenuity rather than nihilism. The difficulty is real, but it should be addressed head-on, not ignored.

NOTES

1. It is worth noting, however, that the IAD framework does not have these limitations. It works the same for any kind of assumptions about the goals of institutional design.

2. According to the mean-adjusted Rand criterion of cluster stability, a cluster of five is more stable.

3. Of course, in practice these two are not unrelated. The reason that technology transfers often do not happen is that the mechanism for technology transfers typically involves foreign investment, and weak property protections hamper foreign investment.

REFERENCES

Aligica, Paul Dragos. 2003. "Analytic Narratives and Scenario Building." *Futures Research Quarterly* 19 (2): 57–71.

———. 2018. "Constructivism and the Realm of the Artifactual: The 'Two Basic Articles of Faith' of James M. Buchanan and Vincent Ostrom's Social Philosophy." History of Economics Society conference, June 14–17, 2018, Chicago.

Aligica, Paul Dragos, and Vlad Tarko. 2014a. "Crony Capitalism: Rent Seeking, Institutions, and Ideology." *Kyklos* 67 (2): 156–76.

———. 2014b. *Capitalist Alternatives: Models, Taxonomies, Scenarios*. London: Routledge.

Bates, Robert H., Avner Greif, Margaret Levi, Jean-Laurent Rosenthal, and Barry R. Weingast. 1998. *Analytic Narratives*. Princeton, NJ: Princeton University Press.

———. 2000. "The Analytical Narrative Project." Response to Jon Elster, "Rational Choice History: A Case of Excessive Ambition," review of Bates et al., *Analytic Narratives*, 1998. *American Political Science Review* 94 (3): 696–702.

Capoccia, Giovanni, and R. Daniel Kelemen. 2007. "The Study of Critical Junctures: Theory, Narrative, and Counterfactuals in Historical Institutionalism." *World Politics* 59 (3): 341–69.

Carpenter, Daniel P. 2000. "What Is the Marginal Value of Analytic Narratives?" *Social Science History* 24 (4): 653–67.

Crawford, Sue E. S., and Elinor Ostrom. 1995. "A Grammar of Institutions." *American Political Science Review* 89 (3): 582–600.

Elster, Jon. 2000. "Rational Choice History: A Case of Excessive Ambition." Review of Bates et al., *Analytic Narratives,*1998. *American Political Science Review* 94 (3): 685–95.

Gwartney, James D., Robert Lawson, and Joshua Hall. 2017. *Economic Freedom of the World 2017 Annual Report*. Vancouver, BC, Canada: Fraser Institute.

Hanson, Robin. 2008. "Politics Isn't About Policy." *Overcoming Bias*. September 25, 2008. http://www.overcomingbias.com/2008/09/politics-isnt-a.html.

Hazlitt, Henry. 1946. *Economics in One Lesson*. New York: Harper & Brothers.

Klein, Daniel B., and Stewart Dompe. 2007. "Reasons for Supporting the Minimum Wage: Asking Signatories of the 'Raise the Minimum Wage' Statement." *Econ Journal Watch* 4 (1): 125–67.

McGinnis, Michael D. 2011. "An Introduction to IAD and the Language of the Ostrom Workshop: A Simple Guide to a Complex Framework." *Policy Studies Journal* 39 (1): 169–83.

Olson, Mancur. 1996. "Big Bills Left on the Sidewalk: Why Some Nations Are Rich, and Others Poor." *Journal of Economic Perspectives* 10 (2): 3–24.

Ostrom, Elinor. 1990. *Governing the Commons: The Evolution of Institutions for Collective Action*. Cambridge, UK: Cambridge University Press.

———. 2005. *Understanding Institutional Diversity*. Princeton, NJ: Princeton University Press.

———. 2008. "Developing a Method for Analyzing Institutional Change." In *Alternative Institutional Structures: Evolution and Impact*, edited by Sandra Batie and Nicholas Mercuro. New York: Routledge.

———. 2010. "Beyond Markets and States: Polycentric Governance of Complex Economic Systems." *American Economic Review* 100 (3): 641–72.

———. 2014. "Collective Action and the Evolution of Social Norms." *Journal of Natural Resources Policy Research* 6 (4): 235–52.

Parikh, Sunita. 2000. "Commentary: The Strategic Value of Analytic Narratives." *Social Science History* 24 (4): 677–84.

Poteete, Amy R., Marco A. Janssen, and Elinor Ostrom. 2010. *Working Together: Collective Action, the Commons, and Multiple Methods in Practice*. Princeton, NJ: Princeton University Press.

Ragin, Charles. 1987. *The Comparative Method: Moving Beyond Qualitative and Quantitative Strategies*. Oakland: University of California Press.

———. 1994. *Constructing Social Research: The Unity and Diversity of Method*. Thousand Oaks, CA: Pine Forge Press.

———. 2000. *Fuzzy-Set Social Science*. Chicago: University of Chicago Press.

Simler, Kevin, and Robin Hanson. 2018. *The Elephant in the Brain: Hidden Motives in Everyday Life*. New York: Oxford University Press.

Tarko, Vlad. 2015. "The Challenge of Empirically Assessing the Effects of Constitutions." *Journal of Economic Methodology* 22 (1): 46–76.

———. 2017. *Elinor Ostrom: An Intellectual Biography*. London: Rowman & Littlefield.

Tarko, Vlad, and Andrew Farrant. 2019. "The Efficiency of Regulatory Arbitrage." *Public Choice* (online January 2019). https://doi.org/10.1007/s11127-018-00630-y.

Tilly, Charles. 2006. *Why? What Happens When People Give Reasons . . . and Why*. Princeton, NJ: Princeton University Press.

Vogel, Steven K. 1996. *Freer Markets, More Rules: Regulatory Reform in Advanced Industrial Countries*. Ithaca, NY: Cornell University Press.

Wagner, Richard E. 1989. *To Promote the General Welfare: Market Processes vs. Political Transfers*. San Francisco: Pacific Research Institute for Public Policy.

———. 2016. *Politics as a Peculiar Business: Insights from a Theory of Entangled Political Economy*. Cheltenham, UK: Edward Elgar Publishing.

Wilson, David Sloan, Elinor Ostrom, and Michael E. Cox. 2013. "Generalizing the Core Design Principles for the Efficacy of Groups." *Journal of Economic Behavior & Organization* 90 (Supplement): S21–S32.

METHODOLOGICAL TENSIONS

CHAPTER SIX

WHOSE PROBLEMS ARE
BEING SOLVED?

POLYCENTRIC GOVERNANCE AND "THE POLITICAL"

ANDREAS THIEL AND ERIK SWYNGEDOUW

T he thoughts and arguments laid out in this chapter unfolded throughout
a series of conversations between one who some would call a "Work-
shopper" (Andreas Thiel, an affiliate of the Vincent and Elinor Ostrom
Workshop in Political Theory and Policy Analysis, who visited the workshop
until 2013) and a Marxist critical geographer (Erik Swyngedouw). It was only
through long-established mutual respect and trustful relations that the conversations could occur; the tensions that surfaced are obvious for anyone vaguely
familiar with what the Workshop and Critical Geography stand for.

The invitation to write this chapter provides the opportunity for putting
these conversations on paper and deepening some of the aspects raised. This
discussion also brought to the fore that a wide range of political perspectives and
theories are customarily neglected in debates of the Ostroms' work and require
attention. Clearly, this chapter cannot possibly achieve a comprehensive inclusion
of all relevant fields of political scholarship. However, for scholars from the fields
of collective action theory on the one hand and critical geography on the other,
this chapter is intended to highlight an important blind spot in the concept of

polycentric governance and a related research gap. The blind spot concerns the way polycentric governance considers marginalized claims by individuals and collectives in daily governance practice, and the research gap concerns how different ways of addressing such marginalized claims affect the performance and assessment of polycentric governance. At the same time, this chapter does not really engage with the very different assumptions that underpin these approaches, with a positivist, functionalist orientation that adheres to methodological individualism on the side of the Bloomington School and a critical, material-structuralist or constructivist perspective on the side of critical geography.

The chapter examines the ideal conception of polycentric governance in relation to a particular argument in critical geography. Nonetheless, our conversation may be of broader interest also to scholars who aim to spell out the common ground between the broader notion of political ecology on the one hand (and its predominant interest in social justice (Robbins 2012)) and polycentric governance on the other (Clement 2013; Gruby and Basurto 2014; Armitage 2008).

We will organize the cross-evaluation of approaches through the question of how what post-foundationalists call "the political" relates to "politics" as constituted in polycentric governance. Our guiding question is, Do marginalized, noninstitutionalized claims play a role in polycentric governance and, if so, how? Or in other words, What is the relationship between those included in existing governance arrangements and those who remain on the outside—excluded or marginalized? In relation to the "how" of representing the political, we posit the value-driven claim that humans as political beings are assumed to be equal and to have an equal voice. On a conceptual level, we evaluate the corresponding performance of polycentric governance.

Essentially, we corroborate that "the political" and "politics," as organized in polycentric governance, conceptually refer to mutually exclusive spheres. In this chapter, we refer to politics as the formal and informal—usually instituted—modalities of governing, including the actions of recognized actors (like parties, nongovernmental organizations, unions, lobbying groups, and similar) and the procedures of representation, negotiation, and policy implementation or policing. Politics, in other words, is the sensible reality of what produces a relatively stable social constellation. But any existing political order is predicated upon forms of exclusion, domination, or marginalization. Consider, for example, issues of minority rights, abortion control, rights and treatment of asylum seekers, the role of homeless people in healthcare, activities of illegal squatters, and landless movements, which regularly challenge the norms and rules that organize politics and claim respect. Occasionally, the rules and norms that organize institutionalized politics are reconfigured in response to those issues. The political, therefore, refers to the moments or events of interruption that may open a politicizing procedure to change the existing instituted order in the direction of a great inclusive equality. For example, the civil rights movement in the United States was precisely such a politicizing process. Thus, we consider it promising to think through how the concept of polycentric governance relates to the political. Recently, scholarly debates have more prominently featured polycentric governance as a framework to think about an upscaling of bottom-up collective action, particularly as an organizing principle of affairs concerning large numbers of people (Aligica 2014; Aligica and Boettke 2009; McGinnis 2016; McGinnis and Ostrom 2012; Wall 2014). In our view, this trend justifies deeper treatment of polycentric governance. As the outcome of our pragmatic and somewhat eclectic argument, we argue that polycentric governance requires discussing access to arenas in which values of collectives and their politics are structured. Further, it requires engaging with structural and redistributional measures to cater to equalizing endowments necessary for self-organization.

We develop this argument in the following sections: First, we introduce our understandings of the democratic political and polycentric governance. Second, we elaborate on institutional change in polycentric governance. Third, we synthesize these elements by discussing what conceptual options polycentric governance suggests for dealing with the political. Finally, to conclude, we discuss the cross-evaluation of the two approaches and our overarching question before summarizing our findings.

"THE POLITICAL" AND "THE DEMOCRATIC" IN POST-FOUNDATIONAL THOUGHT

In this chapter, we use the notion of the political to critically evaluate the concept of polycentric governance as it has been detailed by Vincent and Elinor Ostrom. The political, as emphasized in this chapter, is epistemologically rooted in what is generally referred to as post-foundational political thought. The argument developed centers on the difference between "politics" on the one hand and "the political" on the other (Swyngedouw 2011, 2018).

In post-foundational political thought (see Marchart 2007), the political is a signal of the absence of a foundational or an essential point (in social, cultural, or political philosophy) on which to base a polity or a society. The political, therefore, stands for the radical heterogeneity that cuts through "the people." The political is the signifier that affirms that the people, as a coherent or cohesive collection, does not exist. On the contrary, the people are cut through by all manner of differences along class, gender, ethnic, ideological, or other lines. Politics, in contrast, refers to the power plays between political actors and the everyday choreographies of policy making within a given institutional and procedural configuration in which individuals and groups pursue their interests. Politics contingently institutes society and gives society some (instable) form and temporal, but spatialized, coherence and semblance of order (and, in a "democratic" polity, does so in the name of the people as a whole). It is entailed in the institutions and technologies of governing and in the tactics, strategies, and power relations related to conflict intermediation and the furthering of particular partisan interests. It is through politics that society comes into being. But it is also politics that sutures or colonizes the space of the political, and through this, disavows the political origins of the politics. In other words, politics aims at suture, closure, and the disavowal of the radical splits that cut through the people.

Differentiation between *le politique* (as the political) and *la politique* (politics or policy) has been the orienting framework of much of post-foundational political thought (see Hewlett 2007; Marchart 2007). There are significant differences between authors (in particular, with respect to the strategic significance of this analysis; see, among others, Stavrakakis 2000; Marchart 2007). Still, they share the view that the political marks the antagonistic differences that cut through the social, signaling the absence of a principle on which a society, a political community or "a people" can be founded. For these reasons, they distinguish the politics from politics or policy.

In contrast to foundational perspectives that assume that politics is the way through which society realizes itself, post-foundational thought insists on the impossibility of the social, the nonexistence of the people. The people do not preexist the political sequence through which it is called into being as a procedure of living-in-common. It is through institutionalization that the people, as an assumedly cohesive social category, comes into being. There is no given, foundational or irreducible basis (like language, religion, or nation) upon which to found a society. It is this lack of a conclusive foundation in the social that renders its founding impossible and that inaugurates the political as the name for the heterogeneities that cut through the social. Therefore, all social orders are profoundly contingent and are structured to conceal their own absent ground. In these terms, political difference is between politics as the contingent and an incomplete attempt to ground a particular set of power relations on an ultimately absent foundation, and the political as the ineradicable presence of this absence itself. The political continually undermines the social orders constructed upon it, and it holds open the possibility of more or less radical change. For instance, the private ownership of nature and the distribution of its metabolized products in the form of commodities for exchange are commonly accepted as the preferred, natural, and universally constituted form of organizing socio-ecological relations. Yet, this organizational principle is continually challenged by those who disagree fundamentally (for example, indigenous communities fighting to maintain nature as commons, or "commonists" struggling for forms of common ownership).

According to post-foundationalists, the field of politics/the political is thus split into two: The political stands for the constitutive lack of ground to constitute society. In contrast, politics stands for the always contingent, precarious, and incomplete attempt to institutionalize and to spatialize the social, offer closure, and let society coincide with community, understood as a cohesive and inclusive whole. Seemingly, also borrowing from anti-communitarian ideas, post-foundationalists hold that politics always harbors totalitarian moments that marginalize and silence the political. Politics replaces the political with community (as an imagined coherent unity such as nation, ethnic group, or another social category—for example, organization, management, good governance). In the realm of politics, problems tend to be dealt with through administrative-organizational-technical means while questioning things as such disappears (Nancy and Strong 1992).

As critique of the current status of democracy, making the political explicit sheds light on the struggles against increasing bureaucratization, legalization, privatization, and economization of social relations (Flügel-Martinsen 2004; Flügel-Martinsen, Heil, and Hetzel 2004). It concerns structuring the system, not only steering and coordinating the system, under an overarching (institutionally inscribed and unquestioned) hegemonic order. It, therefore, aims for a radically democratic process and insists on an ethic of democracy that emphasizes openness, indecisiveness, inconclusiveness, and normative contingency.

The above theorization begs the question regarding what legitimately constitutes the democratic in "the political." For Claude Lefort (1988), the invention of democracy inaugurated the presumption of equality as axiomatically given and presupposed. Although sociologically untrue, the democratic presumes the equality of each and every person. This presumption of equality characterizes any given order, including instituted democratic politics, and stands in strict opposition to the sociologically verifiable inequalities within the social order. Equality interpreted in that way holds that anyone can claim the place of power in democracy: there is no authority (in the social, natural, or divine) that designates the site of power because the presumption is that the social does not exist as a result of the recognition of its own absent ground and heterogeneity. Democracy contingently affirms society's nonexistence. Thus, people constitute community specifically in an antagonistic response to claims by others. Democracy is "founded upon the legitimacy of a debate as to what is legitimate and what is illegitimate—a debate which is necessarily without any guarantor and without any end" (Lefort 1988, 39).

Democracy, therefore, lies in the axiomatic presumption of equality and the free expression of its egalitarian practices. The democratic political requests a universalizing and collective process of emancipation as *égaliberté*—"equality," the first part of the word as the absence of discrimination (*égalité*) and the second part of the word as the absence of repression (*liberté*) (Dikeç 2001). Similarly, for Jacques Rancière (1998), democracy is neither historically nor institutionally limited to modernity. For him, the "democratic" political manifests itself in moments of interruptive acting that address an inegalitarian "wrong" and demonstrate equality. For example, African American activist Rosa Parks, one of the early activists of the civil rights movement, refused to yield her bus seat to a white man when the bus driver told her to do so. Her act inaugurated a political event both by demonstrating the inequality embedded in the existing instituted order (politics) and by symbolically demonstrating equality through her interruptive act. In democratic communities, equality of members implies that those who do not have a share in decision-making can claim their egalitarian share in the instituted order. For Rancière (1998), this characteristic of democracy is more important than what results from it. Political acts consist of two steps. In the first step, a group articulates its vision of equality of its members, which may imply a significant redistribution of assets and means of society. A collective formulates a reason or an issue, the consequences of which concern everyone who is part of that community. The second step is implementing the understanding of equality vis-à-vis others and vis-à-vis the existing order.

Several qualifications and critiques of these perspectives are due at this point. First, in post-foundational thought "the political" and "politics/policy" (or "police," as discussed by Rancière) are inextricably linked. Thus, also following Chantal Mouffe's (2000) assertion, the continuous struggle between the political and the institutionalized order is a necessary paradox. This paradox results from the need to produce some sort of order through institutional arrangements (like the state) on the one hand and the contingent, inherently questionable, and antagonistic forces that order itself produces (or rather excludes and marginalizes) on the other. It is part and parcel of desires for order once we assume an essential common ground constituting society that would legitimately silence contending perspectives (Ritzi 2016). Nonetheless, the macro-oriented perspective hardly addresses the tension that individuals face. Instead, it seems that equality, continuous negotiation on the grounds of equality, and disorder are considered superior a priori. Second, the dichotomous conceptual map with reference to politics on the one hand and the political on the other entails a tendency that makes analysts insensitive to individuals' need for order in social contexts as proposed by institutionalists (Bowles 2004). Therefore, third, it throws different ways of structuring politics "into the same bowl," not considering differences in their potential to transform themselves toward more or less equality (Niederberger 2004).

Clearly, our discussion that follows is only generally inspired by the above discussion of post-political and post-foundational thought. We derive that politics is the attempt to institutionally order societies. It is based on the idea that societies are able to agree on and define something that holds the people together. Then the political becomes contingent and relative to the contents that were struggled for, ordered, and codified in politics. The political is contesting the social order that politics tries to impose, as well as the presumed foundational values it represents and temporarily stabilizes.

In what follows, we examine how an idealizing perspective on polycentric governance as sometimes promoted by the Ostroms relates to post-foundational thought and how it relates to the political. In that context, we presume the legitimacy of corresponding claims based on the assertion of egalitarian rights by humans.

POLYCENTRIC GOVERNANCE

Polycentric governance, as any type of governance, is about establishing order, coherence, and predictable patterns of behavior.[1] Thus, polycentric governance addresses what post-foundational thought describes as politics. It starts from the assumption of shared values. In contrast, what post-political thought signals with the political would concern the allocation and distribution of valued resources toward values that are not (yet) shared by a community and represented through the kinds of polycentric governance it relies on at a particular moment in time (see McGinnis 2011b). The question is, therefore, how values that are not shared by an established collective come to be represented in polycentric governance.

An idealized, normative perspective on polycentric governance holds that information exchange among interdependent actors leads to mutual adjustment in ways that benefit the realization of societal welfare (McGinnis 2016). Most relevant for understanding the role of politics and the political in polycentric governance is understanding the change of polycentric governance and its determinants (for rare treatments of this matter, see Ostrom and Basurto 2011; Ostrom 2014b; Aligica 2014).

In recent decades, the Ostroms and other scholars have elaborated on the concept of polycentric governance in a multitude of publications. In what follows, we want to briefly describe the model of polycentric governance and its context and functioning. We want to start with agency-related features, address principles and values that structure idealized polycentric governance, and discuss the institutional context of polycentric governance. Subsequently, we elaborate on the conception of institutional change in polycentric governance.

AGENTS' CAPABILITIES IN
POLYCENTRIC GOVERNANCE

As paraphrased above, in idealized polycentric governance the fundamental principle of social ordering is self-organization. To allow for theory building, actors are conceptualized as being boundedly but intendedly rational and fallible learners who are able to improve their well-being over time. Thus, actors are presumed to self-organize collective goods provision and production in order to maximize their perceived net benefit in relation to diverse performance criteria. Polycentric governance, therefore, depends on what the Ostroms refer to as democratic capabilities of self-organization (see Ostrom 2014a). They point toward the need for "informed citizens . . . able to challenge efforts to take over their democratic system by powerful autocrats" (Ostrom 2014a, 2). Centrally, citizens need to learn about overcoming social dilemmas, avoiding the tragedy of the commons, and learning about the advantages that arise from conflict and ways to resolve conflicts.

Furthermore, public entrepreneurs are considered necessary (i.e., they exercise leadership in an executive role with certain degrees of autonomy and incentives to constructively engage in conflicts). Such public entrepreneurs create artifacts impregnated by values and "materials" (Ostrom 1999a). Artisanship implies the consideration of shared values in democratic societies as much as it requires a commonly understood and similarly shared theory of constitutional choice (Ostrom 1999a, 2015).

SHARED VALUES, SOCIAL-PROBLEM CHARACTERISTICS, AND OVERARCHING RULES IN POLYCENTRIC GOVERNANCE

A fundamental precondition of self-organization in polycentric governance is a judgment about what is right or wrong, or what is valuable and what is not. This judgment needs to be shared within a community of actors and it provides the basis for what Vincent Ostrom called the Faustian bargain—that is, "the use of instruments of evil to do good" (Ostrom 2008, 34). He sees this judgment as a necessary tradeoff that underpins all human societies and as a system of order that requires the possibility to sanction misbehavior. On certain occasions, individuals who implicitly or even explicitly agreed to membership in a society may themselves be subject to such sanctioning to maintain social order. However, to correct fallibility of societal judgments underpinning sanctions, community members need to be open to communication in order to understand others' perspectives and appreciate tensions resulting from the Faustian bargain (Ostrom 1999a, 2008). We would argue that these are tensions that refer to what we referred to above as the political, which may indeed be repressed in a particular order.

The ingredient of shared values puts polycentric governance close to discussions about communitarianism versus cosmopolitanism or classical liberalism. Communitarians emphasize the importance of the social realm. They assume that individuals who are well integrated into communities are better able to reason and act in responsible ways than are isolated individuals. Communitarians differ in the extent to which their concepts are attentive to maintaining liberty and individual rights. Indeed, as social pressure to conform to a community rises, the result may be to undermine the individual self (Etzioni 2003). Therefore, cosmopolitans and classical liberalists hold that the major flaw of communitarianism is the impossibility to equally maintain individual liberties and uphold community values (Bauman 1995; Dobson 2006). They argue that communities use moral standpoints to oppress people; they are authoritarian in nature and push people to conform (Kymlicka 1993, 208–11; cited in Etzioni 2003).

Vincent Ostrom also speaks about the need that self-organizing actors share common values. Still, he remains fairly unspecific with respect to the type of values actors should share. Instead, he refers to what he calls the "Golden Rule" as underlying the covenantal order of polycentric governance. It implies that people do not do to others what they do not want to suffer from themselves (Ostrom 2008). Ostrom writes, "The golden rule . . . is . . . better . . . conceived as a method of normative inquiry that enables human beings to come to a commonly shared understanding about the meaning of value terms used as norms or criteria of choice" (V. Ostrom 1990, 43). He sees the Golden Rule as a cognitive device—for making interpersonal comparisons and arriving at common understandings of norms and criteria for moral judgment on that which is prohibited versus that which is permitted (V. Ostrom 1990).

The Golden Rule is grounded in equality. Thus, each person should be content with as much liberty as one would allow others against oneself. Effectiveness of such an order depends upon citizens' prioritization of enforcement of the Golden Rule as an overall organizing value. Still, Vincent Ostrom admits to the possibility of conflicts to emerge as a result of unintended consequences or of erroneous assumptions about consequences. Conflict is indicative of ignorance and offers potential for learning. Also, conflict may emerge from the deliberate pursuit of strategies to gain at the cost of others. Dealing with them is the *raison d'être* of politics. Thus, human beings are considered fallible because errors inevitably occur and they can learn from their errors, reconsider problematical situations, and achieve resolutions by using the human imagination to explore new possibilities.

Thus, first, polycentric governance expects that within a population, collectives will exist whose values, orientations, and preferences are heterogeneous but which all subscribe to the Golden Rule. Heterogeneity, in turn, results in diverse ways of providing for and producing collective goods. One expectation is that collectives of actors prioritize different performance criteria (e.g., effectiveness, political representation, equity, resilience, sustainability; Ostrom, Tiebout, and Warren 1961; Aligica and Tarko 2012). Correspondingly, polycentric governance has been proposed as a principle for organizing governance that fares particularly well in contexts of value heterogeneity. For example, spiritual orientations are organized according to different values and preferences affiliated with religious standpoints held by multifaceted, overlapping collectives.

Second, besides shared values and their heterogeneity across communities, polycentricity is structured by presumed variations in perceptions concerning characteristics of social problems that require diverse ways of organizing effective collective action. Characteristics of social problems may refer to the specific level on a spatial scale at which collective goods are provided for cost-effectively, where spillover effects are respectively internalized. Alternatively, characteristics of social problems may refer to institutional features that address opportunistic behavior more or less effectively (e.g., hybrid versus market governance; Williamson 1991), or they may relate to features that determine the performance of coordinating across goods and services, leading to institutional diversity.

Third, in addition to values and their distribution over populations and social-problem characteristics, overarching rules affect polycentric governance. Among other things, they set out how collectives with heterogeneous values and perceptions of social problems aggregate their preferences and come to joint decisions. In one way or another, for self-organization in polycentric governance to function well, rules need to cater to what other authors have referred to as options of exit, voice, and self-organization (Aligica and Tarko 2012). Relating to different ways of legitimizing the way public goods are provided or produced, these ways are exercised by citizens and consumers. On the demand side of public service provision and production, consumers need to buy into certain provisioning ways; alternatively, on the supply side, provisioning actors can similarly voice their concerns or exit from particular ways of collective-goods provision in relation to interrelated providers and producers. Exit, voice, and self-organization are, therefore, ways in which actors can contest the actions of other, functionally interdependent actors. They allow agents in their roles as citizens or consumers to select those features and performances of governance that the agents prefer.

Simultaneous operation of these mechanisms needs support of formal and informal overarching rules (Thiel 2017). Corresponding rules enable numerous actors to be involved with provisioning or producing collective goods. These rules give agents in polycentric governance alternatives for providing and producing specific goods and services, which enable contesting of existing relations. They make threats of citizens and consumers, producers or providers, more credible; at the same time, rules may increase other, for example, coordination-related transaction costs or costs of production, because of economies of scale that are forgone.

From the perspective of polycentric governance, the political tries to achieve institutional change representing values from outside of its realm— that is, outside regulated and institutionalized processes of an organized polity. Thus, in what follows, we expand on how institutional change operates in polycentric governance.

INSTITUTIONAL CHANGE IN POLYCENTRIC GOVERNANCE

Following Ostrom (2014b; see Ostrom and Basurto 2011), we consider implicit or explicit negotiation processes over institutional arrangements to be at the core of institutional change in polycentric governance. The processes can be conceptualized through the Bloomington School's Institutional Analysis and Development (IAD) framework.[2] The IAD framework helps us to analyze what it calls action situations, which are instances in which the well-being of agents at least in part depend on other actors' choices. In analyzing such constellations, the framework particularly focuses on the way institutions shape actors' (interdependent) choices. The approach assumes that actors maximize their perceived net benefit, reflecting their preferences and values and the options available to them. The action situation in the IAD framework usefully operationalizes institutional change as "bargaining problems" between boundedly rational actors and invokes "the asymmetries of power in a society as a primary source of explanation" (Knight 1992, 210). In these action situations, actors implicitly or explicitly bargain over institutions that regulate a collective. In the model, actors are learners who are not only boundedly rational but also fallible and who experiment with rules and, therefore, eventually change them to improve their well-being.

Ostrom distinguishes mechanisms of institutional change as those suggested by classical institutionalists and anthropologists (Ostrom and Basurto 2011; Hodgson 2004; Cleaver 2002). Thus, institutional change becomes an outcome of a combination of social learning, evolution, and emergence (Ostrom 2014b). Conscious forms of institutional change are distinguished from unconscious forms of institutional change (Ostrom and Basurto 2011). Conscious forms express humans' ability to learn. For instance, their ability entails experimenting with institutions, imitating rules, deliberately negotiating favorable institutional arrangements, or competitively selecting consciously devised rules. According to this perspective, institutional change never optimizes but at most improves the situation of actors involved, given the complexity of the choices at stake. From this perspective, it is difficult to conceptualize and incorporate all manner of political action that operates at a distance from any institutional configuration (such as what the political describes) and, in fact, interrupts existing socio-institutional configurations.

In contrast, unconscious rule changes go beyond rational choice. They result from variations in interpretations of rules, from unconscious, slowly developing adaptations or even neglect of rules. Changes of underlying (shared) values and preferences fall into this category. Ostrom and Basurto (2011) highlight that the pace of change of endogenous or exogenous drivers of institutional change could make the difference between conscious and subconscious institutional change. Nonetheless, no theories of institutional change or combinations thereof are considered to help us conclusively understand how the different mechanisms interlink and lead to a renegotiation of institutions (Ostrom 2014b; Schmid 2004; North 2005).

Of the processes described above, we consider conscious institutional change as particularly relevant to the way the political may affect polycentric governance. Concretely, such institutional change can be triggered by changes endogenous or exogenous to the action situation. As a rule, we consider those changes that affect several collective goods as exogenous to an action situation (e.g., socio-economic changes), while those that predominantly affect one collective good would be endogenous (e.g., rules structuring decision-making in a particular action situation).

In idealized polycentric governance, each actor group endogenous to an action situation has potentially three pathways for contesting the way collective goods are provided, expressing their discontent, and triggering institutional change. First, "voice" entails attempts to delegitimize provision and production of collective goods through politics or administrative channels. A second, more radical option is "exit." It involves physically or socially exiting from a relationship with providers and producers, which undermines funding and support. It includes physically moving away or withdrawing from cooperation. Third, consumers, providers, or producers may couple exit with self-organization for providing and producing collective goods. Together with social-problem characteristics, the institutions structuring the action situation determine to what extent actors can exercise the contestation options of exit, voice, and self-organization. Several authors have devised typologies of "power resources" that cut across the institutions that structure action situations and whose change may lead to institutional change through renegotiation of institutions (Knight 1992; Schlüter 2001; Theesfeld 2005). In whatever way they are categorized, endogenous drivers, such as changes in rules and power resources, can lead to institutional change as they reshape the positions of actors in various roles in polycentric governance arrangements.

Exogenous drivers of institutional change are changes in social-problem characteristics, socio-economic and value heterogeneity of collectives, and *de facto* constitutional rules (see Ostrom 1999b). For example, the transaction costs that actors in different roles encounter when they want to change institutions depend on the way social-problem characteristics shape the availability of alternatives to provide for collective goods. Particular, place-based goods cannot be easily offered by multiple ways of provisioning. Second, changes in community features, such as heterogeneity of values, income and other socio-economic characteristics, and changes in perceptions of social problems may trigger institutional change. Heterogeneity of actor groups potentially leads to diverse problem perceptions, preferences, and governance arrangements concerning the way collective goods are provided. Thus, institutional change may be more likely in highly heterogeneous societies because actors have a broader set of governance options to compare with (Bednar 2009). Also, institutional change may occur when levels of heterogeneity change, for example as a result of widening income gaps or because actors in a particular space might encounter new or emerging collectives and actors who promote distinct values. Further exogenous drivers of institutional change include changes in technologies of governance, or factor or product prices (e.g., because of changes in perceptions of scarcity; North 1994; Lin 1989; Thiel 2014). Changes in perceptions of characteristics of social problems, associated net-benefits of particular governance arrangements, and changes in heterogeneity of collectives and changes in their values affect prefer ences of the actors bargaining over institutional change. In contrast, exogenous or endogenous changes in constitutional rules change the positions of the bargaining actors. That way, they potentially lead to institutional change as actors' ability to shape bargaining over institutions changes.

In relation to changes in preferences over particular institutions, according to our conceptualization of decision-making over institutions, exogenous or endogenous factors therefore can affect actors' norms, values, and heuristics or emotional reactions in a way that their preferences for and strategic bargaining over institutional options is affected (see Ostrom 2005). According to Ostrom's model, this effect can operate through personal experience or shifts in broader culture in a way that actors consider institutional alternatives preferable (Ostrom 2005, 105). Through institutional change, the changes in preferences of some are shared (as institutionalized) across a collective. Therefore, the fact that changes are shared by some does not mean that institutional change is aligned with preferences of all members of a collective. Rather, it represents (changes in) preferences of those who dominate decision-making on institutional orders in polycentric governance. Alternatively, preferences of actors regarding particular institutions may be stable, but institutional change may occur because their bargaining position has changed, benefiting or disadvantaging their position.

We, therefore, consider institutional change as driven by exogenous changes in overarching rules, heterogeneity of the community, or perceptions of social-problem characteristics, which may trigger changes in collectively expressed preferences of interdependent actors engaged in polycentric governance. Alternatively, preferences may change endogenously as a result of the way actors evaluate existing polycentric governance. Subsequently, these actors involved in governance may exert pressure to change institutionalized orders through exit, voice, and self-organization if they have the resources and are in a position to do so. Ultimately, independent of whether drivers of institutional change were endogenous or exogenous, whether they translated into changes in preferences of actors, or whether they translated into changes in bargaining positions, an evolutionary path of institutional change develops in which, presumably, at any moment in time, institutions reflect a temporary compromise between bargaining (coalitions of) actors over what they prefer as institutional arrangement (McGinnis 2005; Aligica 2014; see also figure 6.1).

FIGURE 6.1: INSTITUTIONAL CHANGE IN POLYCENTRIC GOVERNANCE

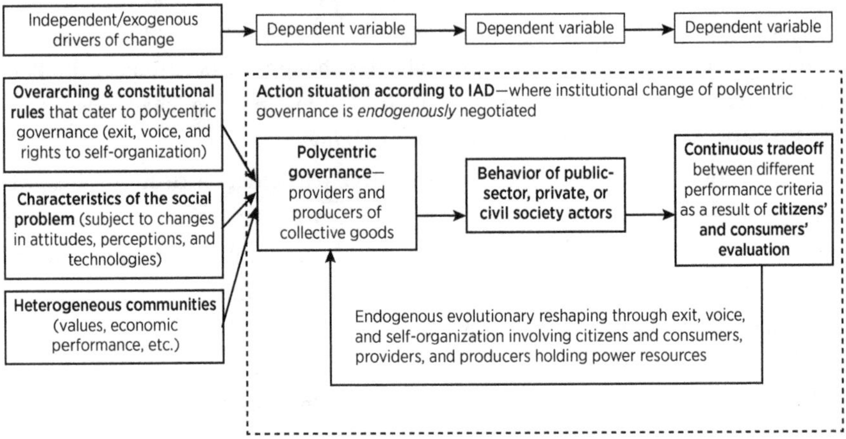

Source: Thiel 2017.

DISCUSSION: POLYCENTRIC GOVERNANCE, INSTITUTIONAL CHANGE, AND "THE POLITICAL"

We have described at length the concept of institutional change in polycentric governance because, ultimately, we have argued that expressions of the political try to achieve institutional change in forms of polycentric governance. The political presents a necessarily exogenous driver of institutional change in polycentric governance; it aims at integrating noninstitutionalized claims and reconsidering what are held to be shared values in polycentric governance and its institutionalized politics. Correspondingly, the substance of the political is changing continuously. Wherever the political successfully shapes polycentric governance, leading to respect for previously unheard and unaddressed claims, it ceases to be political.

Idealized polycentric governance is about a particular form of establishing order in which shared values and understandings provide for the core around which bottom-up self-organization and politics organize collective provision of goods and services. Thus, it is a concept that does not address the political. Equally, from the perspective of idealized polycentric governance, no necessity exists concerning the need to formulate the normative positioning of the political in relation to politics, in the way that the concept of democratic equality described above suggests. In contrast, its principal authors (such as the Ostroms) consider democracy and equality to be realized if agents were enabled to self-organize their affairs and affect politics. They are not explicitly concerned about situations in which actors diverge from shared values. Nonetheless, regardless of how transitory and abstract normative values they advocate may be (as in the case of agreement on the Golden Rule as a method of normative inquiry), they presume that actors share values and engage in self-organization in their name. In contrast, post-foundational thought holds that shared values as foundational to everyday politics do not (and cannot) exist and that focusing our attention on claims that are not represented in politics could cause us to fall victim to the attempts of (polycentric) politics to artificially create shared values.

In the next sections, we first address if and how, on the basis of our concept of institutional change in polycentric governance, the political may become institutionalized. The question is, How do noninstitutionalized claims that contradict predominant, presumed values in which collectives and their politics are grounded affect institutional change in everyday politics? Subsequently, we address broader structural conditions related to equity, access, and higher levels of societal organization required for this change to happen.

As our elaboration of institutional change in polycentric governance highlights, most factors considered in theorizing polycentric governance do not offer entry points for "the democratic representation/integration of the political." Instead, the concept focuses on members of polycentrically structured politics who share certain underlying values. Members of corresponding collectives, in contrast, can shape polycentric politics in multiple ways, such as exit or voice. The way collective goods are provided may change as a result of endogenous or exogenous factors, all of which affect the politics of collective-goods provision.

Similarly, the micro-concept of decision-making that relates culture, values, and mental models to individuals' decisions and institutions hardly offers entry points for actors and issues that are not part of the politics of polycentric governance. One could argue, therefore, that polycentric governance is about solving the problems of established communities that share underlying values but is not about solving problems of unestablished and unrepresented communities and their concerns. That situation becomes particularly problematic where the claims of established communities posit tensions in relation to the political claims of such unestablished and excluded groups and individuals.

Instead, defendants of polycentric governance and its democratic qualities would argue that it offers the additional mechanisms of self-organization to unestablished communities and individuals for introducing political claims into polycentric governance. However, empirically, such rights are often selectively granted, for example exclusively to citizens of a particular nation. Similarly, rights to form a political party may be granted only to citizens, and further conditions may apply. How such selection relates to the guiding Golden Rule that defendants of an idealized polycentric governance advocate thereby remains an open and, most of all, an empirical question subject to what has been called a procedure of "normative inquiry." These, however, are empirical questions that idealized polycentric governance does not address. Considering this aspect, however, is key for assessing the democratic quality of polycentric governance in the sense of its ability to provide each individual with equal rights to have his or her claims heard and treated in an equal manner based on the equality of individuals as humans.

Thus, we will next assess whether the idealized concept of polycentric governance indeed declares itself on the possibility of the political, for example, expressed through changes in the heterogeneity of collectives. We also assess whether members can easily be represented through rights to self-organization in polycentric governance. Also, such claims would need to be in line with higher-level, shared values of the collective, which are inscribed in what polycentric governance conceptualizes as overarching rules that legitimize the organization of current affairs. On the one hand, we expect that such higher-level norms potentially exclude claims of some people. On the other hand, these norms guarantee that existing values and collectives are not undermined in illegitimate ways. Thus, a confrontation between political statements and overarching rules reproduces the tensions between the political, which legitimizes contesting action based on human equality, and rules based on shared values. The latter necessarily distinguish legitimate forms of (self-organizing) engagement into shaping polycentric governance from illegitimate ones. However, rules also avoid violent forms of expressing the political, on which arguments presented above about the political do not declare themselves.

This tension touches upon the open question of how the political will deal with extreme cases of principled, equal representation of the "democratic, political." The question emerges of whether any kind of claim should be represented and how that may be done. To put it differently, the question is whether certain political issues are potentially illegitimate. It may be questioned whether such "pre-selected" issues still address "political issues." This point highlights the necessarily emergent tension between the political and any kind of order such as the one developed in polycentric governance. Polycentric governance considers this tension as reproducing what we have referred to as a Faustian bargain, the fact that individuals need to accept a certain degree of subjugation for improving societal and individual welfare. As a matter of fact, we would argue that answers to questions about admissible claims differ across space and time. Thus, what is admissible is constantly renegotiated between societies and political forces and is reflected in gradual value change, which over time brings change in the content and orientation of politics and polycentric governance. Thus, value change becomes the ultimate indicator of institutional change in polycentric governance that incorporates the political.

The opportunity to self-organize is a precondition for political issues to be able to enter the scene of politics in polycentric governance. However, it not only depends on rights but also on individual capacities and resources, which need to be at the disposal of corresponding actors. Collective action theory made invaluable contributions to understanding the problems involved and the conditions under which self-organization is likely to emerge in a sustainable manner (Ostrom 2007; Olson 1994; Ahn, Ostrom, and Walker 2003; Cleaver 2007; Ostrom 2014a). Particularly, in regard to advocating democratic, equal representation of the political in polycentric governance, the questions emerge whether marginalized groups in all cases have the resources to self-organize their claims, and whether they have access to politics, or whether polycentric governance leads to structural inequalities and de facto dominance of particular issues and values in society. Obviously, these questions concern absolute as well as relative means that actors use in pursuing certain values. Further, we need to factor in influence over the broader debate of political issues. Dramatically unequal distribution of endowments is particularly problematic because it adds to layers of biases favoring institutionalized matters in line with corresponding politics and values over noninstitutionalized ones. This problem is also captured by the concept of path dependence among institutionalist scholars where governance at one point in time necessarily shapes subsequent development paths of governance of collective-goods provision and production (Pierson 2000; Arthur 1994; North 2005; Ostrom 2014b).

At the heart of catering to equal representation of (legitimate) political claims is, therefore, the question of enabling actors to equally represent issues in polycentric politics. On the one hand, this equality requires access to corresponding debates and decision-making forums, which is obviously an important institutional question. As a matter of fact, what are called clear boundaries and rules establishing these (excluding) boundaries have been found to be core to successful self-organization and therefore also to polycentric governance (Cox, Arnold, and Villamayor-Tomás 2010). Thus, how political issues and their representatives relate to existing groups and boundaries and how they manage to establish their own boundaries would be a key aspect of successfully introducing new values inscribed in political issues into politics. Further, plain financial, organizational, and informational resources would be necessary to reconfigure politics of polycentric governance. Thus, it requires resources to engage in corresponding debates on equal terms. On the other hand, we expect that the lack of redistribution to approximately equal endowments for self-organization instills a dynamic that favors the communitarian elements of polycentric governance over the liberal elements inscribed in overarching rules. In other words, if the political and its democratic right to equal representation were structurally disadvantaged concerning resources for representation, then the values around which politics in polycentric governance were organized would structurally dominate, reinforcing "totalitarian" tendencies in societies organized around communitarian principles. One of the few authors addressing this problem in relation to communitarianism is Coughlin (2003, 13), who writes that the instrumental consequence of "extreme inequality undermines civic participation and the sense of community shared by members of the broader society." Etzioni, Volmert, and Rothschilds (2004), for example, made several concrete suggestions in this regard, such as basic minimum income, which would need further examination regarding their compatibility with idealized polycentric governance.

The question that we need to address, therefore, is whether, in writings on polycentric governance, the authors discuss ways to overcome potential structural inequalities between actors who wish to self-organize. This question differs from the mention of fairness as a design principle for successful, sustained collective action in the work of Elinor Ostrom. She refers to fair distribution of the outcomes of politics as opposed to addressing actors who are marginalized and external to collective action (E. Ostrom 1990; Cox, Arnold, and Villamayor-Tomás 2010). The principle is, therefore, grounded within the realm of politics and the realm of outcomes.

In relation to Vincent Ostrom's work, one could argue that the question of democratic as equal representation is present in the performance criterion of political representation (Ostrom, Tiebout, and Warren 1961). It holds that the way that a service is provided to people affects how those people are affected by the transaction. But we see this situation as inspired by the notion of efficiency, except where redistribution of income was sought as a matter of public policy. We would argue that this criterion is interpreted in a far too narrow manner for it to be encompassing the kind of democratic representation of the political in the way that values are settled within and across collectives, as we discuss in this chapter.

Thus, in the concept of polycentric governance, do actors who represent marginalized claims have equal opportunities to self-organize and therefore trigger institutional change in the way democratic equality requires of humans as individuals? Interrelatedly, should democratically equal access to forums that co-shape collective values be granted? Should it be selective? Although the writings of the Ostroms clearly advocate the enablement of individuals, they seem to be deliberately silent on the question of redistribution of resources for the sake of enabling self-organization by the individual and the collectives of actors struggling for political purposes. The underlying problem is that redistribution tables the need for higher-level jurisdictions that make the corresponding decisions. Thus, nonvoluntary redistribution necessarily invokes tensions with polycentric governance, which negates centralized responsibilities for specific tasks, including decisions on redistribution to approximate equality in endowments for the sake of self-organization. Centralizing responsibilities, according to Vincent Ostrom, opens doors for opportunistic behavior and rent-seeking by public agents and long-term undermining of checks and balances exercised by bottom-up self-organization in polycentric governance. Similarly, the Ostroms were relatively silent on the question of access (Klooster 2000; Cleaver and de Koning 2015). In relation to either, the question of redistribution and the question of access, the relatively abstract Golden Rule and the idea of normative inquiry seem to be the most relevant reference of the Ostroms. Nonetheless, we need to keep in mind that using such a self-referential moral standard carries normative content that, in many cases, might reproduce existing values. By extension, using such a standard can be expected to reproduce distinctions between "politics" as presumed legitimate contestation and "the political."

Vincent Ostrom is very clear that polycentric governance needs to be secured in all domains and components of governance (Ostrom 1999c). Thus, the conventional branches of the executive, judicial, and legislative powers need to be organized in polycentric, bottom-up ways. Alternatively, tendencies for monocentric totalitarian regimes in one domain or branch would lead to spillover effects and monocentricity in other domains. This kind of argument would rule out the existence of responsibilities for redistribution at a higher level of government because it instills a dynamic toward monocentrism.

One of the few places where scholars at the Ostrom Workshop addressed issues of equity on a broader level was a report on local governance in the United States (ACIR 1987). This study makes the claim that principles of equity demand limits on the permissible range of disparity. Two solutions are advocated. The first concerns delineating communities in a way that members are heterogeneous regarding income or wealth. However, we note that averaging across members of a community through its consolidation leads to inefficiencies—that is, situations of mismatch between levels of demand and supply for goods and services. Orientation by economic efficiency, therefore, seems to provide a structural argument for homogeneity as opposed to heterogeneity of collectives. Further, in relation to our concern, such upscaling and integrating of heterogeneous collectives do not explicitly enable marginalized, political groups to self-organize. Also, upscaling the rule of collectives does not overcome the problem of continuously integrating the political into politics through institutional change. Instead, it may simply expand particular orders and further sideline political issues.

As an alternative, we suggest permitting disparities among provision units but redistributing goods and services through grants from overlapping, higher-level jurisdictions. For this purpose, a multitude of types of inter-jurisdictional schemes have been advocated by scholars of public finance (Musso 1998). It is suggested that particular standards of equity in endowments should be guaranteed in that way, an argument that is also made from the communitarian side (see Coughlin 2003). Citizens would be enabled to freely allocate resources in a way that maximizes their preferences. The latter is considered advantageous over the rearrangement of the boundaries of actor groups (ACIR 1987). Nonetheless, the fundamental questions regarding who is entitled to benefit from redistribution and how it relates to the political are not addressed. Also, other authors have shown the difficulties that collectives have of actually introducing redistributive rules that benefit the marginalized (Brennan and Buchanan 1993). It is thus unlikely that collectives will democratically agree to introduce rules that enable the kinds of democratic equality that have been discussed here. Rather, by itself, normative polycentric governance seems to face great difficulties to avoid excluding individuals from receiving support that enables self-organization and access to ways of shaping politics. At the very least, how to put such claims for democratic equality into practice is unanswered by theorizing on polycentric governance. It should, therefore, be a matter of further conceptual and empirical research.

CONCLUSIONS

In this chapter, we discussed how the political, which represents values that are not considered in the way communities are ordered, relates to polycentric governance. We specifically evaluated whether the political stood a chance of being represented in a democratic (equal) way in struggles over shared values in the presumed core of communitarian order, as suggested in the Ostroms' conception of polycentric governance. First, we elaborated on the political. We highlighted its origin in post-foundational thought and connected it to an understanding of democracy that calls for equal representation of any claim. Second, we characterized polycentric governance and highlighted the role of preferences, values, and particular agency-related features and capabilities of actors in polycentric governance. Polycentric governance stands for politics as everyday resolution of collective issues in institutionalized orders. From the perspective of post-foundational thought, however, politics is one of two mutually exclusive concepts: politics (institutionalized in governance) and the political (as noninstitutionalized or unrepresented claims to collectives ordered through governance). Further, we mapped what determines the shape of polycentric governance (constitutional rules, social-problem characteristics, and heterogeneity of actors) before we elaborated on exit, voice, and self-organization and interrelated power resources as mechanisms that endogenously shape polycentric governance.

We connected our discussion of the political with that of polycentric governance by examining how the political as a trigger of institutional change is conceptualized in polycentric governance. We argued that the political may trigger institutional change in polycentric governance if corresponding values and associated actors managed to mobilize collective action in a way that their claims were met in polycentric governance. Three issues surfaced in this discussion:

1. It became clear that in our analysis the political could only be addressed in polycentric governance through its institutionalized treatment. In turn, the political would be institutionalized and incorporated into politics, satisfying individuals' needs for social order, at least to some extent, while creating new aspects excluded from politics in a dialectical manner. The struggle over what constitutes the (contested) core of collectives, therefore, ever continues.

2. In negotiations across the dividing lines between politics and the political, higher-level formal or informal norms may play a role in selecting issues that legitimately trigger institutional change. Although discursive treatment of claims as absolutely equal may be desirable for reasons of equality of humans, if order were desired, some way of selection would still need to be institutionalized, re-creating deficiencies in representing the political. As a matter of fact, corresponding struggles about what is allowable and supported in arguments over values of collectives in polycentric governance reproduce tensions between the political and politics.

3. In writings about polycentric governance, little to no attention is paid to the question of what is legitimate political interference and what is illegitimate, and of who gets access to arenas where values are shaped and who doesn't, while, in fact, the importance of boundaries is emphasized.

Similarly, redistribution of relative endowments in order to have approximate equality among capacities of actors and issues for self-organization are not addressed. One might even fear that as long as they are not addressed, corresponding structural inequalities may further deepen as time goes by. Thus, certainly from the perspective of equal representation of political, marginalized interests and claims, we would expect that redistributive measures would need discussion and research in relation to their compatibility with polycentric governance. We interpret the silence of the Bloomington School in this regard as testimony to the difficulties of connecting normative thinking on polycentric governance to approximated equal endowments and opportunities for self-organization of claims marginalized by societies. Admittedly, one could argue that the inclusion of political and marginalized issues into politics of institutionalized redistribution is a contradiction in terms, highlighted by the necessary mutual exclusiveness of the political and politics. From a pragmatic, value- and policy-oriented perspective, however, we would advocate an engagement of scholars working on polycentric governance with the kinds of redistributive measures and problems highlighted in this chapter.

NOTES

1. Polycentric governance has been described as follows:

> Polycentric connotes many centers of decision-making which are formally indepen-
> dent of each other. Whether they actually function independently, or instead con-
> stitute an interdependent system of relations, is an empirical question in particular
> cases. To the extent they take each other into account in competitive relationships,
> enter into various contractual and cooperative undertakings or have recourse to
> central mechanisms to resolve conflicts, . . . the various political jurisdictions . . .
> may function in a coherent manner with consistent and predictable patterns of
> interacting behaviour. To the extent that this is so, they may be said to function as a
> "system." (Ostrom, Tiebout, and Warren 1961, 831)

2. Note that we do not illustrate the IAD in this chapter. We only use its elements to provide theoretical and analytical guidance to help us explain how institutional change would work. We refer readers to fundamental articles on IAD (e.g., McGinnis 2011a).

REFERENCES

Advisory Commission on Intergovernmental Relations (ACIR). 1987. "The Organization of Local Public Economies." ACIR report A-109, Washington, DC.

Ahn, T. K., Elinor Ostrom, and Brian Walker. 2003. "Heterogeneous Preferences and Collective Action: Incorporating Motivational Heterogeneity into Game-Theoretic Models of Collec-tive Action." *Public Choice* 117 (3-4): 295–314.

Aligica, Paul Dragos. 2014. *Institutional Diversity and Political Economy: The Ostroms and Beyond.* New York: Oxford University Press.

Aligica, Paul Dragos, and Peter J. Boettke. 2009. *Challenging Institutional Analysis and Devel-opment: The Bloomington School.* New York: Routledge.

Aligica, Paul Dragos, and Vlad Tarko. 2012. "Polycentricity: From Polanyi to Ostrom, and Beyond." *Governance: An International Journal of Policy Administration and Institutions* 25 (2): 237–62.

———. 2013. "Co-Production, Polycentricity, and Value Heterogeneity: The Ostroms' Public Choice Institutionalism Revisited." *American Political Science Review* 107 (4): 726–41.

Armitage, Derek. 2008. "Governance and the Commons in a Multi-Level World." *International Journal of the Commons* 2 (1): 7–32.

Arthur, Brian W. 1994. *Increasing Returns and Path Dependence in the Economy*. Ann Arbor: University of Michigan Press.

Bauman, Zygmunt. 1995. "Communitarianism, Freedom, and the Nation-State." *Critical Review* 9 (4): 539–53.

Bednar, Jenna. 2009. *The Robust Federation: Principles of Design*. Cambridge, UK: Cambridge University Press.

Bowles, Samuel. 2004. *Microeconomics: Behavior, Institutions, and Evolution.* Princeton, NJ: Princeton University Press. Copublished with Russell Sage Foundation, New York.

Brennan, Geoffrey, and James M. Buchanan. 1993. *Die Begründung von Regeln. Konstitutionelle politische Ökonomie.* Tübingen, Germany: Mohr.

Cleaver, Frances. 2002. "Reinventing Institutions: Bricolage and the Social Embeddedness of Natural Resource Management." *European Journal of Development Research* 14 (2): 11–30.

———. 2007. "Understanding Agency in Collective Action." *Journal of Human Development* 8 (2): 223–44.

Cleaver, Frances, and Jessica de Koning. 2015. "Furthering Critical Institutionalism." *International Journal of the Commons* 9 (1): 1–18.

Clement, Floriane. 2013. "For Critical Social-Ecological System Studies: Integrating Power and Discourses to Move beyond the Right Institutional Fit." *Environmental Conservation* 40 (1): 1–4.

Coughlin, Richard. 2003. "Does Socioeconomic Inequality Undermine Community? Implications for Communitarian Theory." *Responsive Community* 13 (2): 12–24.

Cox, Michael, Gwen Arnold, and Sergio Villamayor-Tomás. 2010. "A Review of Design Principles for Community-Based Natural Resource Management." *Ecology and Society* 15 (4): 8.

Dikeç, Mustafa. 2001. "Justice and the Spatial Imagination." *Environment and Planning* 33 (10): 1785–1805.

Dobson, Andrew. 2006. "Thick Cosmopolitanism." *Political Studies* 54 (1): 165–84.

Etzioni, Amitai. 2003. "Communitarianism." In *Encyclopedia of Community: From the Village to the Virtual World, Vol. 1.*, edited by Karen Christensen and David Levinson, 224–228. Thousand Oaks, CA: Sage Publications.

Etzioni, Amitai, Andrew Volmert, and Elanit Rothschild, eds. 2004. *The Communitarian Reader: Beyond the Essentials.* Lanham, MD: Rowman & Littlefield.

Flügel-Martinsen, Oliver, ed. 2004. *Die Rückkehr des Politischen: Demokratietheorien Heute.* Darmstadt, Germany: Wiss. Buchges.

Flügel-Martinsen, Oliver, Reinhard Heil, and Andreas Hetzel. 2004."Die Rückkehr des Politischen." In *Die Rückkehr des Politischen: Demokratietheorien Heute*, edited by Oliver
Flügel-Martinsen, 7–16. Darmstadt, Germany: Wiss. Buchges.

Gruby, Rebecca L., and Xavier Basurto. 2014. "Multi-level Governance for Large Marine
Commons: Politics and Polycentricity in Palau's Protected Area Network." *Environmental
Science & Policy* 33 (November): 260–72.

Hewlett, Nick. 2007. *Badiou, Balibar, Rancière: Re-thinking Emancipation*. London: Continuum
International Publishing Group.

Hodgson, Geoffrey M. 2004. *The Evolution of Institutional Economics: Agency, Structure, and
Darwinism in American Institutionalism*. London: Routledge.

Knight, Jack. 1992. *Institutions and Social Conflict*. Cambridge, UK: Cambridge University Press.

Kymlicka. Will. 1993. "Some Questions about Justice and Community." In *Communitarianism
and Its Critics,* edited by Daniel Bell, 208–21. Oxford: Clarendon Press.

Lefort, Claude. 1988. *Democracy and Political Theory.* Cambridge, UK: Polity Press.

Lin, J. Y. 1989. "An Economic Theory of Institutional Change: Induced and Imposed Change."
Cato Journal 9 (1): 1–33.

Marchart, Oliver. 2007. *Post-Foundational Political Thought: Political Difference in Nancy,
Lefort, Badiou, and Laclau.* Edinburgh: Edinburgh University Press.

McGinnis, Michael D. 2005. "Costs and Challenges of Polycentric Governance." Paper for
the Workshop on Analyzing Problems of Polycentric Governance in the Growing EU,
Humboldt-Universität zu Berlin, June 16, 2005.

———. 2011a. "An Introduction to IAD and the Language of the Ostrom Workshop: A Simple
Guide to a Complex Framework." *Policy Studies Journal* 39 (1): 169–83.

———. 2011b. "Networks of Adjacent Action Situations in Polycentric Governance." *Policy
Studies Journal* 39 (1): 45–72.

———. 2016. "Polycentric Governance in Theory and Practice: Dimensions of Aspiration and
Practical Limitations." Conference paper presented at the Ostrom Polycentricity Workshop, Bloomington, IN, December 14–17, 2006.

McGinnis, Michael D., and Elinor Ostrom. 2012. "Reflections on Vincent Ostrom, Public Administration, and Polycentricity." *Public Administration Review* 72 (1): 15–25.

Mouffe, Chantal. 2000. *The Democratic Paradox.* London: Verso Books.

Nancy, Jean-Luc, and Tracy B. Strong. 1992. "La Comparution/The Compearance: From the Existence of 'Communism' to the Community of 'Existence.'" *Political Theory* 20 (3): 371–98.

Niederberger, Andreas. 2004. "Aufteilung(en) unter Gleichen: Zur Theorie der demokrati-
schen Konstitution der Welt bei Jacques Rancière." In *Die Rückkehr des Politischen:*

Demokratietheorien Heute, edited by Oliver Flügel-Martinsen, 126–46. Darmstadt, Germany: Wiss. Buchges.

North, Douglass C. 1994. "Institutional Change: A Framework of Analysis." *Economic History* 9412001, University Library of Munich, Germany, revised December 14, 1994.

———. 2005. *Understanding the Process of Economic Change.* Princeton, NJ: Princeton University Press.

Olson, Mancur, Jr. 1994. *The Logic of Collective Action: Public Goods and the Theory of Groups.* Cambridge, MA: Harvard University Press.

Ostrom, Elinor. 1990. *Governing the Commons: The Evolution of Institutions for Collective Action.* Cambridge, UK: Cambridge University Press.

———. 2005. *Understanding Institutional Diversity.* Princeton, NJ: Princeton University Press.

———. 2007. "Collective Action Theory." In *The Oxford Handbook of Comparative Politics,* edited by Carles Boix and Susan C. Stokes, 185–208. Oxford, UK: Oxford University Press.

———. 2014a. "A Frequently Overlooked Precondition of Democracy: Citizens Knowledgeable about and Engaged in Collective Action." In *Elinor Ostrom and the Bloomington School of Political Economy, Vol. 1: Polycentricity in Public Administration and Political Science,* edited by Daniel H. Cole and Michael D. McGinnis, 337–52. Lanham, MD: Lexington Books.

———. 2014b. "Developing a Method for Analyzing Institutional Change." In *Elinor Ostrom and the Bloomington School of Political Economy, Vol. 1: Polycentricity in Public Administration and Political Science,* edited by Daniel H. Cole and Michael D. McGinnis, 281–316. Lanham, MD: Lexington Books.

Ostrom, Elinor, and Xavier Basurto. 2011. "Crafting Analytical Tools to Study Institutional Change." *Journal of Institutional Economics* 7 (3): 317–43.

Ostrom, Elinor, Roy Gardner, and James Walker. 1994. *Rules, Games, and Common-Pool Resources.* Ann Arbor: University of Michigan Press.

Ostrom, Vincent. 1990. "An Inquiry Concerning Liberty and Equality in the American Constitutional System." *Publius: The Journal of Federalism* 20 (2): 3–51.

———. 1999a. "Artisanship and Artifact." In *Polycentric Governance and Development: Readings from the Workshop in Political Theory and Policy Analysis,* edited by Michael D. McGinnis. Ann Arbor: University of Michigan Press.

———. 1999b. "Polycentricity (Part 1)." In *Polycentricity and Local Public Economies: Readings from the Workshop in Political Theory and Policy Analysis,* edited by Michael D. McGinnis, 52–74. Ann Arbor: University of Michigan Press.

———. 1999c. "Polycentricity (Part 2)." In *Polycentricity and Local Public Economies: Readings from the Workshop in Political Theory and Policy Analysis,* edited by Michael D. McGinnis, 119–38. Ann Arbor: University of Michigan Press.

————. 2008. "The Normative and Limiting Factors in a Polycentric Political Order." In *The Struggle to Constitute and Sustain Productive Orders: Vincent Ostrom's Quest to Understand Human Affairs,* edited by Vincent Ostrom, Mark Sproule-Jones, Barbara Allen, and Filippo Sabetti, 29–44. Lanham, MD: Lexington Books.

————. 2015. "Executive Leadership, Authority Relationships, and Public Entrepreneurship." In *Elinor Ostrom and the Bloomington School of Political Economy,* edited by Daniel H. Cole and Michael D. McGinnis, 217–32. Lanham, MD: Lexington Books.

Ostrom, Vincent, Charles M. Tiebout, and Robert Warren. 1961. "The Organization of Government in Metropolitan Areas: A Theoretical Inquiry." *American Political Science Review* 55 (4): 831–42.

Pierson, Paul. 2000. "The Limits of Design: Explaining Institutional Origins and Design." *Governance: An International Journal of Policy and Management* 13 (4): 475–99.

Rancière, Jacques. 1998. *Disagreement.* Minneapolis: University of Minnesota Press.

Ritzi, Claudia. 2016. "Die politische Theorie der Postdemokratie: Jacques Rancière." In *Politische Theorien der Gegenwart III: Eine Einführung,* edited by André Brodocz and Gary S. Schaal, 338–66. Opladen, Berlin: Verlag Barbara Budrich.

Robbins, Paul. 2012. *Political Ecology: A Critical Introduction.* 2nd ed. Malden, MA: J. Wiley-Blackwell.

Schlüter, Achim. 2001. *Institutioneller Wandel und Transformation: Restitution, Transformation und Privatisierung in der Tschechischen Landwirtschaft.* Aachen, Germany: Shaker Verlag GmbH.

Schmid, Alfred Allan. 2004. *Conflict and Cooperation: Institutional and Behavioral Economics.* Malden, MA: J. Wiley-Blackwell.

Stavrakakis, Yannis. 2000. "On the Emergence of Green Ideology: The Dislocation Factor in Green Politics." *Discourse Theory and Political Analysis: Identities, Hegemonies, and Social Change,* edited by David Howarth, Aletta J. Norval, and Yannis Stavrakakis, 100–18. Manchester, UK: Manchester University Press.

Swyngedouw, Erik. 2011. "Interrogating Post-Democratization: Reclaiming Egalitarian Political Spaces." *Political Geography* 30 (7): 370–380.

————. 2018. *Promises of the Political.* Cambridge, MA: MIT Press.

Theesfeld, Insa. 2005. *A Common Pool Resource in Transition: Determinants of Institutional Change for Bulgaria's Postsocialist Irrigation Sector.* Aachen, Germany: Shaker Verlag GmbH.

Thiel, Andreas. 2014. "Rescaling of Resource Governance as Institutional Change: Explaining the Transformation of Water Governance in Southern Spain." *Environmental Policy and Governance* 24 (4): 289–306.

————. 2017. "The Scope of Polycentric Governance Analysis and Resulting Challenges." *Journal of Self-Governance and Management Economics* 5 (3): 52–82.

Wall, Derek. 2014. *The Sustainable Economics of Elinor Ostrom: Commons, Contestation and Craft*. London: Routledge, Taylor & Francis Group.

Williamson, O. E. 1991. "Comparative Economic Organization: The Analysis of Discrete Structural Alternatives." *Administrative Science Quarterly* 36 (2): 269–96.

CHAPTER SEVEN

IN PRAISE OF ECLECTICISM

WHY ELINOR AND VINCENT OSTROM'S WORKS MATTER

AURELIAN CRAIUTU

should like to begin with a few personal remarks about how I became acquainted with the work of Elinor ("Lin" as she preferred to be called) and Vincent Ostrom. In what follows, I shall refer to both of them because their works cannot—and should not—be separated from each other. They were complementary in many ways and, as Lin herself remarked when she got the call from Stockholm in October 2009 ("*We* won!" were her first words to Vincent upon hearing the news that she was awarded the Nobel Prize), the prize was, in fact, a recognition of their joint effort to rethink the foundations of collective action and order in modern society.[1]

For a long time, I had not been able to put their writings on the mental map that I learned in graduate school. At Princeton, where I earned a PhD in politics (political theory) in the 1990s, the Ostroms' work was never discussed in graduate courses. We were asked to study a wide array of authors from John Rawls, Jürgen Habermas, Hannah Arendt, and Samuel Huntington to Theda Skocpol, Juan Linz, Robert Dahl, and Robert Putnam, but not the Ostroms. Therefore, I did not read them at that time. A decade later, from 2001 to June 2012, when both Lin and Vincent Ostrom passed away, I had the privilege of being their junior colleague in the Department of Political Science at Indiana

University, Bloomington. I still remember quite well the job talk I gave in early December 2000, which was attended by both Lin and Vincent. It was a great honor to see them there, but I must confess that it was also a cause of mild concern for me, because I had heard a lot about them and did not expect easy questions from them. In fact, my concern was valid, because Vincent, after listening patiently to my account of Tocqueville's intellectual debts, went on to ask a convoluted and tough question on the concept of civilization in the work of Ibn Khaldūn, a prominent 14th-century Muslim historian and thinker from North Africa. Even though my talk touched on the concept of civilization in the writings of Guizot, the question had apparently no direct link to the main topic of my lecture, which focused on the influence of the so-called French Doctrinaires (Guizot, Royer-Collard, etc.) on Tocqueville. Fortunately, I had a copy of Ibn Khaldūn's masterpiece *Muqaddimah* in my library, but I had not read it. I knew, however, that he had an original theory of civilization and history and had argued that too much bureaucracy, high taxes, and unwise legislation tend to lead to the decline of a society as a whole. I cannot remember what I responded exactly, but the exotic nature of the question remained imprinted in my memory for some time.

After arriving in Bloomington in the summer of 2001, I became affiliated with the Workshop in Political Theory and Public Policy and thus I got to know the Ostroms a little bit better over time. They received me warmly into their circle and followed with interest my work on Tocqueville and French modern political thought. I shared with them their strong appreciation for Tocqueville's new science of politics, which we regarded as a better guide than Marx for understanding the post-1989 world. Nevertheless, for various reasons, I was not a regular participant in the Workshop's weekly seminars, nor was I a close associate of the Ostroms, whose work I only knew imperfectly at that time.

RESPONDING TO TOCQUEVILLE'S CHALLENGE

The fact that both Lin and Vincent had a deep appreciation for Tocqueville did not come as a surprise to me given their strong interest in the science of association and self-government, both major themes in *Democracy in America*. The main questions they pursued in their works were, How can human beings who are fallible and possess limited information practice self-governance and maintain self-governing ways of life over a long period? How do real people go about trying to solve concrete problems regarding common goods? What rules and norms do they follow? Moreover, why do some associations succeed while others fail?

To answer these important questions, the Ostroms examined all kinds of associations—some similar to the ones discussed by Tocqueville, others different from what he saw in America—from suburban municipalities to neighborhood associations and farming associations. In his writings, Vincent often pointed to an observation made by Tocqueville, who noted with surprise that, in America, society governs itself for itself, without much interference from outside. The possibility that a society would exist that would not be governed top-down but would organize itself in such a way that it would govern itself bottom-up was, in the Ostroms' view, the central discovery of Tocqueville in America. It is no surprise then that Tocqueville has always been a sort of patron saint at the Ostroms' Workshop, where his portrait hangs in the room that carries his name. Tocqueville's thoroughgoing critique of despotism and robust defense of civil society provided the Ostroms with a solid background against which they developed their own views on key topics such as self-government, federalism, citizenship, and the science of association.

Nonetheless, the Ostroms' appreciation for Tocqueville went a step further: they also tried to heed the Frenchman's call to create a new political science for a new world. The key concept of Tocqueville's new science of politics was what he called *l'état social* (social condition), seen as a product and cause of political institutions, laws, customs, and ideas. In the footsteps of the French Doctrinaires, Tocqueville highlighted the strong interdependence between social and political order and stressed the centrality of mores to the functioning of a healthy and stable democracy. In a famous letter to Claude-François de Corcelle on September 17, 1853, Tocqueville emphasized again the priority of mores over laws. "Political societies," he wrote, "are not what their laws make them, but what sentiments, beliefs, ideas, habits of the heart, and the spirit of the men who form them, prepare them in advance to be, as well as what nature and education have made them" (Tocqueville 1985, 294). That insight was at the core of his new science of politics, whose ambition was to shape the general ideas and actions in society.[2]

In a memorable speech given a year earlier at the Academy of Moral and Political Sciences in Paris,[3] Tocqueville distinguished between the *art* of government and the *science* of government. The art of government, he argued, closely follows the ever-changing flux of political phenomena and varies according to the diversity of events; in so doing, it seeks to meet the ephemeral needs of changing political circumstances. The true science of government differs from the art of government in several important ways. Situated at the inter-section between several disciplines (philosophy, sociology, and law), it seeks to discover the rights that belong to individuals, the laws appropriate to differ-ent societies, and the virtues and limitations of various forms of government. Anyone who examines the roots of political order, Tocqueville believed, must avoid building an imaginary society in which everything is simple, orderly, uniform, and in accord with reason. Instead, the analyst must remain close to social and political reality and investigate the roots of order and how people associate in order to pursue common goals. As a critic of the French system marked by administrative centralization, Tocqueville admired federalism and decentralization in America and hoped that one day his compatriots would be able to change the centralized pattern of governance that dominated French politics. He understood that a new science of politics was needed for a novel democratic world characterized by an increasing equality of conditions and a new social state. Tocqueville described himself as an impartial spectator situ-ated between two worlds, casting calm glances on both sides and seeking to see further than his contemporaries, animated by partisan concerns.

Inspired by Tocqueville's cross-disciplinary and allegedly nonpartisan outlook, the Ostroms emulated his methodological and political eclecticism. Like Tocqueville, they paid special attention to what happens in the bosom of society, aware that political institutions reflect mores, norms, values, and customs that shape institutions. Their approach aimed at shedding fresh light on how people organize themselves to pursue common goals and create social and political order apart from—or in conjunction with—top-down structures (the state, regulatory agencies, etc.). The Ostroms believed that this agenda could not be pursued within a traditional department of political science but rather in a new cross-disciplinary framework. In particular, they believed that political scientists must be chastised for the "superficial way" they think of citizenship in democratic societies. The Ostroms challenged conventional political scientists to think about the ordinary exigencies of life in these soci-eties in a "much more fundamental way" (Ostrom 1997, 3) than the principle "one person, one vote, majority rule." Vincent, for example, was concerned and worried about what happens when machine politics and boss-rule prevail and stifle the authority of citizens. His writings call into question the minimal procedural definition of democracy and the state-centered perspective still fashionable among contemporary students of comparative politics. According to this view based on the works of, among others, Samuel Huntington and Robert Dahl, the presence of elections and the existence of a multiparty system are the litmus test of democracy; hence the key to assessing the viability of a regime lies in evaluating the capacity of the state to enforce rules of peaceful cohabitation and cooperation among its citizens.[4]

Consequently, the Ostroms sought to carve out a path beyond the procedural definition of democracy or the classical dichotomy of "the state" versus "the market" that had dominated much of conventional social sciences and public policy studies for a long time. Their dissatisfaction with that thinking came to the fore in all their writings, culminating in Vincent's last published book on the meaning and fragility of democracy, a major rethinking of "what it means to govern and function as citizens in democratic societies" (Ostrom 1997, 5). The subtitle of the book is *A Response to Tocqueville's Challenge*, defined as the question of whether democratic societies based on reflection and choice can be viable in the long term. The way in which Ostrom approached this issue was idiosyncratic and unconventional. He did not seem particularly interested in the fact that Tocqueville wrote *Democracy in America* for a French audience, nor did he seem surprised by the fact that Tocqueville worked with more than 10 definitions of democracy to describe what he called "the great democratic revolution" unfolding under his own eyes. Instead, Vincent insisted on the distinction between "stateless" and "state-governed" democracies.

It was only in 2009, when I coedited *Conversations with Tocqueville* with Sheldon Gellar, a longtime collaborator of the Ostroms and former associate of their Workshop, that I came to realize better the ways in which my own research interests overlapped with those of the Ostroms and their collaborators. They were interested in studying the pervasive effects of centralization and the tradition of paternalism, along with various challenges to democratic consolidation across the world that were posed by the legacy of statism and a weak civil society. I shared a similar set of interests and concerns, because I came from a part of the world (Eastern Europe) that had struggled with a long tradition of centralization, low levels of civic interest, and a strong dependence on the state. The idea of using Tocqueville as a guide for understanding how to build a free and open society on the ruins of communism had always been on my intellectual radar screen. In two essays published in Romanian in the weekly *22* (*Twenty-Two*) (Craiutu 1993a and 1993b), I drew upon Tocqueville's ideas on the apprenticeship of liberty to show how we might go about fostering self-governing skills and civic capacities with a view to creating a robust civil society. Two decades later, I revised and developed these ideas in a longer study (Craiutu 2014), which concluded with a few lessons inspired by the philosophy of the Bloomington School. The apprenticeship of liberty, I argued, requires not only separation of powers and administrative decentralization but also learning and practicing what Tocqueville called the art of being free. The rule of law cannot properly exist in a society whose citizens do not have the habit of forming local associations and do not regularly cooperate with each other to pursue common goals. If democracy at the local level is weak, and if society is organized around a monocentric pattern of governance, democratic institutions will not perform well, and trust in them will decline over time, leading to disenchantment and detachment.

The chapters in *Conversations with Tocqueville* discussed those topics at length. Prefaced by Lin, our book opened with an important essay by Vincent on citizen-sovereigns, originally given as an official speech to commemorate the presentation of the John Gaus Award by the American Political Science Association (Ostrom 2009). We regarded Vincent's text as an example of the insight that an appreciation of Tocquevillian analytics and of the wisdom of the Founding Fathers might bring into a discussion of democracy around the world. Most of the essays included in *Conversations with Tocqueville* were contributed by scholars then associated with the Ostrom Workshop and the Bloomington School. They reflected its interdisciplinary and innovative research, along with its astonishing breadth of inquiry. We included chapters on democracy in Guatemala, Mexico, Burma, China, Japan, Russia, and the United States, in addition to Africa and Western Europe. Our eclectic book showed that Tocqueville's new science of politics can still offer a valuable conceptual framework and set of tools for studying the processes of democratization, not only in North America and Western Europe but also in Africa, Asia, and Latin America.

THE ECLECTICISM OF THE OSTROMS' AGENDA

In the fall of 2009, soon after *Conversations with Tocqueville* was published, I founded, with the help of a seed grant from the Philadelphia-based Jack Miller

Center, a small Tocqueville Program at Indiana University, which ended up being located in the Ostrom Workshop. From the outset, we saw it as a natural extension of Vincent's work on Tocqueville and Lin's work on self-governance. The goal of the program (which continues to this day due to the generous funding provided by the Veritas Fund, the Apgar Foundation, Liberty Fund, and Indiana University) has been to foster an understanding of the central importance of principles of freedom and equality for democratic government and moral responsibility, two themes close to the Ostroms' agenda. It has focused on the theoretical foundations of democracy and the development of liberal democratic institutions, particularly in the American historical context. Our guests have been invited to Bloomington to reflect critically on main Tocquevillian themes such as freedom, equality, civil society, religion, citizenship, mores, individualism, democracy, centralization, self-government, despotism, and civil associations.

Locating our Tocqueville Program in the Ostrom Workshop was an easy and obvious choice at that time; our hope is that it will continue to remain there in the future to represent and honor an important part of the Ostroms' rich intellectual legacy. We wanted to be open, eclectic, diverse, and committed to exploring various facets of democracy from a plurality of perspectives—methodological, political, and intellectual. In choosing to pursue an eclectic agenda, we have followed, in fact, a key principle of the Bloomington School as conceived by the Ostroms. At the same time, we have exposed ourselves to a set of critiques similar to what they received over time. They were taken to task for ignoring class, power, conflict, and race, or for working with a simplified understanding of politics; at times, they were criticized for endorsing a particular ideological agenda with libertarian, anti-statist leanings. These critiques were a consequence of their intellectual eclecticism that fits no particular school of thought and no single ideological camp.

The eclecticism of the Ostroms' approach should be properly emphasized and carefully examined. At some point, I was tempted to call it moderation, given the fact that the Ostroms' worldview was pluralistic and diverse, averse to any grand-design blueprint and universal solutions. Moreover, their methodology was never doctrinaire but was based on case studies, surveys, and experiments that emphasized the irreducible heterogeneity of the social and political world. Nonetheless, I was not sure that moderation would be the right term in this case. In his book discussing the intellectual legacy of the Ostroms, Paul D. Aligica devoted an entire chapter to their pragmatism, pointing out some similarities between their approach and the pragmatic philosophy of John Dewey (Aligica 2014a). In the end, I chose to speak about eclecticism because I believe that this term not only applies to the Ostroms' work but also points to some interesting tensions in their writings that must be taken into account.

What kind of eclecticism can be found in the writings of the Ostroms and the Bloomington School in general? At least three important types come to mind: *institutional, methodological* (manifested in the methods, sources, and conceptual apparatus used), and *political.* Taken together, they help explain why there is more than one way to situate the work of the Ostroms and their collaborators in a larger academic and political context. Let us address briefly each of them.

First, I should like to highlight the *institutional* eclecticism as illustrated by the creation of the Workshop in Political Theory and Policy Analysis at Indiana University in the early 1970s. In an interview Lin Ostrom gave to Fran Korten, she openly acknowledged the challenges encountered in trying to find a place for her work that would be suitable, acceptable, and recognizable to others. "I was doing a bunch of research through the years that many people thought was very radical and people didn't like," she said. "As a person who does interdisciplinary work, I didn't fit anywhere."[5] The emphasis on the lack of fit is worth noting because it sheds light on the difficulties the Ostroms had in finding a proper cross-disciplinary home for their research. In another text, Lin remarked that the "disciplinary huts" of many modern universities have always had a hard time enabling scholars to have an effective intellectual exchange across disciplines.[6]

It is no surprise then that the traditional framework offered by a classical department of political science proved insufficiently flexible to advance the Ostroms' research. Their strong commitment to interdisciplinary work made them determined to set up in 1973–74 their own Workshop in Political Theory and Policy Analysis as a research center *sui generis*, independent of the Department of Political Science at Indiana. It was supposed to be a single independent unit located between—and cooperating with—several other academic units on the Bloomington campus, such as the College of Arts and Sciences (where the Department of Political Science was located), the School of Public and Environmental Affairs, and the School of Business. The Workshop, as it came to be known, was committed from the outset to pursuing an original and eclectic agenda using an interdisciplinary team of scholars from various departments. It remained over the years (until the death of the Ostroms in

2012) an eclectic place where scholars from various disciplines came together to study a variety of topics using diverse methodologies under the broad label the "Bloomington School."[7] Lin herself held joint appointments in political science and public policy until the end of her long academic career and led not only the Workshop but also the Center for the Study of Institutions, Population, and Environmental Change (CIPEC).

By emphasizing the need to create a cross-disciplinary science of politics working with a broad view of governance, the Ostroms responded to the risk of becoming irrelevant in a world that is becoming ever more complex and multileveled and that requires new approaches. They rejected factionalism and promoted collaborative work—it is not an accident that *Working Together* was the title of the last published book Elinor coauthored with two junior colleagues in 2010—going to great lengths to welcome collaborators from various departments and countries. The very name chosen for the institution the Ostroms founded in Bloomington is revealing in this regard. They wanted to create a *workshop*, not a center. A workshop is a place in which individual scholars can freely interact with each other, on an equal footing, and work together, as artisans in a workshop, toward solving common problems. There was no pressure to conform to a standard method or toward a single goal; there was only a commitment to free and open inquiry that all participants were expected to honor. It was the cross-disciplinary and collaborative focus of the Workshop that made its research relevant and applicable to a wide array of topics from police departments, the internet, and healthcare reform to reforming international organizations and addressing environmental challenges such as sustainability and climate change.[8]

Second, there is the Ostroms' *methodological* eclecticism as reflected in their sources, concepts, and interpretations. The research carried out within the Workshop brought a seminal contribution to the study of the diversity of institutional forms in economic and political life and their implications for governance. To this effect, the Ostroms and their collaborators in the Bloomington School focused on applied problems and practices, eschewing grand generalizations, universal blueprints, and big concepts such as "the state." They preferred instead to examine contextual situations and the degree to which institutions are matched to the local conditions and norms found in various communities. The Ostroms and collaborators set out to analyze what the term *institution* means and what factors affect the evolution of institutions over time; they were also interested in exploring what is meant when people say that institutions facilitate or discourage effective problem-solving and innovations. The Ostroms aspired to combine scientific rigor and policy relevance and were open to using a variety of methods and nested levels of analysis in their efforts to understand how institutions work in different settings. They were critics of homogenization and simplification and insisted that scholars take heterogeneity seriously to begin understanding the complexity of the social and political world. In their view, this approach required challenging deep-seated academic conventions and called for straddling various disciplines and subfields.

From the outset, the Ostroms' research agenda challenged the common wisdom among their fellow political scientists and public policy scholars. Vincent's critique of public administration as traditionally taught in American universities is a good case in point. Most of the courses in public policy, he noted in *The Intellectual Crisis in American Public Administration* (1973), assumed the existence of a monocentric system of power, while the reality on the ground seems to point to the existence of a polycentric system of governance that should be studied from an interdisciplinary perspective. The Ostroms' agenda can be situated at the intersection of several fields of inquiry, such as political science, political theory, law, economics, public policy, public administration, political economy, anthropology, religious studies, and the sociology of knowledge.[9] It combines economic theory, game theory, public choice theory, transaction cost theory, covenantal theory, and theories of public goods and common-pool resources. The Ostroms and their collaborators developed two models of analysis, known as the Institutional Analysis and Development (IAD) and the Social-Ecological System (SES) frameworks, that required cross-disciplinary work and collaboration, combining formal models and laboratory experiments with extensive fieldwork research.[10] The wide diversity of these fields and perspectives speaks for itself and presents a challenge to all those who are more narrowly trained and inclined to follow conventional lines of research.

The interdisciplinary and eclectic nature of the Ostroms' research agenda was also reflected in the remarkable geographic breadth of the work they carried out and sponsored. Their collaborators studied specific issues regarding collective action and choice in a diversity of settings, some Western, others non-Western. The fact that a good part of these collaborators came from countries situated in Asia (Nepal, India, Burma), Africa (Liberia, Kenya), and Latin America (Mexico, Brazil, and Columbia) was not a mere coincidence. On the contrary, it should be seen as proof of Lin and Vincent's principled commitment to the study of forms of governance in what normal political science would consider "unconventional" settings. Staunch methodological individualists, the Ostroms came to accept ideas that the communities in non-Western parts of the world had a particular holistic spirit, such as solidarity of the village associations, age sets, women's groups, and consensus decision-making, that profoundly influenced daily operations and choices.

Not surprisingly, the sources Lin and Vincent used in their works were equally eclectic. It was not uncommon for them to quote in the same paper from thinkers as diverse as Thomas Hobbes, Alexis de Tocqueville, John R. Commons, James Buchanan, and Friedrich A. Hayek while also drawing upon the writings of Amartya Sen, Daniel Kahneman, Amos Tversky, and Frank Knight. In the case of Vincent Ostrom, for example, one may be surprised to learn that the three seminal texts for him were Hobbes's *Leviathan*, *The Federalist Papers*, and Tocqueville's *Democracy in America*. Tocqueville may have admired James Madison and Alexander Hamilton, but there is a huge difference between Hobbes, Madison, Hamilton, and Tocqueville in their methods, conclusions, and style of writing. It is fair to say that Vincent's interpretation of Tocqueville was *sui generis*; he did not approach Tocqueville as a sociologist or a political philosopher.[11] His exegesis of *Democracy in America* put a premium on self-governance but had little interest in other aspects of Tocqueville's work and life. One wonders then whether Vincent had fully explored the implications of a central idea of Tocqueville—namely, that democracy is primarily a way of social organization that affects all spheres of life in society, from family to economy and religion, albeit in different ways. Moreover, his claim that the awareness of the mysteries of being is "a necessity in the constitution of order in democratic society" (Ostrom 1997, 179) appears as surprisingly obscure. Why not speak of religion in a straightforward manner, as Tocqueville himself did?

Equally surprising, of the three authors of the Federalist Papers, Vincent seems to have been most attracted to Alexander Hamilton, who advocated a strong executive power different from Vincent's preference for local knowledge and self-government. It is paradoxical that he showed little interest in the Anti-Federalist authors with whom he seemingly had many things in common. The Anti-Federalists defended many ideas and commitments that also loom large on the Ostroms' agenda, beginning with the ideal of self-governing communities and ending with the belief that, all things considered, smaller scale can often work better than larger scale. Brutus, Centinel, and the other Anti-Federalists of early US history also believed that creating a federal government and securing political competition for power may not be the best way of expressing the interests of the people in their collective capacity. As such, some of the theses advanced by the Anti-Federalists, strong defenders of federalism, seem to be more in line with the Ostroms' defense of self-governing capabilities and their skepticism toward boss-rule and party politics than the essays in the Federalist Papers. At times, Publius's essays, which justified the need for a strong federal government with wide powers, seem to contradict some of the ideas of the Ostroms.[12]

Finally, anyone who views Dewey as a supporter of active government might be surprised to learn that his form of pragmatism exercised a certain appeal on Vincent Ostrom. He viewed Dewey's theory of democracy as compatible with Tocqueville's science of association and, toward the end of his career, he paid special attention to what Dewey had to say about the education of democratic citizens.[13] The reason for this surprising affinity might have to do with the fact that, as Paul Aligica points out, "Ostrom recognizes in Dewey's take on democracy a vision that goes beyond the mere procedural and formal" (Aligica 2014a, 172) and emphasizes more than simple voting and petitioning. Much like Dewey, Ostrom looked at democracy as a new way of life and form of social organization with implications for all spheres of life. One of the ideas central to Vincent's work was that citizens must be engaged in a continuous process of giving reasons and assessing the reasons and arguments made by others in their effort to achieve common objectives. And yet, all things considered, one can reasonably claim that there are important differences between Dewey's ideas and the framework of the Bloomington School. Dewey was arguably closer to Max Weber's bureaucratic mentality and shared Woodrow Wilson's belief in the power of big and active government, while the Ostroms had no patience for Weber and considered President Wilson as their main intellectual opponent.

Last but not least, I should like to address the Ostroms' *political* eclecticism. Starting from concrete governance dilemmas, which they carefully examined in various social settings, Lin, Vincent, and their collaborators acknowledged the existence of a wide variety of institutional arrangements that go *beyond* the classical concepts of states and/or markets. Some of these arrangements may be more successful than others, but they all testify to humans' capacity for self-government. Conventional wisdom and mainstream academic practices, the Ostroms warned, contain many bad medicines that rely on unsound, ideologically motivated assumptions. Lin Ostrom noted in the introduction to the graduate syllabus on institutional theory she taught for decades at Indiana University that people may talk about "THE" government doing X or Y, but there are individuals who hold positions in a variety of situations within "THE" government. This thinking about governance is flawed, which explains why the Ostroms argued for shifting the focus of inquiry.[14] To understand processes at any level of organization, researchers and analysts must examine the actions of individuals who are participants, along with the incentives they face. There are many factors that can influence these incentives, but a major source, particularly in the public sector, is the rules of the game individual actors are part of. These rules specify what must, may, or may not be done in various contexts; along with formal and informal institutions, they make up economic, social, and political order. The thesis that the Ostroms and their collaborators defended was the following:

> Individuals, who seriously engage one another in efforts to build mutually productive social relationships—and to understand why these are important—are capable of devising ingenious ways of relating constructively with one another. The impossible task, however, is to design entire social systems "from scratch" at one point in time that avoid the fate of being monumental disasters. Individuals who are willing to explore possibilities, consider new options as entrepreneurs, and to use reason as well as trial and error experimentation, can evolve and design rules, routines, and ways of life that are likely to build up to self-governing entities with a higher chance of adapting and surviving over time than top-down designs.[15]

That is why the Ostroms and their collaborators resisted calls for bringing "THE" state back in along with further consolidation of public authority and centralized bureaucratic administration. Those policies imply the existence of omnicompetent public officials, omniscient legislators, and the perfection of a uniform and universal system of laws or total deregulation of the markets. Such conditions are never realized in reality and ignore the complexity and diversity of the world. Instead of old concepts in political science such as "THE" government, "THE" state, left/right or capitalism/socialism, the Ostroms preferred to use new ones such as polycentricity, power-with versus power-over, and constitutional artisanship.[16]

In their writings, the Ostroms celebrated people's capacities for self-government and expressed their strong belief in human creativity and the possibility of gaining mutual trust and understanding to achieve "patterns of social accountability" (Ostrom 1997, 287). At the same time, they also paid attention to cases of institutional failure and weakness, eager to draw the appropriate lessons from them. Their extensive fieldwork and experiments led them to conclude that there is no single form of social and political organization that can be universally valid and good. It is for that reason that their worldview cannot be ascribed to any particular ideological camp and frustrates all attempts to locate it on a traditional ideological map.[17] Creative appropriations (or misappropriations) of their work are also likely to occur. It is no surprise then that their ideas have been used by advocates on opposite sides of policy debates, often defending contradictory positions. In what follows, I would like to single out three such significant themes that are central to the philosophy of what came to be known as the Bloomington School—seeing like a citizen, polycentricity, and the opposition to any form of blueprint thinking—that allow us to better assess the originality and enduring relevance of the Ostroms' approach.

"SEEING LIKE A CITIZEN"

Given the eclecticism of the Ostroms' agenda, it is no accident that scholars on both the Left and the Right have been able to find something valuable and intriguing in the new science of politics of the Bloomington School. On the Left, the Ostroms have been applauded for their focus on democratic citizenship meant to strengthen participatory frameworks and civic practices; they were also praised for insisting that markets are sometimes inefficient in dealing with common-pool resources, which require other forms of governance. Yet they did not challenge the importance of free markets in general; they only refused to idolize them as the miraculous solution to all problems. At the same time, the Ostroms were skeptical toward what they took to be the elitism of a certain part of democratic theory. They denounced "the meaninglessly chattering about democracy" (Ostrom 1994, 130) that focuses only on elections and monocentric systems of governance. Their reluctance to use the term "democracy" has not gone unnoticed either.

On the Right, libertarians and classical liberals have also been correct to argue that there is an undeniable libertarian or classical liberal strain in the Ostroms' agenda. To be sure, Lin and Vincent emphasized that there is a

"Faustian bargain" (Ostrom and Ostrom 2004, 109) at the heart of all societies that explains why the exercise of power is fraught with so many problems and why there will always be many inequalities between the rulers and the ruled. "All organizations," Vincent wrote (1980, 312), "are Faustian bargains where instruments of evil are used to do good." He had read and reflected upon the works of Moisey Ostrogorski (1854–1921)and Robert Michels (1876–1936) about the oligarchic nature of modern political parties and came to denounce in unambiguous terms what he used to refer to as "boss-rule." Governing modern societies poses significant challenges in light of the steady scientific innovation that requires, in turn, constant adaptation and change. As Vincent once put it, "So long as new knowledge continues to accrue, long-term planning is an impossibility. New knowledge contributes to the erosion of technologies based upon prior knowledge" (Ostrom 1980, 311). Consequently, he was deeply skeptical of theories presenting "the State" as "the unique association for the common good" (Ostrom 1997, 285). Writing about American democracy, but possibly extending his observations beyond it, Vincent concluded that "democracy is at risk when 'the government' is presumed 'to govern'" (Ostrom 1994, 259), and when citizens are expected only to obey passively, without active involvement in the administration of their communities. Such a presupposition, he argued, is simplistic and unjustifiable because it does not render justice to the myriad ways in which "it is people who govern in assuming responsibility for managing their own affairs, for learning how to relate to others, for setting the terms and conditions for taking collective decisions and collective actions, and for holding those who exercise authority on behalf of others accountable to fiduciary relationships" (Ostrom 1994, 259).

The Ostroms embraced the perspective of "seeing like a citizen" and emphasized the importance of taking stock of local knowledge and resources when making decisions about using common-pool, limited resources. "Seeing like a citizen" can indeed be regarded as a *motto* for the Ostroms' entire work and career, given their belief in the possibility of building societies that govern themselves for themselves, bottom-up, rather than being state-governed, top-down.[18] "Great Societies," Vincent Ostrom believed, "are not organized by some single center of Supreme Authority exercising tutelage over Society. Knowledgeable, skillful, and intelligible persons build great societies by working with one another and mediating conflicts to achieve conflict resolution in forming coherent patterns of relationships with one another" (Ostrom 1997, 291). Implicit here is a critique of "seeing like a state,"[19] an approach that attempts to govern society top-down and relies on absolute faith in the power and omniscience of a single agent that has the monopoly of sovereign authority. On this view, citizens are seen as passive and helpless recipients of orders, unable to handle complex problems on their own. Such a naïve faith in the power of "the state," Ostrom believed, is not only unable to account for the myriad of institutional frameworks formed by human relationships in everyday life but also is incompatible with the maintenance of republican institutions of local self-government. For the Ostroms, living in a self-governing, open, and free society requires that individuals never view themselves as masters exercising power *over* others. Instead, they must educate and cultivate their imagination and instincts through "due deliberation and reflection" (Ostrom 1994, 131) so that they learn how to exercise power *with* their fellow citizens, as cocreators of social order.

POLYCENTRICITY

Instead of focusing on the state, the Ostroms and their collaborators preferred to analyze the concrete challenges and problems faced by local governments and communities. As Vincent remarked (Cole and McGinnis 2014, 44), "We need not think of 'government' or 'governance' as something provided by states alone. Families, voluntary associations, villages, and other forms of human association all involve some form of self-government. Rather than looking only to states, we need to give much more attention to building the kinds of basic institutional structures that enable people to find ways of relating constructively to one another and of resolving problems in their daily lives." To this effect, the Ostroms insisted on the importance of making necessary distinctions between small and large-scale frameworks of governance and applying different methods of inquiry. The effectiveness of governance depends on scale. Sometimes, governments are too big to handle complex local issues, while at other times, they may be too small to address issues that require a larger scale of cooperation. In other words, size matters when dealing with the allocation and use of limited resources and creating formal and informal institutions and rules to handle such problems. Some issues are best solved locally, while others are best addressed globally. Collective action problems are solvable on multiple scales; there is no simple solution, no single ideological blueprint, left or right, that might solve them. Sweeping theories cannot render justice to small-scale problems of collective actions, while local approaches are often inadequate to tackle large-scale issues.

That is why Lin and Vincent Ostrom relied on the concept of polycentric order borrowed from Michael Polanyi (1891–1976), which they developed and refined into a central concept of their eclectic science of politics.[20] In *The Logic of Liberty* (1951), the Hungarian-born philosopher developed the concept of polycentricity in relation to scientific research and the circulation of information in society; he then drew original connections between polycentricity, the rule of law, and freedom of association and expression, and offered a cogent defense of the principles of open society. In all its forms (market, judicial, economic, and political), polycentricity became for the Ostroms the key to understanding social order in complex societies with its conglomerate of diverse institutions, decision centers, and loci of power, enjoying autonomous prerogatives. Unlike Polanyi's version of polycentric order, which tended to emphasize its spontaneous nature, the concept of polycentricity as developed by the Ostroms was based on a careful study of metropolitan governance and the provision of local services. It involved a myriad of rules, norms, values, incentives, and constitutions, some being the outcome of conscious design, others emerging from individuals' free and spontaneous interaction.[21] This view was the Ostroms' main way of criticizing monocentric theories and their focus on top-down power. Polycentricity also became central to the Ostroms' defense of federalism in the modern age and their staunch critique of the Wilsonian notion of unitary governance directed by experts at the top. The Ostroms believed that centralization with its top-down solutions has important limitations and is often not the right way to go about solving common-pool resource dilemmas. Instead, more freedom must be given to people to try to solve their problems at the local level, by using their specific knowledge, resources, and incentives.

AGAINST BLUEPRINT THINKING

The question remains, Isn't the Ostroms' worldview closer to that of classical liberalism after all? This is an important question that has been addressed elsewhere.[22] Here I want to reflect on the Ostroms' refusal to think ideologically and the fact that they were always skeptical toward all panaceas, including classical liberal ones (less state, more market, etc.). None of these allegedly universal solutions, they argued, may be seen as infallible and none can effectively be used in all contexts. As Lin Ostrom warned, people need to remain skeptical toward the danger of allegedly self-evident truths. "Reforms based on overly simplified views of the world," she used to say (Ostrom 2000, 42), "have led to counterintuitive and counterintentional results in both urban and common-pool resources." Two good examples are decentralization and spontaneous order, both classic tropes in the philosophy of classical liberalism.

Although the Ostroms explored the benefits of decentralization, they did not regard it as *the* key to all the social and political problems people face in their daily lives. As Lin argued in an important paper cowritten with Krister Andersson et al. (2015) on the dangers of too much decentralization,[23] other factors should be taken into account as well before the benefits of decentralization can be properly assessed. They will appear and materialize only when the actors targeted by reforms are downwardly accountable to the citizens they are supposed to serve. Decentralization reforms can fail when this doesn't happen, which explains why decentralization is "an unsatisfactory substitute for a constitutional system of rule based upon federal principles for the concurrent exercise of governmental authority" (Ostrom 1994, 92). The same can be said of another classical liberal concept, spontaneous order. While the Ostroms clearly understood the complexity of social and political order, they were also aware that the concept of spontaneity is misleading, because a good part of social order involves a good dose of "conscious" design. For them, spontaneous order and institutional design were *not* incompatible. The US Constitution, which Vincent often referred to in his writings, was itself the product of such conscious design. There was nothing spontaneous about it because it involved a conscious effort to achieve a certain set of constitutional rules and institutional outcomes.

The Ostroms' misgivings toward the concept of spontaneous order can also be analyzed in light of their affinity with the German tradition of ordoliberalism. Influenced by the Freiburg School of Walter Eucken and his main collaborators (Wilhelm Röpke, Alexander Rüstow, and Alfred Müller-Armack), German ordoliberalism combined a confidence in the virtues of free markets with the belief that "*konforme Eingriffe*"[24] are often needed to maintain free competition in the market. These are state interventions in keeping with the logic of the free market meant to create the institutional framework necessary for the proper functioning of the latter. The Ostroms did not oppose a priori government interventions in all circumstances, although they were critical of specific interventions, in particular the consolidation of public services (schools or police districts) in districts that bring together diverse communities and constituencies.

All this helps to explain why they were reluctant to use the classical dichotomies of state or the market, left or right, capitalism or socialism. Because they believed that there is no single form of organization that can be "good" for all actors and in all circumstances and contexts, they insisted that it is essential to always judge in the context rather than according to general ideas or theories about good governance. The choice of solutions is always context-specific and depends on prudential judgment and local knowledge, necessary complements to theoretical knowledge. What people need are systematic, comparative, institutional assessments to choose what is appropriate in each case. This approach is the opposite of any form of blueprint thinking. As Lin Ostrom wrote in *Understanding Institutional Diversity*, the latter can be found when and where "policymakers, donors, citizens, or scholars propose uniform solutions to a wide array of problems that are clustered under a single name based on one or more successful exemplars. . . . Projects or programs rely on some formula . . . rather than learning the specifics of a particular setting and enabling participants to experiment and learn from their own experience and that of others" (Ostrom 2005, 274–75). Simply put, blueprint thinking is a form of ideological thinking; it can take the form of uncritically advocating more government interventions or defending deregulation at all costs simply because these measures conform to an ideological map, traced in advance, or a litmus test. Advocates of state-led, top-down approaches can fall into the trap of blueprint thinking as much as defenders of community governance. There is no single simple rule that can work perfectly in all circumstances; the real world is complex and heterogeneous, and the actors are individuals who are fallible, unpredictable, and unique. That is why Lin and Vincent Ostrom believed that scientists need to go "beyond markets and states" in order to study polycentric governance of complex social and economic systems. In many instances, the real problem is simply that the blueprint is seen as the "holy grail" recommended for solving a specific problem, thus excluding other possible options. Viewed from this perspective, not even the concept of democracy is (or should be) immune from criticism and contestation; if it is to maintain its robustness, it must remain open to contestation. The same applies even to polycentricity; sometimes monocentric systems of governance are appropriate and might work better than polycentric systems.

MAKING DEMOCRACY WORK

In rejecting the ideological polarization over the size of government as a false and ultimately unproductive dichotomy and shifting the focus of attention toward polycentric forms of governance, Lin and Vincent Ostrom were aware that the essence of politics could not—and should not—be reduced to parties, trade unions, and parliaments, as many of their fellow political scientists thought. Governance, broadly defined, occurs in other settings as well, or, better said, patterns of governance can be found throughout the entire society, nested at various levels. The Ostroms acknowledged that governments are important and perform a vital function in modern society, but they admitted at the same time that governments do not exhaust the concept of governance. Networks of power and governance frameworks can also be found outside of the halls of parliaments and the executive power, in local settings where people develop and use various rules of cooperation. In her work with her collaborators, Lin Ostrom identified seven such types of rules—position, boundary, choice, aggregation, information, payoff, and scope[25]—the formation of which is as important as the process of lawmaking within the halls of parliamentary assemblies or the activity of regulatory agencies. The real essence of politics is not to be found in parties, national assemblies, or cabinets. It should be looked for and examined in the many ways in which ordinary people, rather than political leaders and professional politicians, work together to solve common problems at the grassroots level. It is not a mere coincidence then that the Ostroms insisted on developing citizen capabilities and viewed citizens as constitutional artisans. They stressed the importance of educating an enlightened and active citizenry as an essential prerequisite for a robust democracy. Their focus on "seeing like a citizen" has the advantage that it does not require being wedded to a particular ideological position.

The Ostroms proposed a new vocabulary and a novel paradigm that challenged key tenets of the mainstream political science in the same way Michael Oakeshott's famous distinction between civil and enterprise associations in *On Human Conduct* (1975) sought to offer a new way of thinking about freedom in modern society that went beyond the traditional distinction between capitalism and socialism/communism. Oakeshott distinguished between two ways of looking at the nature and task of government. According to the first view, the government should use its power to impose the pursuit of a single purpose on all citizens; the alternative second view is that the government should be strictly confined to using its power to create and uphold an institutional framework within which citizens can pursue a variety of purposes of their own choice.[26] The Ostroms rejected the first perspective and adopted the second one. They believed that the real challenge is to identify and chart the patterns of order looming underneath the apparent chaos associated with the practice of polycentricity. The point can be taken one step further.[27] What is at stake here is discovering a novel theory of hidden order, a simultaneously visible and invisible hand *sui generis* directing the social mechanism and applicable to many instances of social and political order. The originality of the Bloomington School is to have shown that principles of polycentricity can and should be extended through the whole system of human affairs. This discovery applies not only to public or market sectors but also to local and federal governments, elections, legislative bodies, and political parties.

The Ostroms' work also suggests that scholars ought to conceptualize the very notion of sovereignty, a core concept in political science. Instead of working with a monocentric concept of sovereignty, as political theorists are accustomed to do, it would be better to endorse a complex form of sovereignty, which has both a normative purpose as well as a real basis in the functioning of modern democracies. The issue of complex sovereignty has recently been discussed by French political theorist Pierre Rosanvallon (2006), who criticized the excessive focus on voting and elections among political scientists. He analyzed the emergence of an "indirect" or counter-democracy that seemingly has striking affinities with the concept of polycentricity.[28] In a polycentric system of governance, there are many decision centers and makers, and power and sovereignty are widely diffused and dispersed in the nooks and crannies of the entire society. Unlike Max Weber, who adopted a monocratic principle of government that led to the modern concept of the state as a unitary command structure, the Ostroms believed that no one has the entire monopoly over the legitimate use of force in society. As a result, scientists and researchers need to analyze multiple decision centers and makers whose existence challenges the monopoly of power in society. As already seen, this scrutiny amounts to examining the rules, constitutions, and other mechanisms devised by individuals in their efforts to coordinate their actions to improve their collective well-being in public settings.

That is why claiming that the Ostroms ignored "politics" altogether would be incorrect and would miss the mark. After all, Vincent wrote at length about federalism and participated as an adviser to the Alaska Constitutional Convention.[29] Analysts need to pay special attention to the Ostroms' definition of the political, which was anything but conventional. As Lin Ostrom herself pointed out (Cole and McGinnis 2014, 324):

> Colleagues in political science have frequently chided us for the many studies we have conducted on "dull, unimportant local problems." If one confines political science to the study of national elections, national legislative behavior, and the politics of the presidency, we are missing a great deal at both a local and international level. We must draw on all of the social sciences as well as ecology, biology, history, cultural studies, area studies, and law to slowly build a better, multidisciplinary base for our work on all levels of political organization.

As already noted, the Ostroms' new science of politics sought to carve out a path beyond market and democratic "fundamentalism," which makes their work relevant today, in a highly polarized environment, bitterly divided between pro-market and pro-statist camps that think in black-and-white, either/or terms.[30] They resisted ideological complacency and refused simplistic dichotomies. "They are better lenses, I hope, than those that compel us to perceive social reality in terms of just two ideal types: states and markets," Vincent Ostrom once remarked. "Dichotomies should be avoided in the social sciences" (Cole and McGinnis 2014, 43). They did not believe that a robust market economy and a representative democracy are self-creating or self-sustaining. As such, they parted company not only with those who argued that "the less government, the better," but also with those who believe that all that would be needed for democracy to work would be to grant more power to the state and its agents. The real issue, Lin and Vincent remarked, lies elsewhere and cannot be decided with the aid of any ideological blueprint. There are no panaceas. Everything depends on scale, formal and informal institutions, and incentives that ought to be tailored to different contexts and actors. Although individuals are called to reaffirm the seminal importance of freedom, equality, and pluralism, they also need to reiterate two undeniable truths: this social and political world is immensely complex, and the knowledge about it, for all the great progress already made, remains inevitably limited and fallible.

The eclectic and complex nature of the Bloomington School came to the fore in a recent book on this topic published by Derek Wall. Writing from the Left, he summarized the Ostroms' lessons as follows: "Think about institutions; Pose social change as problem solving; Embrace diversity; Be specific; Listen to the people; Self-government is possible; Everything changes; Map power; Collective ownership can work; Human beings are part of nature too; All institutions are constructed, so can be constructed differently; No panaceas; Complexity does not mean chaos" (Wall 2017, n.p.). This list is interesting and intriguing for several reasons. First, it shows how eclectic the agenda of the Bloomington School is, given its penchant for experimentalism, fallibilism, and pluralism. Second, the list also points to its democratic implications for rethinking collective ownerships and the role of co-ops. Third, it shows that it is possible to claim that, taken as a whole, the Ostroms' eclecticism may not be entirely coherent on several levels, or is incompletely theorized. There are several tensions between their work and classical liberalism, conventional political science, and public administration.

Lin and Vincent would have wholeheartedly agreed with that last point, which they could have seen as a vindication of their worldview. An eclectic approach, selectively borrowing various themes and concepts from both the Left and the Right, may contain contradictions and tensions, but this is precisely what a heterogeneous world in constant flux demands and needs. The Ostroms believed that the world itself is eclectic and complex—it consists of governments, local associations, families, neighborhoods, churches, markets, customs, ecosystems, and informal institutions—and, as a result, requires a multiplicity of methods and approaches to make sense of its diversity.

In the end, the eclecticism of the Ostroms' approach can be interpreted as a form of epistemic humility and an open acknowledgment of human fallibility. Yet, much like moderation,[31] eclecticism is a two-edged sword. On the one hand, it gives those in this field the independence and flexibility to draw on a wide variety of sources, and it opens up space for dialogue and cooperation with all sides. On the other hand, eclecticism risks satisfying no side and might be seen as not rigorous enough. As such, it might condemn people to marginality and, sometimes, relative isolation, especially when they are reluctant to use their research to endorse any particular ideological camp in partisan debates. This was exactly the Ostroms' case.

Reflecting on the academic influence and reception of *Governing the Commons* (Ostrom 1990) in a symposium published in *Perspectives on Political Science* in 2010, Frank Baumgartner remarked that Elinor Ostrom's work was placed "in the crosshairs" of a powerful ideological divide. By concluding that neither states nor markets can be trusted alone, she fell "in between the

intellectual fault lines of those believing any state intervention would necessarily fail and those who think that top-down bureaucratic control . . . is the
obvious solution to any market failure" (Baumgartner 2010, 575, 576). Both
Lin and Vincent have been criticized for working with an etiolated understanding of the political or for ignoring class, power relations, and inequalities. Another alleged limit is their treatment of context simply as exogenous
circumstances under which individuals choose. Other scholars, like Peregrine
Schwartz-Shea, pointed out possible tensions between the universalizing
assumptions of the rational-actor model[32] and Lin's desire to understand the
perspectives of actors in the field. Similar tensions were detected between her
preference for self-organizing systems and her policy-analytic role of advis-
ing governmental and other decision makers, or between her advocacy for
a general framework and a unifying language of research and her critique of
universal solutions. Still others, like Jane Mansbridge, noted with surprise
that democracy is a term that appears nowhere in *Governing the Commons*
and rarely in Lin Ostrom's other work. In Mansbridge's view, she was vague
about the ways in which people might be included in the design process and
has little to say about political regimes in general. Moreover, as Jeffrey C.
Isaac, the editor of the 2010 symposium on Ostrom's work, argued, articles
and other writings by Lin and Vincent displayed a striking "indifference" to
the state and much of what most political scientists consider "politics" (Isaac
2010, 569). It is not clear what the Ostroms would have to say about those
circumstances in which people disagree about ends and means and what is
just and unjust, or in which some of the proposed ends are viewed as unjust.[33]

Moreover, Vincent held an original view of citizens as *constitutional artisans*, a perspective which might strike their critics as simultaneously romantic
and highly demanding, leaving out to some extent an important dimension
of social and political life—leadership. "A self-governing society," he wrote,
"would presumably turn on a universality of artisanship in which each person
first becomes one's own governor—one's own master—and then, in the course
of coping with problems that inevitably arise in interdependent patterns of
artisanship-artifact relationships, becomes capable of working out associated
arrangements with others" (Ostrom 1997, 202).[34] To some, this view might
seem too good to be true, because it glosses over the many challenges of citizenship as well as over the many inequalities of power existing in all societies,
including Western ones. Moreover, Ostrom did not fully address the question
of the extent to which the pathologies associated with a culture of top-down

command rather than collaborative inquiry might be in good part the out-come of the modern division of labor that leaves citizens too little time to govern themselves. One is left wondering whether the problems detected by the Ostroms might not be entrenched in and inseparable from the nature of modern society, whose iron cage had been analyzed by Max Weber, the Ostroms' nemesis.

CIVIC STUDIES

Those are open questions that I cannot fully answer here. I should like to conclude with a final point, which is supposed to mirror and complement the optimism undergirding their work, an optimism badly needed in our cur-rent polarized environment.[35] I believe that the Ostroms' methodological and political eclecticism makes them particularly relevant to reformers, starting with those who seek to improve any education system. Free and open societ-ies that call themselves democratic need to pay special attention to educating citizens so that they can learn how to practice the art of association. Habits of self-governance cannot be obtained overnight, nor can they be spread through hastily designed civics courses. They can be achieved only by "first living in the traditions of family, neighborhood and community" (Ostrom 1997, 299) and through a carefully thought-out system of education of citizens as artisans. By paying attention to the Ostroms' message, citizens might—by examining various levels of democratic governance—be able to avoid the shortcomings of minimalist or purely formal definitions of democracy (based on free elections, the existence of the rule of law, and political competition) that ignore the chal-lenges posed by machine politics and money. Looking back at the work she and Vincent undertook during their careers, Lin Ostrom confessed (Aligica 2014a, 164):

> One of our greatest priorities has been to ensure that our research contrib-utes to the future of citizens, entrepreneurs in the public and private spheres, and officials at all levels of government. We have a distinct obligation to participate in this educational project as well as to engage in the research enterprise so that we build a cumulative knowledge base that may be used to sustain democratic life. Self-governing, democratic systems are always fragile enterprises. Future citizens need to understand that they participate in the

constitution and reconstitution of rule governed polities and to learn the "art and science of association." If we fail in this respect, all our investigation and theoretical efforts are useless.[36]

Needless to say, this call to action is far from being an easy task. The Ostroms' theory of polycentric social order is predicated not only on the existence of key freedoms (freedom of association, freedom of the press and thought) and federalism but also on the presence of an active body of citizens-artisans, participating in local associations and skilled in the art and science of association. In the footsteps of Tocqueville, the Ostroms raised the bar quite high in their attempt to go beyond the tenets of mainstream political science. "Democracy conceptualized as an open public realm," Michael Fotos noted (2015, 75), "demands more of theory and of its citizens than the mainstream conceptualization of democracy as essentially electoral, a realm wherein 'nearly universal suffrage and competitive and fair elections for most of the primary offices of government' are sufficient for maintaining a self-governing polity." Such polycentric systems of government do not emerge spontaneously; on the contrary, they need constant nurturing. Political apathy, powerlessness, or dys-functionalities can be analyzed not only in terms of inequalities of power but also in terms of deprivation of capabilities. Intelligent measures can be taken to cultivate citizens' capabilities for self-governance, a priority on the agenda of the Ostroms. In this regard, their contribution overlaps with Amartya Sen and Martha Nussbaum's important work on capabilities; it is no accident that Lin Ostrom, for example, referred to Sen's writings on this topic.[37] Without such capabilities, there can be no practice of self-governance, but only a system in which there is a constant struggle to dominate and capture scarce resources in a ruthless competition for power.

Tocqueville was among the first to understand this point. Although believing that the cure for the ills of democracy is more democracy, he emphasized at the same time that democracy must be educated, moderated, and puri-fied of its revolutionary instincts. Citizenship—that is, working with others to pursue common projects—is an art that can be learned through practice and a long apprenticeship. The Ostroms were right to follow in Tocqueville's footsteps in this regard. Their normative commitments relied upon a model of human beings as boundedly rational and of fallible learners who, through reflection and choice, can improve the conditions under which they live. Polit-ical theories, Lin Ostrom remarked in *Governing the Commons*, should not describe people as prisoners; the challenge is how to work toward enhancing the capabilities of the people so that they can change and devise better rules for collective action. Democracy may not be the best form of government, but it does have a clear advantage over all other forms of government. The citizens of a democratic regime are prone to making many errors, but they tend to be more enlightened and more alert than those who live under other forms of government; they have the luxury of making what Tocqueville called "retrievable mistakes." They can learn by doing and thus realize the extent to which they depend on cooperating with others on equal terms to pursue common goals. In this process, they also learn about the importance of civic spirit and become aware of their rights and duties. Moreover, they learn to respect the laws because laws promote the general interest and can be changed peacefully through a process of deliberation and contestation. As a result, under the dominion of democracy, as Tocqueville put it (2010, 399):

> It is, above all, not what public administration executes that is great, but what is executed without it and outside of it. Democracy does not give the people the most skillful government, but it does what the most skillful government is often impotent to create; it spreads throughout the social body a restless activity, a superabundant force, an energy that never exists without it, and that, if only circumstances are favorable, can bring forth marvels. Those are its true advantages.

This quote has always been one of my favorites in *Democracy in America* and I consistently use it in my own work and teaching. It is an optimistic and refreshing insight in a fast-paced age in which books with resounding titles such as *How Democracies Die, Against Democracy, The Retreat of Western Liberalism*, or *Why Liberalism Failed* become best sellers overnight and are widely discussed in the mass media.[38] To many critics of democracy, the image of the vibrant democratic society described by Tocqueville is at best utopian and at worst incoherent. The voters are ignorant and unable to understand the complexities of most political problems. Many are simply uninterested in politics or unwilling to devote time to participating in politics. Viewed from this perspective, as Jason Brennan provocatively put it (2016, 3), "the "decline in political engagement is a good start, but we still have a long way to go. We should hope for even less participation, not more. . . . Ideally, most people would fill their days with painting, poetry, music, architecture, statuary, tapestry, and porcelain, or perhaps football, NASCAR, tractor pulls, celebrity gossip, and trips to Applebee's. Most people, ideally, would not worry about politics at all."

The Ostroms would have opposed (but not dismissed!) such a cynical view of civic competence because it works with a problematic and ultimately simplifying understanding of what "politics" is all about. Politics is not primarily or only about parties and voting, as Brennan and others imply; it occurs in many settings and forms, some of which may appear as apolitical at first sight. That is why, if they were alive today, Lin and Vincent would renew their efforts to steer political scientists away from "seeing like a state" toward "seeing like a citizen." They would reaffirm their confidence in the possibility of building self-governing, rather than state-governed, societies. The Ostroms would remind scientists and policymakers that they have few other choices except to explore and try to improve step by step, while learning from what has worked and what has failed in the past. At the same time, they would insist that people must remain skeptical toward buzzwords, allegedly self-evident truths, and theories that promise to simplify the complex world of today. Once again, there are no panaceas to rely upon in efforts to make democracy work. Some things begin at the grassroots level and can be solved only there; others depend on larger frameworks of governance and can be solved only in those contexts.

Those are some of the insights that make Lin and Vincent Ostrom's eclectic work relevant today. Far from being a limitation, their methodological, institutional, and political eclecticism shows why their writings still matter and why it is likely that they will continue to inspire new generations of scholars struggling to improve democratic practices and institutions.

ACKNOWLEDGMENTS

An earlier version of this chapter was originally presented at a conference organized by the Mercatus Center at George Mason University (July 31–August 1, 2018). I would like to thank the organizers of the conference and the editors of the present book for inviting me to attend this event and contribute to this volume. Also thanks to Barbara Allen, Dan Cole, Sheldon Gellar, Michael McGinnis, Filippo Sabetti, and Vlad Tarko for their comments and suggestions.

NOTES

1. On this issue, see Fotos 2015, 70–71.

2. On Tocqueville's new science of politics, also see Craiutu (2015) and Zuckert (2014).

3. On this topic, see Tocqueville's important speech given in April 1852 at the Academy of Moral and Political Science in Paris, translated in Danoff and Hebert, eds., 2010, 17–29.

4. For an interesting comparison between Huntington and Tocquevillian analytics, see Gellar's chapter in Craiutu and Gellar (2009, 33–54).

5. Used as an epigraph in Wall (2017). For an intellectual biography of Lin Ostrom, see Tarko (2016).

6. As quoted by Robert Axelrod in his contribution to the 2010 symposium on Lin Ostrom's work in *Perspectives on Politics* (Isaac 2010, 580). On Lin's intellectual journey, see her own account in Ostrom (2010).

7. For some, such a label is problematic and open to question. One of the skeptical voices in this regard has been Lee J. Alston, who became the director of the Ostrom Workshop in 2014. For many others across the world, the label "Bloomington School" has worldwide value, as illustrated by these two excellent documentaries by filmmaker Barbara Allen: *Elinor and Vincent Ostrom—International Studies of Choice, Cooperation, Governance*; https://vimeo.com/121608252; *Elinor Ostrom's Governing the Commons and the Cooperative Enterprise Movement*, https://vimeo.com/163633853.

8. For more details, see Cole and McGinnis (2014) and Sabetti (2011). The diversity of the outlets in which the Ostroms and their collaborators published their research must also be duly underscored. These included both major presses and arguably marginal journals open to their interdisciplinary approaches.

9. Vincent and Elinor were agnostics but they respected, appreciated, and cooperated with people inspired or influenced by religious norms. They often cited Tocqueville's point of departure—equality—which contains a religious norm, the image of men made in the image of God and equal among themselves.

10. Vincent Ostrom described the methodology of the Bloomington School as follows: "We try to combine formal approaches, fieldwork and experiments in order to penetrate social reality rather than to use formal techniques to "distance" ourselves from it, as Walter Eucken once expressed the difference. [. . .] The researcher or observer needs to take into account the way people think about and experience themselves and their situation" (Cole and McGinnis 2014, 42). Also see Michael McGinnis's chapter in this book and his unpublished integrated introduction to the three volumes published in 1999–2000 by the University of Michigan Press, collecting papers written by scholars associated with the Workshop in Political Theory and Policy Analysis at Indiana University, Bloomington (McGinnis 1999a, 1999b, and 2000).

11. The interpretation of Tocqueville that I eventually came to espouse was different in some important respects from Vincent's. I was more interested in Tocqueville's analysis of democracy and how democracy changes the human condition. Vincent was known for ignoring most secondary sources and he always sought to interpret the original source afresh.

12. One exception here would be the Anti-Federalists' skepticism toward the complex system of checks and balances provided by the Constitution.

13. I note in passing that Aristotle played a minor role for Vincent, in spite of the fact that some of the Ostroms' ideas have affinities with Aristotle's political thought, in particular with his comparison of democracy to a potluck dinner in Aristotle's *Politics* (Book III, chap. 11).

14. Here is how one of the Ostroms' collaborators described their approach:

> Instead of assuming the expert "best" option, the Ostroms taught students and colleagues to discover the institution within the community, as community members understood it. They noted that there was a not a single "best solution" as often assumed in political science and public administration of the time. There were many available solutions whose potential success depended on factors beyond the simpler decision situation of most models. They asked, "What would people select for themselves?" This focus on self-governing was key to understanding decisions in a federalist society. (Herzberg 2015, 97)

Herzberg's article provides a clear and useful outline of the originality of the Bloomington School. It complements Mitchell's classic article (1988), which compares the Bloomington School with the Virginia (Buchanan/Tullock) and Rochester (Riker) schools. Mitchell described the importance and influence of the Bloomington School as follows: "Because of its low-keyed operation Bloomington has achieved less notoriety but in some respects, perhaps, more lasting influence in political science. The Ostroms have chosen the less dramatic role of testing middle-level ideas, relating them to our philosophical past and, of waging an educational campaign in public administration—a somewhat thankless task" (Mitchell 1988, 114). On the Bloomington School, also see the special issue of the *Good Society* 20, no. 1 (2011), almost entirely dedicated to Lin and Vincent Ostrom's works.

15. From the introduction to POLS Y673, Institutional Analysis and Development: Micro, taught by Lin Ostrom at Indiana University, Bloomington (Fall 2011).

16. In a conversation with Paul Aligica, Vincent Ostrom summarized the political vision undergirding the Bloomington School as follows (Aligica 2014b, 40):

> Probably the best way to characterize our approach would be to start with one of our most influential themes: the idea that broad concepts such as "markets" and "states" or "socialism" and "capitalism" do not take us very far in thinking about patterns of order in human society. For example, when some "markets" economists speak of "capitalism," they fail to distinguish between an open, competitive market economy and a state-dominated mercantile economy. In this, they follow

Marx. He argued that "capitalism" has a competitive dynamic that leads to market domination by a few large monopoly or monopoly-like enterprises. [. . .] Instead, we should expect to find some combination of market and nonmarket structures in every society, and we should recognize the complex configuration of institutions behind labels such as "capitalism." We might usefully think about combinations of private and public economies existing side by side. However, it's important to stress that not all forms of public enterprise are, or need to be, state-owned and operated. Various forms of communal or public ownership may exist apart from state owner-ship. Markets are diverse and complex entities. Markets for different types of goods and services may take on quite different characteristics. Some may work well under the most impersonal conditions. Others may depend upon personal considerations involving high levels of trust among trading partners. In other words, the options are much greater than we imagine, and we can see this is true if we don't allow our minds to be trapped within narrowly constrained intellectual horizons.

17. As Cole and McGinnis remarked in their introduction to the first of the four volumes on the Bloomington School they edited a few years ago, the Ostroms' own politics were "impossible to pigeonhole in any standard ideological position, except for a long-standing commitment to academic freedom" (Cole and McGinnis 2014, 16).

18. On this topic, see Levine (2011) and Soltan (2011), who discuss Lin and Vincent Ostrom's contributions to the development of "civic studies." These articles were published in a special issue of the *Good Society* 20, no. 1 (2011), dedicated to the Bloomington School, which also featured articles by Filippo Sabetti, John Groenewegen, Hartmut Kliemt, Viktor Vanberg, Harry Boyte, Paul Aligica, and Peter Boettke.

19. I borrow here the title of James C. Scott's book (Scott 1998). It would be worth studying in further detail the similarities and differences on this issue between Scott and the Ostroms.

20. On this topic, see Aligica and Tarko (2012) and Cole and McGinnis (2014, xxi–xxii).

21. On the conditions of polycentricity, see Aligica 2014a, 51–52.

22. See, for example, Boettke and Aligica (2009).

23. It might be argued that what the Ostroms were after—though unstated in their work—was something like the notion of "subsidiarity," not in its institutionalized sense in the European Union, but in its original meaning.

24. The term, which designates interventions compatible with the functioning of the free mar-ket, is Wilhelm Röpke's from his important book, *Die Gesellschaftskrisis der Gegenwart* (1942).

25. As Ostrom (2014, 319) stated:

Position rules create positions (e.g., member of a legislature or a committee, voter, etc.). Boundary rules affect how individuals are assigned to or leave positions and how one situation is linked to other situations. Choice rules affect the assignment of particular action sets to positions. Aggregation rules affect the level of control that individual participants exercise at a linkage within or across situations. Information rules affect the level of information available in a situation about actions and the link between actions and outcome linkages. Payoff rules affect the benefits and costs assigned to outcomes given the actions chosen. Scope rules affect which outcomes must, must not, or may be affected within a domain.

26. Here is what Oakeshott (1975, 314) wrote:

> Civil associates are persons (*cives*) related to one another, not in terms of a substantive undertaking, but in terms of the common acknowledgment of the authority of civil (not instrumental laws), specifying conditions to be subscribed to in making choices and in performing self-chosen actions. A state understood in these terms is identified as a system of law and its jurisdiction. The office of the government is to be the custodian of a *respublica* composing a system of civil law, to adjudicate disputes about the meanings of its component laws . . . and to redress injury. . . . The mode of association here is . . . therefore formal . . . in terms of the conditions to be observed in seeking the satisfaction of wants.

There is a striking similarity between Oakeshott's views and the Ostroms' perspective on civil associations.

27. On this topic, see Fotos (2015) and Aligica and Tarko (2012, 244).

28. The possibility of a comparison between the Ostroms' conception of polycentricity and Rosanvallon's complex sovereignty was raised by Marco Chimini, who took my master of arts course at Pompeu Fabra University in Barcelona (May 2018), in which he wrote a short seminar paper on this topic.

29. On this issue, see Herzberg (2015, 103).

30. See, for example, the affinity between the philosophy of the Bloomington School and the philosophy of moderation undergirding the policy vision proposed by the Niskanen Center as outlined in a recent manifesto, "The Center Can Hold: Public Policy for an Age of Extremes," (December 13, 2018), https://niskanencenter.org/blog/niskanen-center-releases-new-policy-vision-paper/.

31. I commented on the complexity of the concept of political moderation in Craiutu (2017).

32. It is true that the Ostroms generally agreed with a form of the rational-actor model—namely, Herbert Simon's model of boundedly rational humans—but they also recognized that it would be undesirable to reject completely the rational-actor model.

33. On the Bloomington School, see Boettke and Aligica (2009). Peter Levine's chapter in the present book makes an interesting argument for the complementarity between the Bloomington School, the second generation of the Frankfurt School (represented by Jürgen Habermas), and the tradition of nonviolent social movements (Mahatma Gandhi, Martin Luther King Jr.).

34. I would also like to stress here the importance of covenanting in Vincent Ostrom's ideas about the art of association; these ideas should be related to his insistence on the need for a new vocabulary and language of politics capable of addressing this art of association.

35. Lin maintained a robust form of optimism in the prospects for democracy to the end of her life. Vincent's last book (1997) was a bit less optimistic and insisted more on the vulnerability and fragility of democracy.

36. On Ostrom's contribution to "civic studies," see Levine (2011) and Soltan (2011).

37. On the relation between capabilities and development, see Sen (1999), Nussbaum (2013), Shivakumar (2005), and Peter Levine's contribution to this volume.

38. For a critique of this literature, see Cole and Craiutu (2018).

REFERENCES

Aligica, Paul D. 2014a. *Institutional Diversity and Political Economy: The Ostroms and Beyond*. New York: Oxford University Press.

———. 2014b. "Rethinking the Terms of Choice: Interview with Vincent Ostrom." In *Lin Ostrom and the Bloomington School of Political Economy, Vol. 1: Polycentricity in Public Administration and Political Science*, edited by Daniel H. Cole and Michael D. McGinnis. Lanham, MD: Lexington Books.

Aligica, Paul. D., and Vlad Tarko. 2012. "Polycentricity: From Polanyi to Ostrom, and Beyond." *Governance* 25 (2): 237–62.

Andersson, Krister P., Forrest Fleischman, Pamela Jagger, Marty Luckert, Ruth Meinzen-Dick, Esther Mwangi, and Elinor Ostrom. 2015. "Unpacking Decentralization: A Case Study of Uganda's Forestry Reforms." University of Colorado Institute of Behavioral Science, Boulder.

Baumgartner, Frank R. 2010. In "Beyond the Tragedy of the Commons: A Discussion of *Governing the Commons: The Evolution of Institutions for Collective Actions*," edited by Jeffrey C. Isaac. *Perspectives on Politics* 8 (2): 575–77.

Boettke, Peter, and Paul Dragos Aligica. 2009. *Challenging Institutional Analysis and Development: The Bloomington School*. London: Routledge.

Brennan, Jason. 2016. *Against Democracy*. Princeton, NJ: Princeton University Press.

Cole, Daniel H., and Aurelian Craiutu. 2018. "The Many Deaths of Liberalism." Aeon Magazine (June 28, 2018). https://aeon.co/essays/reports-of-the-demise-of-liberalism-are-greatly-exaggerated\.

Cole, Daniel H., and Michael D. McGinnis. 2014. Introduction to *Lin Ostrom and the Bloomington School of Political Economy, Vol. 1: Polycentricity in Public Administration and Political*

Science, edited by Daniel H. Cole and Michael D. McGinnis. Lanham, MD: Lexington Books.

Craiutu, Aurelian. 1993a. "Tocqueville, Our Contemporary I." *22* 26 (July 5–11): 13.

———. 1993b. "Tocqueville, Our Contemporary II." *22* 27 (July 12–18): 14–18.

———. 2014. "Tocqueville and Eastern Europe." In *Tocqueville's Voyages*, edited by Christine D. Henderson, 390–424. Indianapolis, IN: Liberty Fund.

———. 2015. "Tocqueville's neue politische Wissenschaft wiederentdecken: Einige Lektionen für zeitgenössische Sozialwissenschaftler. In *Alexis de Tocqueville: Analytiker der Demockratie*, edited by Harald Bluhm and Skadi Krause, 33–51. Paderborn, Germany: Wilhelm Fink Verlag.

———. 2017. *Faces of Moderation: The Art of Balance in an Age of Extremes*. Philadelphia: University of Pennsylvania Press.

Craiutu, Aurelian, and Sheldon Gellar, eds. 2009. *Conversations with Tocqueville: The Global Democratic Revolution in the Twenty-First Century*. Lanham, MD: Rowman & Littlefield: Lexington Books.

Danoff, Brian, and Joseph L. Hebert, eds. 2010. *Alexis de Tocqueville and the Art of Democratic Statesmanship*. Lanham, MD: Lexington Books.

Fotos, Michael A., III. 2015. "Vincent Ostrom's Revolutionary Science of Association." *Public Choice* 163 (1-2): 67–83.

Herzberg, Roberta Q. 2015. "Governing Their Commons: Elinor and Vincent Ostrom and the Bloomington School." *Public Choice* 163 (1-2): 95–109.

Isaac, Jeffrey C., ed. "Beyond the Tragedy of the Commons: A Discussion of *Governing the Commons: The Evolution of Institutions for Collective Actions*." *Perspectives on Politics* 8 (2): 569–93.

Levine, Peter. 2011. "Seeing Like a Citizen: The Contributions of Elinor Ostrom to 'Civic Studies.'" *Good Society* 20 (1): 3–14.

McGinnis, Michael D., ed. 1999a. *Polycentric Governance and Development: Readings from the Workshop in Political Theory and Policy Analysis*. Ann Arbor: University of Michigan Press.

———. 1999b. *Polycentricity and Local Public Economies: Readings from the Workshop in Political Theory and Policy Analysis*. Ann Arbor: University of Michigan Press.

———. 2000. *Polycentric Games and Institutions: Readings from the Workshop in Political Theory and Policy Analysis*. Ann Arbor: University of Michigan Press.

Mitchell, William. 1988. "Virginia, Rochester, and Bloomington: Twenty-five Years of Public Choice and Political Science." *Public Choice* 56 (2): 101–19.

Nussbaum, Martha. 2013. *Creating Capabilities: The Human Development Approach*. Cambridge, MA: Belknap Press of Harvard University Press.

Oakeshott, Michael. 1975. *On Human Conduct*. Oxford, UK: Clarendon Press.

Ostrom, Elinor. 1990. *Governing the Commons: The Evolution of Institutions for Collective Action*. Cambridge, UK: Cambridge University Press.

———. 2000. "The Danger of Self-Evident Truths." *PS: Political Science & Politics* 33 (1): 33–44.

———. 2005. *Understanding Institutional Diversity*. Princeton, NJ: Princeton University Press.

———. 2010. "A Long Polycentric Journey." *Annual Review of Political Science* 13 (June): 1–23.

———. 2014. "Converting Threats into Opportunities." In *Lin Ostrom and the Bloomington School of Political Economy, Vol. 1: Polycentricity in Public Administration and Political Science*, edited by Daniel H. Cole and Michael D. McGinnis. Lanham, MD: Lexington Books.

Ostrom, Elinor, and Vincent Ostrom. 2004. "The Quest for Meaning in Public Choice." *American Journal of Economic and Sociology*, 63 (1): 106–47.

Ostrom, Vincent. 1973. *The Intellectual Crisis in American Public Administration*. Birmingham, AL: University of Alabama Press.

———. 1980. "Artisanship and Artifact." *Public Administration Review* 40 (4): 309–317.

———. 1994. *The Meaning of American Federalism: Constituting a Self-Governing Society*. San Francisco: Institute for Contemporary Studies.

———. 1997. *The Meaning of Democracy and the Vulnerabilities of Democracies: A Response to Tocqueville's Challenge*. Ann Arbor: University of Michigan Press.

———. 2009. "Citizen-Sovereigns: The Implications of Hamilton's Query and Tocqueville's Conjecture about the Democratic Revolution." Reprinted in Craiutu and Geller, eds., 2009: 19–30.

Polanyi, Michael (1951). *The Logic of Liberty*. Chicago: University of Chicago Press.

Röpke, Wilhelm. 1942. *Die Gesellschaftskrisis der Gegenwart*. Erlenbach: Eugen Rentsch Verlag.

Rosanvallon, Pierre. 2006. *La Contre-démocratie: La politique à l'âge de la défiance*. Paris: Éditions du Seuil.

Sabetti, Filippo. 2011. "Constitutional Artisanship and Institutional Diversity: Elinor Ostrom, Vincent Ostrom, and the Workshop." *Good Society* 20 (1): 73–83.

Scott, James C. 1998. *Seeing Like a State: How Certain Schemes to Improve the Human Condition Have Failed*. New Haven, CT: Yale University Press.

Sen, Amartya. 1999. *Development as Freedom*. New York: Alfred Knopf.

Shivakumar, Sujai. 2005. *The Constitution of Development: Crafting Capabilities for Self-Governance*. New York: Palgrave Macmillan.

Soltan, Karol. 2011. "A Civic Science." *Good Society* 20 (1): 102–18.

Tarko, Vlad. 2016. *Elinor Ostrom: An Intellectual Biography*. London: Rowman & Littlefield.

Tocqueville, Alexis de. 1985. *Selected Letters on Politics and Society*. Edited by Roger Boesche. Translated by James Toupin. Berkeley: University of California Press.

———. 2010. *Democracy in America*. Edited by Eduardo Nolla. Translated by James T. Schleifer. Indianapolis, IN: Liberty Fund.

Wall, Derek. 2017. *Lin Ostrom's Rules for Radicals: Cooperative Alternatives Beyond Markets and States*. London: Pluto Press.

Zuckert, Catherine H. 2014. "Tocqueville's New Political Science." In *Tocqueville's Voyages*, edited by Christine Dunn Henderson, 142–76. Indianapolis, IN: Liberty Fund.

CONTRIBUTORS

ABOUT THE EDITORS

Paul Dragos Aligica is senior fellow with the F. A. Hayek Program for Advanced Study in Philosophy, Politics, and Economics at the Mercatus Center at George Mason University.

Peter J. Boettke is University Professor of Economics and Philosophy at George Mason University and director of the F. A. Hayek Program for Advanced Study in Philosophy, Politics, and Economics at the Mercatus Center at George Mason University.

Roberta Q. Herzberg is distinguished senior fellow with the F. A. Hayek Program for Advanced Study in Philosophy, Politics, and Economics at the Mercatus Center at George Mason University.

ABOUT THE AUTHORS

Aurelian Craiutu is professor of political science at Indiana University, Bloomington.

Peter Levine is associate dean of academic affairs and the Lincoln Filene Professor of Citizenship & Public Affairs at the Jonathan M. Tisch College of Civic Life at Tufts University.

Adam Martin is associate professor of agricultural and applied economics in the College of Agricultural Sciences and Natural Resources and political economy research fellow at the Free Market Institute at Texas Tech University.

Michael D. McGinnis is professor emeritus of political science and former director of the Ostrom Workshop at Indiana University, Bloomington.

Adrian Miroiu is professor of political science at the National School of Political and Administrative Studies in Bucharest, Romania.

Erik Swyngedouw is professor of human geography in the School of Environment, Education and Development at the University of Manchester, United Kingdom.

Vlad Tarko is assistant professor in the Department of Political Economy and Moral Science at the University of Arizona.

Andreas Thiel is professor of international agricultural policy and environmental governance at the University of Kassel and a senior fellow with the Käte Hamburger Kolleg Centre for Global Cooperation at the University of Duisburg-Essen, Germany.

INDEX

Page numbers in *italics* indicate tables (*t*)
and figures (*f*).

A

Acemoglu, Daron, 140
action cycle, 60
action situations
  adjacent action situations, 39–41, *39f*, 49
  concurrent action situations, 38–39, 45
  consequential action situations, 53
  defined, 192
  emerging challenges and, 53
  focal action situations, 43, 123n1
  as game model generalization, 27, 38
  in IAD framework, 36–41, *37f*, *39f*, 43,
    45, 51, 53, 192
  interconnected action situations, 40
  in E. Ostrom's case studies, 43–44
  policy process and, 53, 60–61
  polycentric governance, 194
  in SES framework, 21, 40, 45–51, *46f*
  socialization agents, 58
  types of, 37–38
agent-based models, 97n12
aggregation rules, 241n25
Agrawal, Arun, 44
Agreement on Trade-Related Aspects of In-
    tellectual Property Rights (TRIPS),
    141
Alaska Constitutional Convention, 231

Aligica, Paul Dragos
  on Dewey's influence on V. Ostrom, 222
  end state social theories distinguished
    from process theories, 107
  on heuristic role of theoretical scenarios,
    97n13
  on IAD framework, 76
  on E. Ostrom's pragmatist perspective,
    88
  on E. Ostrom's use of models, 85
  on V. Ostrom's political vision, 240n16
  on Ostroms' intellectual legacy, 217–218
  on Ostroms' normative stance, 107
  on polycentric systems, 139
Allen, Barbara, 239n7
Alston, Lee J., 239n7
American Political Science Association, 113,
    216
analytical landscape, defined, 48
Andersson, Krister P.
  on decentralization, 228
  diagnostic approach, 60
  policy-relevant research, 26
  The Samaritan's Dilemma (with Gibson et
    al.), 30–31, 57
Anti-Federalism, 221–222, 240n12
anti-realism, 88, 97n15
Apgar Foundation, 217
"Appeal to the Nation" (Indian political
    leaders), 108

Argentina: economic policy evolution, *163f*
Aristotle, 240n13
art of association, 243n34
Australia
  economic freedom, *156t*
  economic policy evolution, *163f*

B

Basurto, Xavier, 58, 193
Baumgartner, Frank, 26, 233–234
Berardo, Ramiro, 64n5
"Beyond Positivism" (E. Ostrom), 31–33
Bloomington School
  analytical perspective, 51
  citizen's core question, 10, 105–125
  collective action, 107
  compared to other traditions, 116–120,
    117t–118t
  contributions to scholarship, 62
  core civic action, 119
  core problem, 118
  criticism of, 54
  critique of government-centered theory,
    113
  exploring new ways forward, 56–63
  focus on means, not ends, 107–109
  foundation, 13
  in Gandhi tradition, 108
  importance of, 240n14
  introduction, 8–9
  as label, 219, 239n7
  linking the IAD framework and *Govern-
    ing the Commons*, 36–44
  on local governance in the US, 202
  methodology, 239n10
  navigating institutional landscapes in a
    polycentric system, 50–56
  policy analysis and, 113–116
  policy-relevant research, 26
  political vision, 240n16
  polycentricity concept, 64n5
  revealing ecologies of governance with the
    SES framework, 45–50

rigor-relevance balance, 5–9, 24–31
rigor-relevance improvement, 5–9, 19–72
seeing like a citizen, 5, 110–113,
    224–226, 230
strategic rigor, 31–36
synthesis with other traditions, 120–123
See also Workshop in Political Theory and
    Policy Analysis (Ostrom Workshop)
blueprint thinking
  defined, 229
  necessary assumptions, 92
  E. Ostrom's rejection of, 84, 92–93,
    98n24, 227–229
Boettke, Peter J., 3, 139
Botswana: economic policy evolution, *163f*
boundary choices, 59–60
boundary rules, 241n25
Boynton, George R., 33
Boyte, Harry, 107
Brennan, Jason, 237–238
Buchanan, James
  The Calculus of Consent (with Tullock),
    131
  "constitutional attitude" about institu-
    tions, 147–148
  Virginia School of public choice, 240n14

C

The Calculus of Consent (Buchanan and
    Tullock), 131
California: water governance, 138
Canada
  economic freedom, *156t*
  economic policy evolution, *163f*
Capabilities Approach (Nussbaum), 110, 111
Capitalism and Freedom (Friedman), 111
cartel federalism, 141
Chile
  economic freedom, *156t*
  economic policy evolution, *163f*
Chimini, Marco, 242n28
China: economic policy evolution, *163f*
choice rules, 241n25

citizens
    as actors in government, 223
    as constitutional artisans, 234
    defined, 105
    education systems, 235
    identity and exclusion problems, 116
    institutional forms and, 3–4
    rational motivations, 3
    role in government, 230–231
    seeing like a citizen, 5, 110–113,
        224–226, 230
    See also self-governance; "what should we
        do?"
civic education, 113
civic studies, 107, 235–238, 241n18
civil associations, 242n26
civil disobedience, 109
Civil Rights Act (1964), 123
civil rights movement, 183, 186
    See also King, Martin Luther, Jr.; nonvio-
        lent social movements
classical liberalism, 189–190, 224–225,
    227–228
Claude-François de Corcelle, 213
Clement, Floriane, 42
cluster analysis, 159–162, 175–176, 176n2
Cole, Daniel H., 64n4, 241n17
collective action, 107, 226–227
collective action theory, 199
collective-choice process, 4
collective-choice settings, 38, 47
combinatorial complexity, 152–167
    cluster analysis, 159–162
    constraints on institutional choices,
        158–159
    evaluating outcomes, 164–167
    factor analysis, 156–158
    mapping the diversity of paths, 162–164
    research design and, 175
common-pool resources (CPR)
    citizens' resolution of conflicts, 5
    examples, 4
    IAD framework, 2

introduction, 1, 4, 7
E. Ostrom's design principles, 94–95,
    130–131
E. Ostrom's legacy, 20
E. Ostrom's research, 130–131
principle of participation, 109
SES framework, 45
communication
    formalized language, 78
    need for clarity in, 34, 35
    from scientists to policymakers, *22t*, 23,
        28–29
    vernacular language, 77–78
communitarianism, 189–190, 200, 202
communities
    community policing, 25
    competing interests within, 35
    creative problem solving, 62
    interjurisdictional spillovers and, 137–138
    member participation in coproduction of
        governance, 52–53
    See also local governance
concurrent action situations, 45
Constitution, US, 228, 240n12
constitutional-choice settings, 38, 47
contracting. *See* social recontracting
contracting down, 129, 140, 142, 143
contracting up, 128, 129, 134, 140–141,
    143
Conversations with Tocqueville (Craiutu and
    Gellar, eds.), 215, 216
coproduction, 30
cosmopolitanism, 189–190
Coughlin, Richard, 200
Cox, Michael, 81
CPR. *See* common-pool resources
Craiutu, Aurelian
    background, 211–212, 215–216
    Conversations with Tocqueville (with
        Gellar), 215
    Ostroms and, 211–212, 215
    Tocqueville Program at Indiana Univer-
        sity, 216–217

Tocqueville's influence on, 215–216,
240n11
See also eclecticism: of the Ostroms'
agenda
Crawford, Sue, 27, 57–58
critical geography, polycentric governance
and, 182
Cyprus: economic freedom, *156t*

D
Dahl, Robert, 215
de Loë, Rob C., 59–60
decentralization, 228
The Delivery of Urban Services (E. Ostrom,
ed.), 56–57
democracy
current status of, 185
foundation, 186
litmus test, 215
making democracy work, 230–235
optimism concerning, 237, 243n35
Ostroms' contributions, 215, 224, 225,
230–235
pessimism concerning, 237–238
"the political" and, 185–186
polycentric governance, 197, 198,
200–201
"stateless" *vs.* "state-governed," 215
Tocqueville on, 58, 236, 237
Democracy in America (Tocqueville), 212–
213, 215, 237
"the democratic," in post-foundational
thought, 183–187
Denmark: economic freedom, 152, *156t*
deontic logic, 96n5
design principles
common-pool resources, 94–95, 130–131
conflicts in implementation of, 120
fairness, 200
focal action situations, 123n1
in *Governing the Commons* (E. Ostrom),
36, 43–44
need for normative standards, 106

Dewey, John, 89, 218, 222
diagnostic approach, 59–60
Dickens, Charles: *Great Expectations,* 111
Dompe, Stewart, 151

E
eclecticism
institutional, 218–219
introduction, 13
methodological, 218, 219–222
of Ostroms' agenda, 216–224
political, 218, 222–224, 240n14
in praise of Ostroms' work, 211–246
types of, 218
ecological change, interjurisdictional
spillovers and, 138
ecologies of governance, SES framework
and, 45–50
economic freedom. *See* Fraser Institute's
Economic Freedom of the World
(EFW) index
economic policies
basic components, 152
changes over time, *164f*
diversity of paths, 162–164
evaluating outcomes, 164–167
evolution by country, *163f*
statistical analysis, 149–150
See also policy analysis
economists, as "truth seekers," 35
ecosystem services, 58
education systems, 235
EFW. *See* Fraser Institute's Economic
Freedom of the World (EFW) index
Elinor and Vincent Ostrom (documentary
film), 239n7
*Elinor Ostrom's Governing the Commons and
the Cooperative Enterprise Movement*
(documentary film), 239n7
Elkin, Stephen, 107
end state social theories, 107
endogeneity
of group goals, 35

in IAD framework, 37
institutional change, 193–194, 195
Epstein, Graham, 64n4
equality
  civil rights movement, 186
  Golden Rule, 190–191, 198, 201
  political acts, 186–187
  polycentric governance, 182, 197,
    199–200, 202, 204
  presupposed in democracy, 186
  redistribution of endowments, 201, 202,
    204
  religious norms, 239n9
Estonia: economic freedom, *156t*
ethics
  justice and, 107–108
  political, 107–109, 214–215, 222
Etzioni, Amitai, 200
Eucken, Walter, 228, 239n10

F

factor analysis, 156–158
failure, E. Ostrom on, 56–57
Faustian bargain, 189, 199, 225
federalism, 141, 227
The Federalist Papers, 221–222
Feiock, Richard C., 25
Finland: economic freedom, 152, *156t*
firms, in IAD framework rules, 173–174
Fischer, Alexandra Paige, 48, 60
focal action situations
  IAD framework, 41, 43, 51, 53–55
  E. Ostrom's case studies, 43, 123n1
  SES framework, 45–50, *46f,* 55
Foldvary, Fred E., 137
forest resources, 28, 60
Fotos, Michael, 236
foundational thought, 184
frameworks
  evaluation criteria for, 76
  institutional grammar, 57–58, 78–79
  introduction, 7
  V. Ostrom on, 75

prescriptive inquiry, 76
  roles of, 42, 75–76
  in triadic scheme, 7, 74–75, 96n3
France
  deregulation, 170
  economic policy evolution, *163f*
Frankfurt School
  compared to other traditions, 116–120,
    117t–118t, 121
  core civic action, 119
  synthesis with other traditions, 120–123
Fraser Institute's Economic Freedom of the
    World (EFW) index
  cluster analysis, 159–162, *160f, 161f*
  components, *153t–155t,* 157–158
  differential outcomes across clusters, *166f*
  factor analysis, *158t*
  factor analysis loading, *157t*
  introduction, 11, 149
  principal component analysis, 156–158,
    157t
  variables, 152, 157, *157t,* 159–162, *160f,*
    161f
Freiburg School, 228
French Doctrinaires, 212, 213
Friedman, Milton: *Capitalism and Freedom,*
    111

G

game models, 27, 38, 98n24
Gandhi, Mohandas K.
  addressing problems of inclusion and
    exclusion based on identities, 107
  on civil disobedience, 109
  denying determinism, 120
  India's independence struggle, 108–109
  khadi campaign, 109
  on means as everything, 108, 123n2
  nonviolent social movement, 108,
    116–120, *117t–118t*
  theory and philosophy of, 123nn1–2
Gellar, Sheldon: *Conversations with
    Tocqueville* (with Craiutu), 215

Georgia (country): economic freedom, *156t*
Germany: economic policy evolution, *163f*
Die Gesellschaftskrisis der Gegenwart (Röpke), 241n24
Ghana: economic policy evolution, *163f*
Gibson, Clark
  policy-relevant research, 26
  The Samaritan's Dilemma (et al.), 30–31, 57
Giere, Ronald, 97n11, 97n15
Golden Rule, 190–191, 198, 201
governance
  community participation in, 52–53
  defined, 52
  effectiveness and scale, 226
  justice and, 110–112
  Nussbaum on, 110
  as process, 52
  robustness-performance tradeoff, 98n27
  role of, 110–111
  in SES framework, 45
  systems of, 94–95
  Tocqueville on, 213–214
  See also polycentric governance; self-governance; *specific topics*
Governing the Commons (E. Ostrom)
  academic influence and reception of, 233–234
  balance of rigor and relevance in, 20–21, 43
  citizens of democratic regimes, 236–237
  dedication, 1
  design principles in, 36, 43–44
  forest resources, 28
  IAD framework and, 2, 36–44, 50
  local management of critical common resources, 30
  as policy-relevant research, 26
  SES framework and, 50
  symposium on, 26
government-centered theory, critique of, 113
grammar of institutions, 57–58, 78, 94
Great Expectations (Dickens), 111

Greve, Michael, 140–141
group principles, 106, 122
Guizot, François-Pierre-Guillaume, 212

H
Habermas, Jürgen
  compared to other traditions, 116–120, *117t–118t*, 121
  core problem, 118
  denying determinism, 119–120
  "evaluative processes" theory, 123n1
  interactive groups, 109
  synthesis with other traditions, 120–123
Hamilton, Alexander, 221
Hanson, Robin, 151
Hardin, Garrett
  ideal model, 76–77, 85
  impossibility results, 76–77
  E. Ostrom on, 119
  tragedy of the commons, 49, 62, 77, 119
Hayek, F. A., 136
Hazlitt, Henry, 150–151
Heikkila, Tanya, 60
Hempel, Carl, 74
Herzberg, Roberta Q., 240n14
Hobbes, Thomas: *Leviathan,* 221
homo economicus (model), 81
Hong Kong: economic freedom, *156t*
Huntington, Samuel, 215

I
IAD framework. *See* Institutional Analysis and Development (IAD) framework
Ibn Khaldūn, 212
ICA (Institutional Collective Action) framework, 25
The Idea of Justice (Sen), 84–85, 111
ideal theory, 110
IFRI (Institute for Forestry Resources and Institutions), 28
impossibility results, 76–77
inclusion and exclusion, identity-based, 107
incommensurability thesis, 97n21

India: independence struggle, 108–109
Indiana University. *See* Bloomington School;
    Tocqueville Program; Workshop in
    Political Theory and Policy Analysis
Indianapolis, Indiana: police services, 25
individuals. *See* citizens
Institute for Forestry Resources and
    Institutions (IFRI), 28
institution
  as shared concept, 79
  as theoretical concept, 79–80, 96n9
Institutional Analysis and Development
    (IAD) framework, *37f, 168f*
  action arena, 167, *168f,* 169
  action situations, 36–41, *37f, 39f,* 43, 45,
    51, 53, 169, 170, 192
  adjacent action situations, 39–41, *39f*
  Aligica on, 76
  analytic narrative, 169, 170–171
  applicability in policy settings, 42
  applicability to other statistical tools, 11
  balance of rigor and relevance in, 20–21
  in broader integrative framework, 64n4
  Clement's variables, 42
  concurrent action situations, 45
  contextual conditions, 37, *37f,* 38–39
  as cross-disciplinary and collaborative, 220
  development of, 2–3, 27, 31, 34
  diagnostic approach, 60
  evaluation stage, 174–175
  exploring new ways forward, 56–63
  focal action situations, 41, 43, 51, 53–55
  focus on social-institutional side of policy
    problems, 45
  general template, 170–171
  Governing the Commons and, 2, 36–44, 50
  identification of institutions and configu-
    rations, 169
  institutional design and, 165, 176n1
  introduction, 2–3, 7, 11
  landscape navigation mode of analysis, 58
  level-shifting strategies, 41
  McGinnis's guide to, 42–43

  E. Ostrom's case studies, 43
  E. Ostrom's design principles, 43–44
  E. Ostrom's "map" metaphor, 97n14
  policy failures, analysis of, 57
  political economy analyses, 150
  polycentric governance, 51
  for public choice analysis, 148, 167–175
  purpose, 49
  quality of outcome, 49–50
  rules, 170–174, *171f*
  scientific rigor, 28
  SES comparisons, 45
  sources of error, 169
  statistical tools and, 148
  strategic rigor, 55
  suggested use of, 50–51, 55–56
  value to researchers and policy analysts,
    41–42
institutional challenges, of social
    recontracting, 10–11, 139–141
institutional change
  conscious forms, 193
  endogenous, 193–194, 195
  exogenous, 193, 194–195, 196
  E. Ostrom on, 192, 193
  polycentric governance, 192–196, *196f,*
    197
  polycentric governance, "the political,"
    and, 196–203
  unconscious forms, 193
institutional choices, constraints on,
    158–159
Institutional Collective Action (ICA)
    framework, 25
institutional complexity
  evaluating combinatorial complexity,
    152–167
  evaluation difficulties, 148–149
  IAD framework for public choice analysis,
    148, 167–175
  introduction, 11, 147–150
  is institutional design about institutions?,
    150–151

public choice analysis and, 147–178
institutional design
  cluster analysis, *167t*
  constraints on, 160, 162
  developed countries, *163f,* 165
  developing countries, *163f,* 165
  differential outcomes across clusters,
    166f
  evaluating outcomes, 164–167
  IAD framework, 169
  is institutional design about institutions?,
    150–151
institutional eclecticism, 218–219
institutional forms, citizen interests and,
  3–4
institutional grammar, 57–58, 78, 94
institutional landscapes
  defined, 48–49
  landscape navigation mode of analysis, 58
  navigating in polycentric systems, 50–56
institutional theory
  citizens' self-governance, 5
  Ostrom's design principles, 94–95, 106,
    120
*The Intellectual Crisis in American Public
    Administration* (V. Ostrom), 220
interjurisdictional spillovers, 132–133,
  137–138
Ireland: economic freedom, *156t*
Isaac, Jeffrey C., 234

J

Jack Miller Center, 216–217
Jacobs, Lawrence R., 63n2
Janssen, Marco
  on econometric analyses, 149
  Working Together (with Poteete and E.
    Ostrom), 28, 50, 219
Japan: economic policy evolution, *163f*
John Gaus Award, 216
justice
  created through interaction, 109
  as end state, 107

political ethics and, 107–109
Rawls on, 110
role of government in, 110–112
theories of, 84–85

K

Kim, Seo Young, 25
Kimmich, Christian, 59
King, Martin Luther, Jr.
  addressing problems of inclusion and
    exclusion based on identities, 107
  denying determinism, 120
  dispute resolution, 123n1
  nonviolent social movement, 116–120,
    117t–118t
  Stride Toward Freedom, 119
Kiser, Larry, 31, 34
Klein, Daniel B., 137, 151
Korten, Fran, 218
Kuhn, Thomas, 75, 97n21

L

landscapes. *See* institutional landscapes
Latvia: economic freedom, *156t*
Lefort, Claude, 186
Leviathan (Hobbes), 221
Levine, Peter, 107, 241n18
  See also "what should we do?"
Levy, David M., 35
Libecap, Gary, 138
liberalism, classical, 189–190, 224–225,
  227–228
libertarianism, 111, 224–225
Liberty Fund, 217
Lien, Aaron M., 58
linguistic theory of institutions, 78
Lithuania: economic freedom, *156t*
local governance, 26, 31, 62, 202
  See also communities
The Logic of Liberty (Polanyi), 227
Lona, Ashly, 58
London Underground, in "map" metaphor,
  91–92

M

Madison, James, 221
Mansbridge, Jane, 107, 234
Mantena, Karuna, 108
"map" metaphor, 88, 91–92, 97nn14–15
marginalized groups and claims
    inclusion and exclusion based on identities, 107
    in polycentric governance, 182–183, 197–198, 199, 201
    in post-foundational thought, 185
Mark Lubell, 64n5
markets
    in public economy concept, 135–136
    Structure-Conduct-Performance approach, 135, 143
Martin, Adam, 138, 141
    See also social recontracting
Marxism, 12, 119–120, 181, 212, 241n16
Mauritius: economic freedom, *156t*
McGinnis, Michael D.
    on IAD framework, 28, 39–40, 42–43, 64n4
    on E. Ostrom's contributions to scholarship, 19–20
    on Ostroms' personal politics, 241n17
    policy-relevant research, 26
    on SES framework, 64n4
    See also scientific rigor and policy relevance of Bloomington School
The Meaning of Democracy and the Vulnerabilities of Democracies (V. Ostrom), 215
methodological eclecticism, 218, 219–222
methodological tensions, 179–246
    introduction, 12–13
    E. Ostrom on, 32–34, 73–74
    Ostroms' eclecticism, 12–13, 211–246
    polycentric governance and "the political," 12, 181–210
methodology, Bloomington School, 239n10
metropolitan political systems, OTW analysis, 30
metropolitan reform debate, 130
metropolitan service delivery, 2, 10
Michels, Robert, 225
Miroiu, Adrian. *See* scientific realism
Mitchell, William, 240n14
models, 80–87
    action situation as, 27, 38
    agent-based models, 97n12
    complexity of constructing, 86–87
    constraints, 82, 96n9
    evaluation of, 88, 89
    families of (*See* scenarios)
    field settings, 86
    frameworks and, 7
    ideal models, 76–77, 84–86, 96–97nn10–11
    as investigative instruments, 83, 88
    laboratory experiments, 86
    "map" metaphor, 88, 91–92, 97nn14–15
    E. Ostrom on, 92–93, 98n24
    pivotal role of, 80–83
    policy-relevant framework, 8
    realm of, 83–86
    structural variables, 86–87
    theories, distinguished from, 80–83
    in triadic scheme, 74–75, 80–87, 96n3
monocentrism, 202, 220
Montreal, Canada: recontracting, 143–144
Mouffe, Chantal, 187
Müller-Armack, Alfred, 228
multiple method approach, 4
Muqaddimah (Ibn Khaldūn), 212

N

Nehemiah, Book of, 120–122
"Neither Gargantua Nor the Land of the Lilliputs" (E. Ostrom and Parks), 133, 134
Netherlands
    economic freedom, *156t*
    economic policy evolution, *163f*
"The New Civic Politics" (Boyte et al.), 107
New Zealand: economic freedom, *156t*

Nigeria: economic policy evolution, *163f*
Niskanen Center, 242n30
Nobel Prize (E. Ostrom's)
    acceptance lecture, 7, 45
    assessment of, 19–20
    award, 1
    corecipient, 1
    criticism of, 27
    Nobel committee's comments, 1
    E. Ostrom's research program, 36, 211
nonideal theory, 110
nonrealism. *See* anti-realism
nonviolent social movements
    civil rights movement, 183, 186
    as cluster of strategies, 108
    compared to other traditions, 116–120,
        117t–118t
    core civic action, 119
    synthesis with other traditions, 120–123
norms
    in design principles, 106
    as fragile common resources, 122
    in policy analysis, 115
    religious norms, 239n9
Nussbaum, Martha, 110, 111, 236

O

Oakerson, Ronald J., 26
Oakeshott, Michael: *On Human Conduct*,
        230–231, 242n26
Oates, Wallace, 133
Oberlack, Christoph, 59
oligarchy, 116, 225
Olson, Mancur, 166
On Human Conduct (Oakeshott), 230–231,
        242n26
operational-choice settings, 37–38
opportunity cost, 139
ordoliberalism, 228
"The Organization of Government in
        Metropolitan Areas" (V. Ostrom,
        Tiebout, Warren (OTW))
    cross-sector coordination, 25

definitions, 29
interjurisdicional dispute resolution, 138
metropolitan political systems in, 30
E. Ostrom's empirical tests on, 24–25
polycentric governance, 24, 51, 111
organization (term), 79
Ostrogorski, Moisey, 225
Ostrom, Elinor
    academic appointments, 24, 219
    American Political Science Association
        address, 113
    awards and honors, 1, 13n1 (*See also*
        Nobel Prize)
    biography (Tarko), 56–57
    career hurdles, 2
    on civic education, 113
    commensurability of theories, 97n21
    contributions to scholarship, 19–20, 62
    Craiutu and, 211–212
    criticism of, 27, 62, 217, 234
    on decentralization, 228
    denying determinism, 119
    on direct action, 31
    on "disciplinary huts" of universities, 218
    on ecological change, 138
    on econometric analyses, 149
    on failure, 56–57
    frameworks, focus on, 26–27
    IAD framework and (*See* Ostrom, Elinor,
        IAD framework and)
    on *The Idea of Justice* (Sen), 84
    on ideal models, 76, 84–86, 96–97nn10–
        11
    importance of (*See* Ostrom, Elinor and
        Vincent, importance of)
    on impossibility results, 76–77
    on institutional change, 192, 193, 195
    on institutional complexity and public
        choice analysis, 148–149
    on international agreements, 31
    irrigation model, 86–87
    legacy, 19–20, 217–218
    "map" metaphor, 97n14

marginality in discipline of political science, 26–27
"no panaceas," 29, 34, 84
normative stance, 107
optimism about prospects of democracy, 243n35
on oversimplification, 3
PhD dissertation, 30, 130
policy-relevant research, 26, 29–30
political ideology, 241n17
on political science methodology, 32–34
on political science theory, 73–74, 96n1
on polycentric governance, 51, 131–134
pragmatist perspective, 88
Public Choice Society addresses, 2, 27
on public sector opportunity costs, 139
rejection of blueprint approaches, 84, 92–93, 98n24, 227–229
religious beliefs, 239n9
rigor-relevance balance, 22, 27–28
robustness-performance tradeoff, 98n27
scientific creed, 92
self-governance and, 127–128, 221–222
on self-organization, 189
SES framework and, 27, 28, 40, 45
strategic rigor, 34
structural realism, 88–89
on theory-reality interplay, 98n29
Tocqueville's influence on, 214
triadic conceptual scheme, 74–77, 80–82, 83, 97n21
See also Bloomington School; design principles; specific topics
Ostrom, Elinor, IAD framework and
action situations, 38, 40, 43
case studies, 43
contextual factors, 38–39
development, 2–3, 27, 31, 34
Governing the Commons links, 36–44
level-shifting strategies, 41
"map" metaphor, 97n14
overview of projects using, 28
revisions, 27

Ostrom, Elinor, research topics of
case selection, 143
collective action, 107
common-pool resource governance, 130–131
community-based management of common-pool resources, 26, 27–28
forested areas, 28
institutional grammar, 57–58, 78–79, 94
police services, 25, 130
priorities, 235–236
water governance, 130
Ostrom, Elinor, works by
Conversations with Tocqueville preface, 216
The Delivery of Urban Services, 56–57
"Neither Gargantua Nor the Land of the Lilliputs" (with Parks), 133, 134
Rules, Games, and Common-Pool Resources, 27
The Samaritan's Dilemma (with Gibson et al.), 30–31, 57
Strategies of Political Inquiry, 31–33
Understanding Institutional Diversity, 28, 50, 61, 229
Working Together (with Poteete and Janssen), 50, 219
See also Governing the Commons
Ostrom, Elinor and Vincent, importance of, 211–246
against blueprint thinking, 227–229
challenging mainstream thinking, 1–2
civic studies, 235–238, 241n18
cross-disciplinary and collaborative focus, 220
on democracy, 224
eclecticism of the Ostroms' agenda, 216–224
institutional eclecticism, 218–219
interdisciplinary approach, 4
introduction, 12–13
legacy, 4
linking theories to practice, 4
making democracy work, 230–235

methodological eclecticism, 218,
  219–222
political, definition of, 231–232
political eclecticism, 218, 222–224,
  240n14
polycentricity, 226–227
responding to Tocqueville's challenge,
  212–216
"seeing like a citizen," 5, 110–113,
  224–226, 230
Ostrom, Vincent
on art of association, 243n34
awards and honors, 14n1
on Bloomington School methodology,
  239n10
Buchanan, correspondence from,
  147–148
career hurdles, 2
on centralization, 34, 201
on citizens as constitutional artisans, 234
collective action research, 107
contextual factors in IAD framework,
  38–39
contributions to scholarship, 62
Conversations with Tocqueville essay, 216
Craiutu and, 211–212
criticism of, 62, 217, 234–235
democracy, optimism concerning, 243n35
on democracy, 215, 225
on Faustian bargain, 189, 225
on frameworks, 75
Governing the Commons dedication to, 1
on Great Societies, 225
importance of (See Ostrom, Elinor and
  Vincent, importance of)
Indiana University faculty position, 24
influences on, 214, 221, 222, 240n11,
  240n13
The Intellectual Crisis in American Public
  Administration, 220
legacy, 217–218
machine politics, concerns about,
  214–215

The Meaning of Democracy and the Vulnerabilities of Democracies, 215
normative stance, 107
performance criterion of political representation, 200–201
policy-relevant research, 26, 29–30
political ideology, 231–232, 241n17
as political theorist, 25–26
political vision, 240n16
on polycentric governance, 137, 201–202
on public economy, 139
religious beliefs, 239n9
research priorities, 235–236
on role of theory, 96n4
self-governance and, 221–222, 226
on self-organization, 189
on shared values, 190
strategic rigor, 34
on truth, 98n29
on uncertainty, 141
See also Bloomington School; "The
  Organization of Government in
  Metropolitan Areas"; Workshop in
  Political Theory and Policy Analysis;
  specific topics
Ostrom Workshop. See Bloomington
  School; Workshop in Political
  Theory and Policy Analysis
OTW. See "The Organization of
  Government in Metropolitan
  Areas" (V. Ostrom, Tiebout, Warren
  (OTW))
oversimplification, 2

P
Parks, Roger: "Neither Gargantua Nor
  the Land of the Lilliputs" (with E.
  Ostrom), 133, 134
Parks, Rosa, 186
Patterson, James J., 59–60
payoff rules, 242n25
Peart, Sandra J., 35
Pennington, Mark, 134

Perspectives on Political Science (symposium), 233–234

Pettit, Philip, 110, 111–112

Philippines: economic policy evolution, *163f*

Poland: economic policy evolution, *163f*

Polanyi, Michael: *The Logic of Liberty,* 227

police services, 25, 130

policy analysis
  Bloomington School and, 113–116
  necessary components, 114–115
  rigor and relevance in, 21–24
  statistical analysis, 149–150
  stereotyped model, 113–116, *114f*
  See also economic policies; public choice analysis

policy cycle, 60–61

policy failures, 56–57

policy relevance and scientific rigor. *See* scientific rigor and policy relevance of Bloomington School

"the political," 181–210
  defined, 183, 187
  democracy and, 185–186
  introduction, 12
  polycentric governance, institutional change, and, 196–203
  polycentric governance and, 3, 9, 12, 181–210
  in post-foundational thought, 182, 183–187, 203

political eclecticism, 218, 222–224, 240n14

political economy analyses, 150, 160

political ethics, 107–109, 214–215, 222

political issues, legitimate/illegitimate, 198–199, 204

political science
  E. Ostrom on, 32–34, 73–74, 96n1
  rigor and relevance in, 21–24
  Tocqueville's new political science, 212, 213

politicians, IAD framework rules, 172

politics
  Ostroms' definition of, 231–232

signaling allegiance to a group, 151
  "politics," 182, 187

Politics (Aristotle), 240n13

Polski, Margaret M., 26

polycentric governance
  action situations, 194
  agents' capabilities in, 188–189
  benefits of, 131–132
  blind spot, 181–182
  Bloomington School research tradition, 64n5
  boundaries, 138, 200
  checks on abuses, 140, 201
  critical geography and, 182
  defined, 128
  democracy and, 197, 198, 200–201
  description of, 205n1
  dissolution of jurisdictions, 143–144
  equality and, 182, 197, 199–200, 202, 204
  error-correction opportunities, 131
  evaluation, 137
  exit option, 194
  Faustian bargain, 189, 199
  freedom of entry and exit, 139
  Golden Rule, 190–191, 198, 201
  IAD framework, 51
  idealized, 52, 196–197, 198, 200
  independently constituted jurisdictions, 134
  institutional change, "the political," and, 196–203, *196f*
  interjurisdictional cooperation as collusive, 140–141
  interjurisdictional spillovers, 132–133, 137–138
  introduction of concept to literature, 24
  jurisdictional boundaries, 137–138
  marginalized groups and claims, 182–183, 197–198, 199, 201
  navigating institutional landscapes in, 50–56
  necessary components, 236

opposition to, 24
Ostroms' contributions to, 128–129,
    131–134, 137, 226–227
overlapping publics, 111
"the political" and, 3, 9, 12, 181–210
"politics" and, 183
post-foundational thought and, 187, 188
real-world applications, 51
recontracting and, 10–11, 129–134
redistribution tensions, 201, 202, 204
research gap, 182
rules, 189–193, 198
self-governance and, 128
self-organization, 188–189, 191, 194,
    198, 199–200
SES framework, 51
shared values in, 188, 189–193, 197, 198
social-problem characteristics, 189–193
structural realism, 95
voice in, 194
position rules, 241n25
post-foundational thought
    "the democratic" i, 183–187
    "the political," 182, 183–187, 203
    "politics," 182, 203
    polycentric governance and, 187, 188
    shared values in, 197
Poteete, Amy, 28, 149
    Working Together (Poteete et al.), 50, 219
process theories, 107
production, defined, 29
provision, defined, 29
public administration bureaucracies, 3, 5, 174
public administration tensions, 103–178
    institutional complexity and public choice
        analysis, 11, 147–178
    introduction, 8–11
    social recontracting, 10–11, 127–146
    "what should we do?" (citizen's core ques-
        tion), 10, 105–125
public choice analysis
    evaluating combinatorial complexity,
        152–167

evaluation difficulties, 148–149
framework, *168f*
IAD framework for, 148, 167–175
institutional complexity and, 11,
    147–178
introduction, 11, 147–150
is institutional design about institutions?,
    150–151
rules for politicians, 172
rules for public administration bureaucra-
    cies, 174
rules for voters, 173
Public Choice Society, 2, 27
public economy, 134–139
    coercive sanctions, 142–143
    difficulties with, 136–137
    mutual coordination, 135, 136
    opportunity cost, 139
    Ostroms' concept of, 134–136, 142–143
    social recontracting, 134–139
public entrepreneurs, 30, 62, 189
public-sector institutions, social
    recontracting and, 129
Putnam, Hilary, 90

R
Ragin, Charles, 175
Rancière, Jacques, 186, 187
rational-actor model, 234, 242n32
Rawls, John, 84–85, 98n25, 110, 111
realism, 90, 97n21
    See also anti-realism; scientific realism;
        structural realism
received (syntactic) view of theories, 73–74,
    77–78, 90
recontracting down, 129, 140, 142, 143
recontracting problem, 134–139, 142, 143
relevance. *See* scientific rigor and policy
    relevance of Bloomington School
religious norms, 239n9
republicanism, defined, 110
Research & Creative Activity, 30
resource system, in SES framework, 45

resource units, in SES framework, 45
resource users, in SES framework, 45
rigor. *See* scientific rigor; strategic rigor
Riker, William H., 240n14
Robinson, James A., 140
Rochester school, 240n14
Romania
 economic freedom, 155, *156t*
 economic policy evolution, *163f*
Röpke, Wilhelm, 228, 241n24
Rosanvallon, Pierre, 231, 242n28
Rothschild, Elanit, 200
rules
 government frameworks, 230, 241n25
 IAD framework template, 170–174, *171f*
 in polycentric governance, 189–193, 198
Rules, Games, and Common-Pool Resources (E.
 Ostrom et al.), 27–28
Rüstow, Alexander, 228

S
The Samaritan's Dilemma (Gibson et al.),
 30–31, 57
Sargent, Thomas, 159
scenarios, in triadic scheme, 74–75, 86–87,
 96n2
Schlager, Edella, 58
Schroeder, Larry, 26
Schwartz-Shea, Peregrine, 234
scientific realism, 73–101
 defined, 90
 introduction, 8–9
 models, 80–87
 semantic approach, 74–80
 way to structural realism, 87–95
 See also structural realism
scientific research, primary goal, 34, 88
scientific rigor and policy relevance of
 Bloomington School, 19–72
 communication problems, *22t*, 23, 28–29
 exploring new ways forward, 56–63
 finding balance in the Bloomington
 School, 24–31

introduction, 5–9, 19–21
Jacobs and Skocpol on, 63n2
linking the IAD framework and *Governing the Commons,* 36–44
navigating institutional landscapes in a
 polycentric system, 50–56
policy relevance, distinguishing characteristics, *22t*, 23
revealing ecologies of governance with the
 SES framework, 45–50
rigor and relevance in political science and
 policy analysis, 21–24
rigor-relevance tensions, 20
scientific rigor, 22–23, *22t*, 28–29
strategic rigor and rigor-relevance balance,
 31–36
scope rules, 242n25
Scott, James C., 241n19
secure markets, welfare states and, 158, *158f,
 163f, 164f,* 165, 170
"seeing like a citizen," 5, 110–113, 224–226,
 230
self-governance
 benefits of, 127–128
 as bottom-up social contracting, 128,
 129–130
 challenges in, 106
 citizens as constitutional artisans, 234
 defining collective "we," 106
 forms of, 226
 as fragile enterprise, 140
 human fallibility and, 212–213
 importance of, 127
 introduction, 2, 5, 10
 meaning of, 127
 E. Ostrom on, 127–128, 129–130, 140
 Ostroms' support for, 9, 221–222, 223–224
 polycentricity and, 128, 188–189
 role of national government in, 133–134
 Tocqueville on, 212–213
 See also "what should we do?"
self-organization, 188–189, 191, 194, 198,
 199–200

semantic conception of theories, 74–80
    core claim, 82
    structural realism and, 87–88, 93
    on theories, 77–80
    three levels (triadic) approach, 74–77
Sen, Amartya, 77, 84–85, 111, 236
SES framework. *See* Social-Ecological
        System (SES) framework
SESMAD (Social-Ecological System Meta-
        Analysis Database), 44
shared values
    in polycentric governance, 188, 189–193,
        197, 198
    in post-foundational thought, 197
    in post-political thought, 188
Shivakumar, Sujai: *The Samaritan's Dilemma*
        (with Gibson et al.), 30–31, 57
Siddiki, Saba, 58
Simler, Kevin, 151
Simon, Herbert, 242n32
simplification, criticism of, 2
Singapore: economic freedom, *156t*
Skocpol, Theda, 63n2
Smith, Rogers, 107
Sneed, John D., 96n9
social choice theory, 96n9
social contracting. *See* social recontracting
Social-Ecological System Meta-Analysis
        Database (SESMAD), 44
Social-Ecological System (SES) framework,
        46f
    action situation adjacency, 40
    action situations, 21, 40, 45–51, *46f*
    actor attributes as pointers, 47–48
    applicability, 45, 55–56
    in broader integrative framework, 64n4
    broader social-political-economic settings,
        45
    concurrent action situations, 45
    as cross-disciplinary and collaborative,
        220
    ecologies of governance and, 45–50
    exploring new ways forward, 56–63

focal action situations, 45–50, *46f,* 55
    governance system, 45
    IAD comparisons, 45
    interactions and outcomes, 45
    introduction, 7
    landscape navigation mode of analysis, 58
    E. Ostrom's introduction of, 27
    polycentric governance, 51
    purpose, 49
    quality of outcome, 49–50
    related ecological systems, 45
    strategic rigor, 55
    variables, 45–48
social-problem characteristics, 189–193
social recontracting, 127–146
    contracting down, 129, 140, 142, 143
    contracting up, 128, 129, 134, 140–141,
        143
    defined, 128–129
    institutional challenges, 139–141
    introduction, 10–11
    made difficult by public-sector institu-
        tions, 129
    E. Ostrom's views, 128–129
    polycentric social contracting, 129–134
    recontracting problem, 134–139, 140,
        142, 143
socialization processes, 58
Solow model, 166–167
Soltan, Karol, 107, 241n18
South Korea: economic policy evolution,
        163f
sovereignty, 231
spiraling approach, 59–60
spontaneous order, 228
statistical tools, 11, 148, 149–150
    See also combinatorial complexity
Stigler, George, 147–148
strategic rigor
    analytical pathfinding, 54
    defined, 7, 20, 34
    goal, 35
    outline, 55

rigor-relevance balance, 31–36
Strategies of Political Inquiry (E. Ostrom, ed.),
    31–32
Stride Toward Freedom (King), 119
structural realism
    defined, 8
    impetus for, 87–95
    introduction, 8
    "map" metaphor, 91–92
    E. Ostrom's view and, 74, 88–89, 92–95
    reference, truth, and structure, 89–92
    semantic conception of theories and,
        87–88, 93
    versions of, 90–91
structural variables, 86–87
Structure-Conduct-Performance approach,
    135, 143
subsidiarity, 241n23
Swann, William L., 25
Sweden
    deregulation, 170
    economic policy evolution, *163f*
Swedish International Development Agency,
    31
Switzerland: economic freedom, *156t*
Swyngedouw, Erik. *See* "the political"
syntactic (received) view of theories, 73–74,
    77–78, 90

T

Tarko, Vlad, 56–57
    See also institutional complexity: public
        choice analysis and
technological change, interjurisdictional
    spillovers and, 137
technology transfers, 165, 176n3
tensions. *See* methodological tensions; public
    administration tensions; theoretical
    tensions
theoretical scenarios. *See* scenarios
theoretical tensions, 17–101
    introduction, 4, 5–9
    scientific realism and E. Ostrom, 73–101

scientific rigor and policy relevance of
    Bloomington School, 5–9, 19–72
theories
    correspondence principle, 90–91
    functions of, 77
    models distinguished from, 80–83
    observational terms, 79
    E. Ostrom on, 77
    realist view of, 97n21
    received (syntactic) view of, 73–74,
        77–78, 81, 90
    semantic approach, 77–80, 82
    theoretical concepts, 79–80, 96n6
    in triadic scheme, 7, 74–75, 86–87
    See also semantic conception of theories
The Theory of Justice (Rawls), 110, 111
Thiel, Andreas. *See* "the political"
three levels (triadic) approach, 7, 74–77,
    86–87
Tiebout, Charles M. *See* "The Organization
    of Government in Metropolitan
    Areas"
Tocqueville, Alexis de
    apprenticeship of liberty, 216
    on art of government, 213–214
    on democracy, 58, 236, 237
    Democracy in America, 212–213, 215,
        221, 237
    Indiana University Tocqueville Program,
        216–217
    interpretations of, 240n11
    introduction, 12–13
    new political science, 212, 213–214, 216
    Ostroms' response to, 212–216
    on science of government, 213–214
    on self-governance, 212–213
    socialization's role in sustainable democ-
        racy, 58
Tocqueville Program, Indiana University,
    216–217
Tollison, Robert D., 140
totalitarian tendencies, 200, 202
tragedy of the commons, 49, 62, 77, 119

TRIPS (Agreement on Trade-Related Aspects of Intellectual Property Rights), 141
Tullock, Gordon, 131, 240n14

U

Understanding Institutional Diversity (E. Ostrom), 28, 50, 61, 229
UniGov institutions, 3
United Kingdom: economic freedom, *156t*
United States
  economic freedom, 155, *156t*
  economic policy evolution, *163f*
  local governance report, 202

V

values
  discourse about, 107, 116
  shared values, 188, 189–193, 197, 198
van Fraassen, Bas C., 79, 88
variables
  combinatorial complexity, 175
  EFW index, 152, 157, *157t*, 159–162, *160f, 161f*
  IAD framework, 42
  as pointers, 46, 47–48, 54
  in SES framework, 45–48
  structural variables, 86–87
Veritas Fund, 217
vernacular language, E. Ostrom on, 77–78
Villamayor-Tomás, Sergio, 59, 60
Virginia School of public choice, 35, 240n14
Volmert, Andrew, 200
voters, IAD framework rules, 173

W

Wagner, Richard E., 140
Walker, Jimmy, 19–20
Wall, Derek, 232–233
Warren, Robert. *See* "The Organization of Government in Metropolitan Areas"

water governance, 59, 130, 138
Weber, Max, 222, 231, 235
Webster, D. G., 60
welfare states, secure markets and, 158, *158f, 163f,* 165, 170
"what should we do?" (citizen's core question), 10, 105–125
  Bloomington School and policy analysis, 113–116
  focus on means, not ends, 107–109
  introduction, 10
  other traditions, 116–120
  seeing like a citizen, 5, 110–113, 224–226, 230
  synthesis of traditions, 10, 105–125
Williamson, Oliver E., 1
Wilson, Woodrow, 222, 227
Working Together (Poteete et al.), 50, 219
Workshop in Political Theory and Policy Analysis (Ostrom Workshop)
  community leaders and ordinary citizens, importance of, 26
  cross-disciplinary and collaborative focus, 218–219, 220
  establishment, 24, 218
  goals, 218, 219
  institutional eclecticism, 218–219
  introduction, 4
  methodological eclecticism, 218, 219–222
  name of, 219
  police services, as research topic, 25, 30
  political eclecticism, 218, 222–224, 240n14
  publications, 239n8
  Tocqueville Program, 216–217
  See also Bloomington School
World Trade Organization, 141
Wynne, Susan, 26

Printed in the USA
CPSIA information can be obtained
at www.ICGtesting.com
BVHW052249300723
667995BV00007B/18